THE PAYROLL TOOLKIT

Nuts and Bolts Techniques to Help You Better Understand and Manage a Payroll

REVISED SECOND EDITION

TIMOTHY F. CARSE, CPA
JEFFREY SLATER
North Shore Community College

P&P — PENN & PEARL PUBLISHERS LLC

BIRMINGHAM • ALABAMA • USA

The Payroll Toolkit
Nuts and Bolts Techniques to Help You Better Understand and Manage a Payroll
Revised Second Edition

Dedicated in memory of U.S. Route 66

A volume in "The Best of the Basics"™ series published by:
Penn & Pearl Publishers LLC
P. O. Box 310298
Birmingham, AL 35231-0298
www.pennpearl.com

ISBN 0-9703838-0-0

This book may be purchased in bulk quantity for business or sales promotion purposes. For information please write: Penn & Pearl Publishers LLC, Attention: Special Markets, P. O. Box 310298, Birmingham, AL 35231-0298.

Important Note:
This publication is designed to provide accurate and authoritative information in regard to the subject matter covered. It is sold with the understanding that neither the authors or the publisher is engaged in rendering legal, accounting, tax, or other professional services. If legal advice or other expert assistance is required, the services of a competent professional person should be sought.

From a Declaration of Principles jointly adopted by a Committee of the American Bar Association and a Committee of Publishers.

Please see the *Important Note* in the Preface for more details about the use of this publication.

Publisher's Cataloging-in-Publication Data
Provided by Quality Books, Inc.
Carse, Timothy F.
   The payroll toolkit : nuts and bolts techniques to
help you better understand and manage a payroll /
Timothy F. Carse, Jeffrey Slater. -- Rev. 2nd ed.
   p. cm.
   Includes index.
   LCCN: 00-111488
   ISBN: 0-9703838-0-0

   1. Payrolls--Management.   I. Slater, Jeffrey, 1947-
II. Title.

HG4028.P5C37 2001   658.3'21
                                 QBI01-200132

PREFACE

AN OVERVIEW OF PAYROLL ACCOUNTING AND ADMINISTRATION

The idea of hiring workers and paying them for their time and labor is an ancient one. It is as basic a concept to a business as that of making a profit. Unfortunately, the task of employing workers and paying them is becoming more complex in today's business environment due to increasing government regulations at the federal, state, and local levels. The reality is that the notion of paying employees has turned into a complicated and specialized area of operating a business—an area that is essential to a firm's functioning, growth, and longevity.

The Payroll Toolkit: Nuts and Bolts Techniques to Help You Better Understand and Manage a Payroll is written for the entrepreneurial businessperson who wants to better understand the essential function of payroll administration and management in today's business world.

Whether you are a manager, accountant, bookkeeper, human resources professional, entrepreneur, or president of your company, you will find this book valuable when dealing with the subject of payroll accounting and administration. You don't have to be a CPA, MBA, or tax attorney to understand this book. If you've taken a basic accounting course, you'll feel comfortable reading *The Payroll Toolkit* and will have all the background necessary to utilize it.

This book has been written and designed to be reader-friendly. Its goal is to provide you with a sound understanding of the essentials of payroll accounting and administration. We present a practical "how-to" approach in dealing with the tasks and issues involved with maintaining a payroll. Think of this book exactly as the title implies—a toolkit that you can use to better understand and manage your payroll. It is our belief that a thorough understanding of the basics of payroll is an essential ingredient to managing any business.

THE "PAYROLL ROAD MAP"

We have structured this book around what we call the *payroll process* which is outlined below. By thinking about payroll as a process, you can link together tasks that might seem to be unrelated to each other, helping you to better understand the cyclical steps of payroll accounting and administration. Think of this process as a "payroll road map" that will guide you to the destination you want to reach. Our "payroll road map" has been divided into seven major sections:

A: The payroll administration process.
B: Tracking working time and calculating earnings.
C: Calculating withholding taxes, other deductions, and tips.
D: Paychecks and record-keeping activities.
E: Employer payroll taxes and tax deposits.
F: Payroll reporting requirements.
G: Payroll resources.

Within each section are several chapters that focus on a specific topic or procedure that is an integral part of the payroll accounting and administration process. Our goal in structuring this book into seven sections is to minimize your time and effort to find an answer to a particular question and gain an improved understanding of a specific topic or method.

A glossary, payroll tax calendar, various payroll information summary tables, and information resources can be found in Section G at the back of the book. This section will help your understanding and knowledge of payroll accounting as well as providing a rendezvous where you can find out more about the various resources available for this area of business. Whenever possible, information has been organized so that your efforts to find answers to questions are minimized.

Throughout each chapter, we have included selected payroll questions and answers (which we call Q&A) to situations encountered by professionals. These Q&As are designed to help you focus on practical aspects of our topics and to reenforce your grasp of important concepts.

HOW YOU CAN BENEFIT FROM THIS BOOK

This book has been written to help increase your knowledge and understanding of payroll. In order to help you, we suggest that as you read and study the chapters you actively participate in the process by working through all of the examples you find using pencil, paper, and a calculator. We believe you will better understand and retain the information by "working along" as you read. Of course, you can use this book as a general desk reference, but our goal here is to make this book more than another volume that sits on your shelf at your office, so please try our suggestion.

A NOTE ABOUT DATES AND RATES IN THIS BOOK

This book has been written to accurately reflect the current federal rates and threshold minimums found for various payroll taxes as of the date of publication. Our writing approach utilizes this information in the same way you would if you are working on preparing a payroll for a small business. The various tax rates, dollar minimums, and threshold amounts used for withholding and reporting requirements will change with the passing of time. For your own benefit, we strongly encourage you to obtain the latest information from the IRS and state and local taxing authorities if you are involved with a payroll after the date of this publication.

In order to help you stay current with payroll matters, Appendices 2 and 3 feature the Internet web addresses for the IRS and state government tax authorities. The links listed have been tested as of the date of publication, but such addresses could change without notice. In the event the appendix has listed a web address that has changed since the publication of this book, you can use an Internet search engine to find the new web address.

The IRS and most state government agency web sites offer Adobe® "pdf file" downloads to the public for frequently used payroll forms and tax returns. Take advantage of this convenient way to look at the most current version of the forms we discuss in this book.

THE TERM *PAYROLL PROFESSIONAL*

Throughout the book we refer to the person who is working with a payroll as *the payroll professional.* Our use of this term is intentional because our view is that anyone who maintains a payroll for a business is not merely a clerk or a bookkeeper. We believe the payroll professional is a person who must be both an analyst and manager involved with a very essential function of operating a business.

Depending on your situation and reason for reading this book, the payroll professional could be you or someone with whom you work in your business. The payroll professional could also be a third party to your business who maintains your books or just your payroll (such as a bookkeeper, CPA, or an attorney). Our point here is that in our book, we address this person as the *payroll person* or *payroll professional.*

IMPORTANT NOTE

As noted on the copyright page of this book, this work is not designed or intended to replace or be a substitute for the advice and judgment of an attorney, accountant, or other professional consultant or expert who is knowledgeable about payroll accounting and administration. If you need legal advice or the assistance of an expert regarding a particular payroll matter, do not delay in seeking help from such a professional. That is your best recourse to help resolve a payroll matter that is unique to you and your circumstances. Do not expect or rely on this book to solve any such matter for you alone—it is impossible for any book to take the place of the sound advice and judgment of professionals and experts in an area such as payroll accounting and administration. When you have any doubts about a payroll matter, seek professional guidance.

USE OF PERSONAL PRONOUNS IN THIS BOOK

We have elected to use masculine personal pronouns throughout this book. Due to the awkward nature of the English language, we have found the text to be more readable by minimizing the use of "he/she" and "his/her" in our sentence structure. We intend no offense as obviously both men and women are connected with payroll accounting and administration in today's business world.

AS WE GO TO PRESS—NEW FEDERAL INCOME TAX WITHHOLDING TABLES

As we go to press, we want to mention that new *mid-year* federal tax withholding tables have been created for any payrolls paid during July through December, 2001. With Congressional passage of the George W. Bush administration's **Economic Growth and Tax Relief Reconciliation Act of 2001**, the IRS has issued the new federal tax withholding tables for this six-month time period. These tables can be found in **Publication 15-T** (printed in June, 2001). This special mid-year IRS publication has amended and slightly lowered tax rates and amounts in keeping with the statutes of the new federal law. The examples and illustrations found in Chapter 7 of Section C and the glossary definitions have been revised to reflect these new tax rate changes.

We also note here that the newly enacted law lowers the amount of withholding for supplemental wages (from 28% to 27.5%) and backup withholding (from 31% to 30.5%). The effective date of these two tax withholding rate decreases is August 6, 2001. These taxes are further discussed within this book.

MANY THANKS

We would indeed be remiss as authors if we omitted the names of those individuals who have made the second edition of this work a reality. First we want to extend our thanks to Jeff Shelstad and Laura Liberetti of the McGraw-Hill Companies for their help in granting us permission to publish the second edition. We also want to thank Stuart Hoffman of the Star Publishing Company for his invaluable assistance in this area.

We are deeply indebted to our Penn & Pearl book project team who graciously helped with "the hard stuff": many thanks to Judy Brown of Brown Enterprises for her outstanding electronic pre-press editing and printer coordination. A special note of appreciation goes to Mrs. Connie Ridgeway for copyediting of the manuscript. We are also deeply indebted to Beth M. Woods for a thorough and complete accuracy check of the book prior to its publication, and a warm thank you to Lance and Terrell of Photo Creations in Birmingham, Alabama, for the unique coffee cup appearing in our cover photo—great cup of coffee guys!

STARTING ON YOUR TRIP

It's now time to begin your trip in the area of payroll accounting and administration. We hope that our efforts to chart your journey by using our unique payroll road map will provide you with the knowledge you need and answers you are seeking in this often underemphasized area of managing a business. Have a pleasant trip!

Timothy F. Carse
Jeffrey Slater

CONTENTS

SECTION E

EMPLOYER PAYROLL TAXES AND TAX DEPOSITS

Chapter 12

Unemployment Taxes   237

Chapter 13

Payroll Tax Deposits   251

SECTION F

PAYROLL REPORTING REQUIREMENTS

Chapter 14

Forms 940-EZ and 940   269

The Payroll Administration Process

CHAPTER 1

Introduction to Payroll Accounting and Administration

Payroll accounting and administration today is a challenging area of business that has earned professional status and recognition. Payroll accounting is an ongoing process that involves federal, state, and local law, knowledge of accounting and company policies, and a desire to "get the job done right the first time." This chapter will provide you with a general overview of payroll accounting in today's business world.

1 DEFINING PAYROLL ACCOUNTING

Payroll accounting is an essential accounting activity of any business that employs workers. Whether a business employs one worker or a thousand, it must properly account for employee earnings and comply with the rules and laws that affect the hiring and paying of its employees.

What Is Payroll Accounting and Administration?

In any academic or professional area, it is customary to begin the subject with a definition or two. Definitions are particularly important in the area of payroll accounting and administration because there is some confusion as to what constitutes each activity.

Payroll accounting can be defined as the activities of calculating the earnings of employees and the related withholding for taxes and other deductions, recording the results of payroll activities, and preparing required payroll tax returns. It is not merely the "number crunching" of dollar amounts to arrive at an appropriate journal entry to record the paychecks issued for a payday. We extend the definition to include the essential task of reporting the results of payroll activities to the federal, state, and local governments. An example of such a reporting requirement is the annual event of preparing and issuing Form W-2s (called the *Wage and Tax Statement*).

Payroll administration deals with the managerial aspects of maintaining a payroll, many of which are not directly related to the accounting aspect of payroll. **Payroll administration** can be defined as the activities of (1) managing employee personnel and payroll information and (2) complying with federal, state, and local employment laws. This may encompass interviewing and hiring workers, maintaining personnel records, and seeing that a business complies with labor and antidiscrimination laws in relating to its employees. From a practical standpoint, payroll administration may on some level involve managing the human resource functions within a business.

In analyzing these definitions, the payroll accountant or administrator (who we refer to as the *payroll professional*) needs a working knowledge of accounting, the various laws that affect the payroll activities of a company, and specific company policies. Figure 1–1 illustrates the fact that payroll accounting combines knowledge from these different areas in forming the basic operating rules that must be followed by the payroll professional.

GAAP

The circle on the top left side of Figure 1–1 represents the accounting rules that a payroll accountant must follow. This set of accounting standards or rules is commonly referred to as GAAP or **Generally Accepted Accounting Principles.** These standards, known as *assumptions* or *concepts,* play a major role in how the payroll professional accounts for business and payroll transactions.

Employment Law

The circle on the right side of Figure 1–1 illustrates the various federal, state, and local employment laws that the payroll professional must know about and follow.

The Categories of Rules and Laws That Affect Payroll
Accounting and Administration

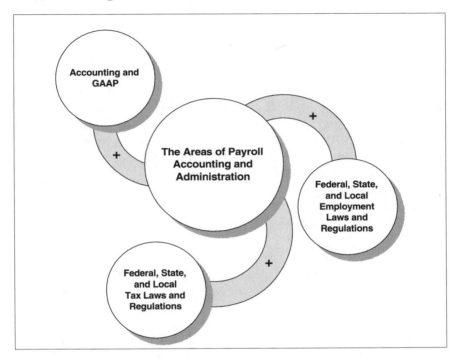

Tax Law

The circle on the lower left side of Figure 1–1 indicates that the payroll professional must be knowledgeable about the various sections of the Internal Revenue Code that apply to payroll activities. The **Internal Revenue Code** (also called the *IRC* or *Code*) is the body of federal law that requires the income of individuals and corporations to be taxed. The IRC applies to payroll accounting in that employers are required to withhold federal income taxes from most employees as required by the code. The code also sets forth specific timetables for federal payroll tax deposits and reporting requirements. Failure of an employer to comply with such laws will result in the levying of fines and penalties by the **Internal Revenue Service (IRS)**. The payroll professional must keep up with changes in the code and comply with them.

Payroll professionals must also be familiar with corporate rules and policies and any labor union agreements that affect the paying of employees. Corporate policies and labor union agreements will vary from company to company. Such policies could directly affect the calculations for working hours and paying of benefits to employees.

Payroll Road Map

Like any accounting activity, payroll accounting is a process that involves a number of tasks to be performed according to specific timetables. Think of this process as a "payroll road map" that will guide you to the destination you want to reach. Payroll accounting as a process has its own cycle, or series of activities, that takes place on a recurring basis. Figure 1–2 shows the payroll accounting process.

In looking at Figure 1–2, you will see that our *road map* begins with hiring employees (A). This process is governed by various federal, state, and local employment laws, corporate policies, and labor union agreements.

Once an employee is hired and begins working, the next step in the process (B) is to keep track of the hours worked and pay the employee. This step in the process, *the cycle of paying employees,* is explained in Segment 2 of this chapter.

Consider the fact that the taxes withheld from employee paychecks must be remitted to the government. The payroll accountant must comply with specific rules for payroll tax deposits (C) and has the responsibility for making deposits on a timely basis. The employer is also responsible for calculating, paying, and reporting its portion of social security taxes and federal and state unemployment taxes for each employee on its payroll.

The payroll professional will prepare a number of federal, state, and local payroll tax returns at various times during each calendar year (D). These reports include the W-2 form, with which you are probably familiar.

Many people think of payroll accounting as merely figuring an employee's paycheck. The reality is that payroll accounting is a process that is very involved and can be time consuming.

About Payroll Tax Deposits

The employer is responsible for remitting the taxes withheld from employee paychecks on a timely basis. These taxes are often referred to as *trust*

F I G U R E   1–2

The Payroll Road Map—A General Overview of the
Payroll Accounting Process

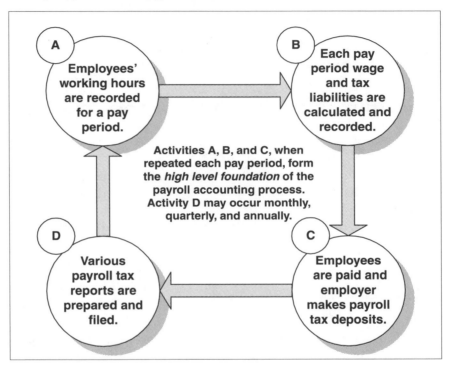

fund taxes because the employer is in the position of being a trustee of the taxes that employees have paid.

Employer Payroll Tax Liabilities

The employer is also responsible for calculating and paying certain payroll taxes that employees generally do not pay. Taxes such as *federal and state unemployment taxes* are the sole responsibility of the employer in most states.

Employers (along with employees) are also responsible for their share of social security taxes. Social security taxes are broken down by programs that benefit certain individuals in specific situations with monetary support. Currently there are four programs that these taxes fund: old age, survivors, disability insurance, and Medicare.

Reporting Payroll Tax Activities

A final and important part in the payroll accounting process is the employer's responsibility to prepare and submit various payroll tax returns to federal, state, and local governments. Such returns will be prepared according to different timetables and must be accurate in all respects. Because payroll tax return preparation can be complicated, we have devoted three chapters in Section F to these tasks.

2 JOB DUTIES OF THE PAYROLL PROFESSIONAL

The Cycle of Paying Employees

This stage in the payroll accounting process can be broken into five steps that occur each time employees are paid. Figure 1–3 describes each step in this cycle.

Consider, for example, the activities that are involved with calculating your paycheck before you are paid.

EXAMPLE 1

You work for U.S. Route 66 Trucking, Inc., a fictitious company that is a common carrier of freight in the southwestern and Midwestern United States. You are paid on an hourly basis every week. The company keeps track of your working hours by having you "punch" (or use) a time clock. Route 66 withholds amounts for your social security, federal income tax, and city taxes as well as a voluntary deduction for medical insurance. Your payday is Friday. There is no withholding for state taxes since U.S. Route 66 Trucking, Inc. is located in Texas, a state which does not tax income.

Q&A

Q: What steps are involved in preparing your paycheck every week?

A: The company must follow the steps illustrated in Figure 1–3. These steps will be discussed in detail in the chapters found in Sections B, C, and D of this book.

Here is a synopsis of the steps found in the cycle of paying employees:

FIGURE 1-3

Summary of the Steps Taken in the Cycle of Paying Employees

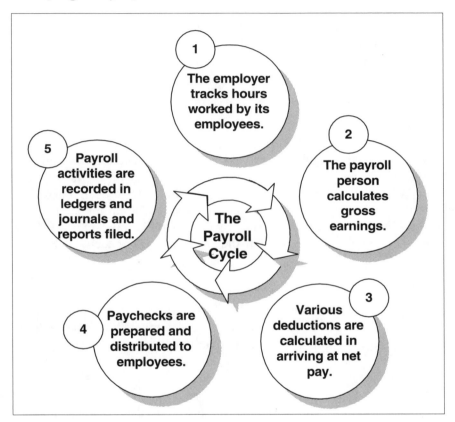

Step 1

U.S. Route 66 Trucking, Inc., like most employers, must keep track of the hours that each employee works. To accomplish this, the company uses a mechanical time clock to track hours worked.

Some companies will use time clocks while others will keep a written timesheet for tracking hours. Many companies have computerized this task, using an employee's ID badge instead of a time card to record the time worked directly into a computer system. Regardless of which method is used, employers will have to track most employees' hours worked in some way.

Usually a department manager or supervisor will be responsible for verification of employee hours worked. After verification, the payroll professional could be responsible for totaling the hours worked in Step 1 of the cycle of paying employees.

The hours employees work are tracked using a predetermined, recurring length of time that has specific starting and ending dates. This length of time is defined in payroll accounting as a *pay period.*

Step 2

At the end of the pay period, the total of the hours worked for each employee will be used in arriving at his *gross earnings.* Calculating gross earnings can be as simple as finding the total of the hours worked and then multiplying the rate of pay per hour by total hours. As we show in Chapter 4, this basic formula is more complicated when overtime hours have been worked or when the employees are paid a fixed salary or when the earnings are calculated using some other method. Usually the payroll accountant is involved at this step in the cycle to calculate the gross earnings of each employee.

Step 3

The employee's gross earnings are then used as the base amount in calculating the federal, state, and local income tax to be withheld for the pay period. Gross earnings are used in determining the amount of social security taxes (FICA taxes) to be withheld from each employee's paycheck. Amounts are also withheld for any voluntary deductions the employee wishes to have taken from gross pay.

The reason for making these calculations is to determine the amount the employee will actually receive for the pay period. Gross earnings less amounts withheld for taxes and other deductions equal the employee's *net earnings (take-home pay).*

Step 4

Employee paychecks are prepared, signed, and given to employees on their payday. At U.S. Route 66 Trucking, Inc., the terminal manager distributes paychecks to drivers. It is important that the payroll professional maintain **confidentiality** when calculating and preparing employee paychecks and when distributing the checks on payday. It is also essential that sensitive payroll information remain confidential within a company.

Step 5

The payroll accountant then records the earnings and deductions for each employee on a pay-period basis. Two accounting records used in recording payroll activities are the *payroll register* and the *employee earnings record.*

The **payroll register** lists by employee the payroll activity for a pay period. Each employee who receives a paycheck for any given pay period will be listed along with amounts for gross earnings, all deductions withheld, and the employer's portion of payroll taxes.

The **employee earnings record** documents each individual employee's pay history on a calendar year basis. The employee earnings record will be updated each pay period. A new record is started for each employee when hired and on January 1 of each successive year.

In addition to keeping these accounting records current and up to date, the payroll accountant records and posts the appropriate journal entries into the company's general ledger.

3   PROFESSIONAL RESPONSIBILITIES OF THE PAYROLL PERSON

We have discussed some of the specific duties of the payroll professional in the area of payroll accounting. Each individual job will have its own unique combination of responsibilities, which may include some or all of the ones discussed. In addition to these specific duties, people who are involved in the payroll accounting profession have broader responsibilities to their employer and to the profession itself.

The payroll professional is placed in a *fiduciary position* in that he deals on a daily basis with confidential employee data and company information. The employer places trust in the payroll professional to maintain confidentiality and a professional attitude at all times when handling and processing payroll information.

The need for **confidentiality** cannot be overemphasized in payroll accounting. Serious problems could result if sensitive payroll information is disclosed. Anyone working in the area of payroll accounting or administration must be aware of this fact when dealing with employee and personnel data and must use great care when working with this information.

Professional Attitude and Standards

Another responsibility of a payroll person is to maintain a professional attitude toward job duties and tasks. We have summarized these responsibilities as four *job goals* or *standards* that the payroll professional should strive toward as part of maintaining a professional attitude. These four payroll accounting objectives are

- Accuracy
- Compliance
- Confidentiality
- Timeliness.

Payroll professionals should do their very best to be **accurate** when computing earnings and deductions. Errors are costly and time-consuming so, as in any area of accounting, one should always strive to "do the job right the first time."

The payroll accountant must make every effort to **comply** with the many rules and laws that directly and indirectly affect the payroll accounting process. It is also the responsibility of the payroll professional to keep up with changes, additions, and modifications to existing rules and laws to ensure that taxes are properly calculated. Complying with the rules governing payroll accounting is a key goal of the payroll professional.

As we have mentioned before in this chapter, it is of the utmost importance that the payroll professional keep employee information **confidential** at all times both on and off the job. Discussing salaries, work schedules, or an employee's personal problems casually with co-workers could lead to company wide rumors and discontent. Competent payroll professionals maintain the confidential nature of information about employees' management matters. Payroll people should strive for this goal at all times.

The area of payroll accounting is subject to many **time deadlines** that must be met. If paychecks are due on Friday afternoon, the employees expect to receive them on time. A late payroll could cause embarrassment, discontent, and poor morale among the employees and must be avoided. Likewise, payroll tax deposits should be made on schedule and tax returns filed by their due dates to avoid penalties, interest, and fines.

You can remember these four goals or standards by memorizing the acronym *ACCT* (as in "accounting"). *A* stands for accuracy, *C* for compliance, *C* for confidentiality, and *T* for timeliness. Thus, if you *ACCT* (account) on a professional level, you can *count* on achieving these four standards!

4 PAYROLL AS A PROFESSION

The area of payroll accounting and administration is now recognized as a legitimate profession in the business world. This is an important step for individuals who have career ambitions in this area as well as those working in other areas of business. Recognition of payroll accounting as a profession helps to promote growth and allows standards to be set in order to further professionalism and competency in the area.

The Origins of Payroll Accounting

The area of payroll accounting has grown and evolved due to the enactment of federal and state laws governing paying employees and tax withholding. In the early part of this century, the task of paying employees was the function of an individual commonly known as a paymaster. Employees were often paid in cash without any taxes being withheld.

Since the 1930s and the enactment of the Social Security Act of 1935, the Fair Labor Standards Act of 1938, the Current Tax Payments Act of 1943, and the Internal Revenue Code, there has been a need to carefully track employee earnings and the deductions for taxes.

When employers became responsible for withholding taxes on earnings, calculating a company's payroll became the principal task of the payroll clerk. Payroll at this time was considered a bookkeeping function and little more. Today the job duties and knowledge required to properly maintain a payroll have elevated the "payroll clerk" to a "payroll professional."

With each new federal or state labor law, the payroll profession is affected. This trend is expected to continue in the future.

Professional Organizations

In 1982 a professional organization was formed that deals exclusively with payroll accounting and administration. The **American Payroll Associa-**

tion (APA) was formed to help promote payroll accounting as a profession and to help payroll accountants/professionals keep up with current changes in the laws and rules that affect payroll accounting. The APA, a nationwide society of payroll professionals, has three objectives:

1. To increase the payroll professional's skill level through education and mutual support.
2. To obtain recognition for payroll work as practiced in today's business and legislative environments and as a professional discipline.
3. To represent the payroll professional in Washington, D.C.

The APA has established a testing program for payroll professionals that provides the individual with recognition for competence in the area of payroll accounting and administration. The **Certified Payroll Professional examination (CPP)** is administered through the APA on an annual basis. Individuals who pass the exam are recognized with the designation CPP. This certification is now considered to be a professional goal that payroll accountants and administrators seek—such certification lends professional status to their occupations. To be eligible to sit for the CPP examination, an individual must have three years of verifiable job experience in the area of payroll accounting or administration out of his last five years of job experience.

Other Payroll Organizations

Another society that has been established to promote the field of payroll accounting and administration is the American Society for Payroll Management (ASPM). The group works with payroll professionals and businesses in a variety of areas. The society also produces publications and newsletters and conducts educational seminars. The society offers memberships to payroll professionals and an affiliate membership to others interested in the field. The ASPM can be reached by calling (800) 684-4024.

In Canada, a group known as the Canadian Payroll Association (CPA) works to promote payroll administration within Canada. The association offers support for Canadian payroll professionals and those who have businesses in Canada. For more information call (416) 487-3380.

Individuals involved in payroll accounting find that networking with other professionals in the field helps them to keep up with current trends and changes. Professionals with common goals who share information and knowledge with each other benefit not only themselves but also the profession as a whole.

With the increase of government regulation in the areas of taxation and employment, computerization in the workplace, and the changing environment of business itself, the payroll professional of the future will need to be highly knowledgeable in many areas. As we have pointed out, competency in the area of accounting coupled with a good working knowledge of employment laws and the Internal Revenue Code will be essential in mastering payroll accounting.

Computer and Communication Skills

Computer literacy is practically a requirement in today's business environment. Due to the unprecedented popularity and acceptance of the personal computer (PC) as a standard office machine in businesses of all sizes, professionals must be proficient in operating a PC and using software. To efficiently utilize the capabilities of PCs, many companies require their employees to possess typing and 10-key keyboard skills. This is especially true of today's payroll and accounting professionals.

The aspiring professional must know how to write clearly and communicate well with others in person and over the telephone. Courses in business letter writing and person-to-person communication skills are always useful to help the payroll professional become adept and feel at ease with both verbal and written communication in the business world.

Payroll Accounting and Human Resources

Human resource management (HRM) professionals have responsibilities in the hiring process and administering of employee benefits programs in a business. Typical duties of an HRM professional include:

- Administering employee benefit programs (medical insurance or pension plans).
- Conducting searches for candidates for employment.
- Developing employee training programs and seminars.
- Screening the applications and résumés of potential employees.
- Writing and revising job descriptions for a business.

In the past, payroll accounting and human resource management were viewed as separate and distinct functions of operating a business. Today this is not altogether true. In many companies, a payroll professional may be delegated some HRM duties (such as creating or updating job descriptions), and HRM professionals often must use and rely on information about employees that is obtained as part of the payroll accounting process (such as marital status or what an employee earns in a week or a month). Since payroll and human resource professionals often require the same information about employees, they often access and use the same computer software programs.

Due to the need to share common employee information and the fact that some payroll accounting and human resource management job duties complement each other, a new type of professional—one dedicated to human resource management and personnel matters as well as payroll accounting and administration—is developing in many companies. Associations such as the APA, ASPM, and CPA will take the lead in establishing the guidelines and knowledge that this new breed of professional will require in the years to come.

CHAPTER 2
The Hiring Process

This chapter covers an important stop on the payroll road map—the legal issue of worker classification. Here we deal with the tasks involved in hiring employees; use of the Forms SS-4, SS-5, and SS-8; the need for maintaining personnel files and documentation; and Form I-9 and Form W-4 and their state versions.

1 INDEPENDENT CONTRACTORS AND EMPLOYEES

What Is an Employee?

For payroll accounting purposes, workers generally are classified as either **employees** or **independent contractors**. How a worker is classified will directly affect withholding and remitting income and social security taxes and will also affect how the earnings are reported to the government. Classification is an important matter to the worker, employer, and government. Classification has become a controversial issue over the last decade and still stirs political debate.

Classifying a worker depends on how **employee** is defined. The common law test is a legal test to which many refer when classifying a worker. The common law test is used for purposes of determining if social security taxes should be withheld, matched, and paid by an employer.

This test will also determine if federal, state, and local income taxes should be withheld from the worker and then remitted to the government by the employer. The results of the common law test will also determine if an employer must pay federal and state unemployment taxes on a worker's earnings. The key issues in the common law test are 1) the amount of control the employer has over the worker (i.e., the worker's behavior and financial control); and 2) the type of relationship established between the employer and the worker (i.e., "Is the relationship temporary or permanent and on-going?"). Several major points in the common law test determine if the worker can be called an employee:

- Does the employer have the power to fire or terminate the worker at will?

- Does the employer provide a place for the worker to work, such as a workbench in a shop or a desk in an office?

- Does the employer provide the worker with tools, supplies, uniforms, or other items used on the job?

- Does the employer have a voice and responsibility in *what* the worker does and *how* the worker does a job?

- Are the services provided by the worker to the employer integral to the operation of the employer's business?

If all of these questions can be answered "yes" by an employer, the worker should be classified as an employee. If there are "no" responses to all of the questions, the worker should be classified in another way, such as an independent contractor.

There are two final questions that should be asked by an employer when classifying a worker as an employee or independent contractor:

- Does the worker offer his services to other employers or to the general public?

- Is there a written agreement between the worker and the employer as to job specifics and duties, payment for services, or an ending date for services?

If the answers to these last two questions are "yes," the worker is most likely an independent contractor. Likewise, if the answers to both questions are "no," the workers would more appropriately be classified as employees.

E X A M P L E   1

> You are familiar with the rules regarding working for an employer. You report to a particular individual, you have set hours on the job, and you are told when to take breaks and lunch hours. You and your employer call you an *employee.*

Defining you as "an employee" means that your employer must at a minimum:

- Withhold income and social security taxes.
- Match the social security taxes you pay.
- Pay federal and state unemployment taxes on your earnings.
- Issue a Form W-2 to you after the end of each calendar year.

The IRS uses other tests as well to classify a worker. The agency will also apply what is known as *Section 530* or *safe-harbor rules* to aid in determining worker status. These rules are found in *Section 530* of a federal tax law known as the **Revenue Act of 1978** (which was amended as a part of *The Tax Equity and Fiscal Responsibility Act* of 1982). Section 530 allows an employer to treat a worker as an independent contractor based on established industry practices or legal precedents. For example, if the job duties of a worker are classified by those in the industry as the duties of an independent contractor, the employer may rely on this and classify an individual worker accordingly. If the worker later is classified as an employee, the employer using the *safe harbor* provision provided by Section 530 will not be subject to penalties for the error in classification. There are other guidelines found in Section 530 that are not discussed here.

A third measure the IRS uses is a form known as the **SS-8,** called *Determination of Employee Work Status for Purposes of Federal Employment Taxes and Income Tax Withholding* (see Figure 2–1). This four-page form can be completed by either the employer or a worker. There are 20 questions which the preparer must answer. Based on the answers to these questions, the IRS will make a determination of the status of a worker. The IRS will notify the form's preparer of the determination.

Q&A:

Q: If an employer submits a Form SS-8 to the IRS for worker determination, how should the worker be classified while the IRS is analyzing the form?

FIGURE 2-1

20

Form SS-8
(Rev. June 1997)
Department of the Treasury
Internal Revenue Service

Determination of Employee Work Status for Purposes of Federal Employment Taxes and Income Tax Withholding

OMB No. 1545-0004

Paperwork Reduction Act Notice

We ask for the information on this form to carry out the Internal Revenue laws of the United States. You are required to give us the information. We need it to ensure that you are complying with these laws and to allow us to figure and collect the right amount of tax.

You are not required to provide the information requested on a form that is subject to the Paperwork Reduction Act unless the form displays a valid OMB control number. Books or records relating to a form or its instructions must be retained as long as their contents may become material in the administration of any Internal Revenue law. Generally, tax returns and return information are confidential, as required by Code section 6103.

The time needed to complete and file this form will vary depending on individual circumstances. The estimated average time is: **Recordkeeping**, 34 hr., 35 min.; **Learning about the law or the form**, 12 min.; and **Preparing and sending the form to the IRS**, 48 min. If you have comments concerning the accuracy of these time estimates or suggestions for making this form simpler, we would be happy to hear from you. You can write to the Tax Forms Committee, Western Area Distribution Center, Rancho Cordova, CA 95743-0001. **DO NOT** send the tax form to this address. Instead, see **General Information** for where to file.

Purpose

Employers and workers file Form SS-8 to get a determination as to whether a worker is an employee for purposes of federal employment taxes and income tax withholding.

General Information

Complete this form carefully. If the firm is completing the form, complete it for **ONE** individual who is representative of the class of workers whose status is in question. If you want a written determination for more than one class of workers, complete a separate Form SS-8 for one worker from each class whose status is typical of that class.

Location:

Alaska, Arizona, Arkansas, California, Colorado, Hawaii, Idaho, Illinois, Iowa, Kansas, Minnesota, Missouri, Montana, Nebraska, Nevada, New Mexico, North Dakota, Oklahoma, Oregon, South Dakota, Texas, Utah, Washington, Wisconsin, Wyoming

Alabama, Connecticut, Delaware, District of Columbia, Florida, Georgia, Indiana, Kentucky, Louisiana, Maine, Maryland, Massachusetts, Michigan, Mississippi, New Hampshire, New Jersey, New York, North Carolina, Ohio, Pennsylvania, Rhode Island, South Carolina, Tennessee, Vermont, Virginia, West Virginia. All other locations not listed

American Samoa, Guam, Puerto Rico, U.S. Virgin Islands

Send to:

Internal Revenue Service SS-8 Determinations P.O. Box 1231, Stop 4106 AUSC Austin, TX 78767

Internal Revenue Service SS-8 Determinations Two Lakemont Road Newport, VT 05855-1555

Internal Revenue Service Mercantile Plaza 2 Avenue Ponce de Leon San Juan, Puerto Rico 00918

Name of firm (or person for whom the worker performed services)

Name of worker

Address of firm (include street address, apt. or suite no., city, state, and ZIP code)

Address of worker (include street address, apt. or suite no., city, state, and ZIP code)

Telephone number (include area code) | Firm's employer identification number

Telephone number (include area code) | Worker's social security number

Check type of firm for which the work relationship is in question:
☐ Individual ☐ Partnership ☐ Corporation ☐ Other (specify) ▶

Important Information Needed To Process Your Request

This form is being completed by: ☐ Firm ☐ Worker

If this form is being completed by the worker, the IRS **must** have your permission to disclose your name to the firm.

Do you object to disclosing your name and the information on this form to the firm?
If you answer "Yes," the IRS cannot act on your request. Do not complete the rest of this form unless the IRS asks for it.   ☐ Yes ☐ No

Under section 6110 of the Internal Revenue Code, the information on this form and related file documents will be open to the public if any ruling or determination is made. However, names, addresses, and taxpayer identification numbers will be removed before the information is made public.

Is there any other information you want removed?
If you check "Yes," we cannot process your request unless you submit a copy of this form and copies of all supporting documents showing, in brackets, the information you want removed. Attach a separate statement showing which specific exemption of section 6110(c) applies to each bracketed part.   ☐ Yes ☐ No

Cat. No. 16106T

Form **SS-8** (Rev. 6-97)

Form SS-8 (Rev. 6-97)

Page **2**

This form is designed to cover many work activities, so some of the questions may not apply to you. **You must answer ALL items or mark them "Unknown" or "Does not apply." If you need more space, attach another sheet.**

Total number of workers in this class. (Attach names and addresses. If more than 10 workers, list only 10.) ▶ _____

This information is about services performed by the worker from _____ (month, day, year) to _____ (month, day, year)

Is the worker still performing services for the firm? . . . .   ☐ Yes ☐ No

● If "No," what was the date of termination? ▶ _____ (month, day, year)

1a Describe the firm's business . . . .

b Describe the work done by the worker . . . .

2a If the work is done under a written agreement between the firm and the worker, attach a copy.
If the agreement is not in writing, describe the terms and conditions of the work arrangement . . . .

c If the actual working arrangement differs in any way from the agreement, explain the differences and why they occur . .

3a Is the worker given training by the firm? . . . .   ☐ Yes ☐ No
● If "Yes," what kind? . . . .
● How often? . . . .

b Is the worker given instructions in the way the work is to be done (exclusive of actual training in 3a)? . .   ☐ Yes ☐ No
● If "Yes," give specific examples . . . .

c Attach samples of any written instructions or procedures.

d Does the firm have the right to change the methods used by the worker or direct that person on how to do the work? . . . .   ☐ Yes ☐ No
● Explain your answer . . . .

e Does the operation of the firm's business require that the worker be supervised or controlled in the performance of the service? . . . .   ☐ Yes ☐ No
● Explain your answer . . . .

4a The firm engages the worker:
☐ To perform and complete a particular job only
☐ To work at a job for an indefinite period of time
☐ Other (explain)

b Is the worker required to follow a routine or a schedule established by the firm? . . . .   ☐ Yes ☐ No
● If "Yes," what is the routine or schedule? . . . .

c Does the worker report to the firm or its representative? . . . .   ☐ Yes ☐ No
● If "Yes," how often? . . . .
● For what purpose? . . . .
● In what manner (in person, in writing, by telephone, etc.)? . . . .

d Does the worker furnish a time record to the firm? . . . .   ☐ Yes ☐ No
● If "Yes," attach copies of time records.

5a State the kind and value of tools, equipment, supplies, and materials furnished by:
● The firm . . . .
● The worker . . . .

b What expenses are incurred by the worker in the performance of services for the firm? . . . .

c Does the firm reimburse the worker for any expenses? . . . .   ☐ Yes ☐ No
● If "Yes," specify the reimbursed expenses . . . .

Form **SS-8** (Rev. 6-97)

FIGURE 2–1 Concluded

6a Will the worker perform the services personally? . . . . ☐ Yes ☐ No
  b Does the worker have helpers? . . . . ☐ Yes ☐ No
    ● If "Yes," who hires the helpers? ☐ Firm ☐ Worker
    ● If the helpers are hired by the worker, is the firm's approval necessary? . . . . ☐ Yes ☐ No
    ● Who pays the helpers? ☐ Firm ☐ Worker
    ● If the worker pays the helpers, does the firm repay the worker? . . . . ☐ Yes ☐ No
    ● Are social security and Medicare taxes and Federal income tax withheld from the helpers' pay?
             ☐ Firm ☐ Worker
    ● If "Yes," who reports and pays these taxes? ☐ Firm ☐ Worker
    ● Who reports the helpers' earnings to the Internal Revenue Service? ☐ Firm ☐ Worker
    ● What services do the helpers perform?

7 At what location are the services performed? ☐ Firm's ☐ Worker's ☐ Other (specify)

8a Type of pay worker receives:
    ☐ Salary ☐ Commission ☐ Hourly wage ☐ Piecework ☐ Lump sum ☐ Other (specify)
  b Does the firm guarantee a minimum amount of pay to the worker? . . . . ☐ Yes ☐ No
  c Does the firm allow the worker a drawing account or advances against pay? . . . . ☐ Yes ☐ No
    ● If "Yes," is the worker paid such advances on a regular basis? . . . . ☐ Yes ☐ No
    ● How does the worker repay such advances?

9a Is the worker eligible for a pension, bonus, paid vacations, sick pay, etc.? . . . . ☐ Yes ☐ No
    ● If "Yes," specify
  b Does the firm carry worker's compensation insurance on the worker? . . . . ☐ Yes ☐ No
  c Does the firm withhold social security and Medicare taxes from amounts paid the worker? . . . . ☐ Yes ☐ No
  d Does the firm withhold Federal income tax from amounts paid the worker? . . . . ☐ Yes ☐ No
  e How does the firm report the worker's earnings to the Internal Revenue Service?
    ☐ Form W-2 ☐ Form 1099-MISC ☐ Does not report ☐ Other (specify)
    ● Attach a copy.
  f Does the firm bond the worker? . . . . ☐ Yes ☐ No

10a Approximately how many hours a day does the worker perform services for the firm? . . . . . . ☐ Unknown
  b Does the firm set hours of work for the worker? . . . . ☐ Yes ☐ No
    ● If "No," explain
  c Does the worker set his own hours of work? . . . _____ a.m./p.m. to _____ a.m./p.m. (Circle whether a.m. or p.m.)
    ● If "Yes," what are the worker's set hours? _____ a.m./p.m. to _____ a.m./p.m.
  d Does the worker perform similar services for others? . . . . ☐ Yes ☐ No ☐ Unknown
    ● If "Yes," are these services performed on a daily basis for other firms? . . . . ☐ Yes ☐ No ☐ Unknown
    ● Percentage of time spent in performing these services for:
      This firm _____ % Other firms _____ %
    ● Does the firm have priority on the worker's time? . . . . ☐ Yes ☐ No
    ● If "No," explain

11a Is the worker prohibited from competing with the firm either while performing services or during any later
    period? . . . . ☐ Yes ☐ No
  b Can the firm discharge the worker at any time without incurring a liability? . . . . ☐ Yes ☐ No
    ● If "No," explain
  c Can the worker terminate the services at any time without incurring a liability? . . . . ☐ Yes ☐ No
    ● If "No," explain

12a Does the worker perform services for the firm under:
    ☐ The firm's business name ☐ The worker's own business name ☐ Other (specify)
  b Does the worker advertise or maintain a business listing in the telephone directory, a trade
    journal, etc.? . . . . ☐ Yes ☐ No ☐ Unknown
    ● If "Yes," specify
  c Does the worker represent himself or herself to the public as being in business to perform
    the same or similar services? . . . . ☐ Yes ☐ No ☐ Unknown
    ● If "Yes," how?
  d Does the worker have his or her own shop or office? . . . . ☐ Yes ☐ No ☐ Unknown
    ● If "Yes," where?
  e Does the firm represent the worker as an employee of the firm to its customers? . . . . ☐ Yes ☐ No ☐ Unknown
    ● If "No," how is the worker represented?
  f How did the firm learn of the worker's services?

13 Is a license necessary for the work? . . . . ☐ Yes ☐ No ☐ Unknown
    ● If "Yes," what kind of license is required?
    ● Who issues the license?
    ● Who pays the license fee?

---

14 Does the worker have a financial investment in a business related to the services
    performed? . . . . ☐ Yes ☐ No ☐ Unknown
    ● If "Yes," specify and give amount of the investment

15 Can the worker incur a loss in the performance of the service for the firm? . . . . ☐ Yes ☐ No
    ● If "Yes," how?

16a Has any other government agency ruled on the status of the firm's workers? . . . . ☐ Yes ☐ No
    ● If "Yes," attach a copy of the ruling.
  b Is the same issue being considered by any IRS office in connection with the audit of the worker's tax
    return or the firm's tax return, or has it been considered recently? . . . . ☐ Yes ☐ No
    ● If "Yes," for which year(s)?

17 Does the worker assemble or process a product at home or away from the firm's place of business? ☐ Yes ☐ No
    ● If "Yes," who furnishes materials or goods used by the worker? ☐ Firm ☐ Worker ☐ Other
    ● Is the worker furnished a pattern or given instructions to follow in making the product? . . . . ☐ Yes ☐ No

18 Is the worker required to return the finished product to the firm or to someone designated by the firm? ☐ Yes ☐ No
    Attach a detailed explanation of any other reason why you believe the worker is an employee or an independent contractor

Answer items 19a through o only if the worker is a salesperson or provides a service directly to customers.

19a Are leads to prospective customers furnished by the firm? . . . . ☐ Yes ☐ No ☐ Does not apply
  b Is the worker required to pursue or report on leads? . . . . ☐ Yes ☐ No ☐ Does not apply
  c Is the worker required to adhere to prices, terms, and conditions of sale established by the firm? ☐ Yes ☐ No
  d Are orders submitted to and subject to approval by the firm? . . . . ☐ Yes ☐ No
  e Is the worker expected to attend sales meetings? . . . . ☐ Yes ☐ No
    ● If "Yes," is the worker subject to any kind of penalty for failing to attend? . . . . ☐ Yes ☐ No
  f Does the firm assign a specific territory to the worker? . . . . ☐ Yes ☐ No
  g Whom does this customer pay? ☐ Firm ☐ Worker
    ● If worker, does the worker remit the total amount to the firm? . . . . ☐ Yes ☐ No
  h Does the worker sell a consumer product in a home or establishment other than a permanent retail
    establishment? . . . . ☐ Yes ☐ No
  i List the products and/or services distributed by the worker, such as meat, vegetables, fruit, bakery products, beverages (other
    than milk), or laundry or dry cleaning services. If more than one type of product and/or service is distributed, specify the
    principal one.
  j Did the firm or another person assign the route or territory and a list of customers to the worker? . ☐ Yes ☐ No
    ● If "Yes," enter the name and job title of the person who made the assignment
  k Did the worker pay the firm or person for the privilege of serving customers on the route or in the territory? ☐ Yes ☐ No
    ● If "Yes," how much did the worker pay (not including any amount paid for a truck or racks, etc.)? $ _____
    ● What factors were considered in determining the value of the route or territory?
  l How are new customers obtained by the worker? Explain fully, showing whether the new customers called the firm for service,
    were solicited by the worker, or both
  m Does the worker sell life insurance? . . . . ☐ Yes ☐ No
    ● If "Yes," is the selling of life insurance or annuity contracts for the firm the worker's entire business
      activity? . . . . ☐ Yes ☐ No
    ● If "No," does the worker sell other types of insurance for the firm? . . . . ☐ Yes ☐ No
    ● If "Yes," state the percentage of the worker's total working time spent in selling other types of insurance . _____ %
  n At the time the contract was entered into between the firm and the worker, was it their intention that the worker sell life
    insurance for the firm:
    ☐ On a full-time basis ☐ on a part-time basis
    ● State the manner in which the intention was expressed
  o Is the worker a traveling or city salesperson? . . . . ☐ Yes ☐ No
    ● If "Yes," from whom does the worker principally solicit orders for the firm?
    ● If the worker solicits orders from wholesalers, retailers, contractors, or operators of hotels, restaurants, or other similar
      establishments, specify the percentage of the worker's time spent in the solicitation _____ %
    ● Is the merchandise purchased by the customers for resale or for use in their business operations? If used by the customers
      in their business operations, describe the merchandise and state whether it is equipment installed on their premises or a
      consumable supply

Under penalties of perjury, I declare that I have examined this request, including accompanying documents, and to the best of my knowledge and belief, the facts presented are true, correct, and complete.

Signature ▶ _____ Title ▶ _____ Date ▶ _____

If the firm is completing this form, an officer or member of the firm must sign it. If the worker is completing this form, the worker must sign it. If the worker wants a written determination about services performed for two or more firms, a separate form must be completed and signed for each firm. Additional copies of this form may be obtained by calling 1-800-TAX-FORM (1-800-829-3676).

⑧

A: The worker should be treated as an employee during this time period pending IRS determination.

What Is an Independent Contractor?

An **independent contractor** is an individual who provides a service or a combination of goods and services to another individual or a business *and who is independent from the individual or business*. The key term in this definition is *independent*. The independent contractor must be independent in all respects from his customers or clients. This means that *independent contractors are truly in business for themselves,* and therefore have the responsibility to pay their own taxes, provide their own tools and supplies, and obtain and pay their own benefits.

Independent contractors generally agree to provide a service or goods to others by a specific date which may be agreed upon by a written or oral contract. The independent contractor is responsible for how the work is performed as well as the quality of the work performed. An independent contractor does not have to sign a written contract in order to be considered a contractor of services.

E X A M P L E 2

If you go to your medical doctor or dentist, that individual is generally providing a service for you without any written agreement. Your doctor or dentist is not your employee but an independent contractor who is providing you with specific services.

However, if you want a carpenter to add a sun deck to your house, both you and the carpenter probably will want to write up a contract that spells out the specific dimensions of the sun deck, what types of materials will be used, and when it is to be completed. In this case the carpenter is an independent contractor operating under a written contract with you.

One of the major payroll administration issues in classifying a worker is simply this: **Who is responsible for withholding and paying income and social security taxes on the worker's earnings?** A secondary issue is that of legal rights under the Fair Labor Standards Act and unemployment and worker's compensation coverage under federal and state unemployment tax acts. A third issue is how a worker's earnings will be reported to the government.

Misclassification of workers by employers has cost the federal and many state governments millions of dollars in lost tax revenue. The government in recent years has vigorously pursued enforcement of proper worker classification in order to recover unpaid payroll taxes, interest, and penalties that otherwise would not be collected and paid.

The employer's responsibilities are different when a worker is classified as an independent contractor. Figure 2–2 contrasts these differences in the areas of withholding and paying taxes and reporting earnings.

F I G U R E   2–2

Classifying a Worker as an Employee or an Independent Contractor

Employer responsibilities and activities	If the worker is classified as an employee	If the worker is classified as an independent contractor
■ The withholding of federal, state, and local income taxes.	Mandatory under federal, state, and local income tax laws.	There is no requirement for the employer
■ Complying with the Fair Labor Standards Act (FLSA).	The employer must follow the provisions of FLSA.	FLSA does not cover a worker classified as an independent contractor.
■ Withholding of FICA taxes and employer matching of FICA taxes.	Required under the federal Social Security Act of 1935.	There is no requirement for the employer. If the workers' earnings are $400 or more when classified as an independent contractor, the worker is subject to self-employment tax (known as SECA).
■ Paying federal and state unemployment taxes on worker earnings.	Required under the Federal Unemployment Tax Act and various state unemployment tax acts.	There is no requirement for the employer.
■ Reporting wages and earnings to the government.	Employer must use Form W-2 after the end of the calendar year.	The business that pays the independent contractor must use Form 1099-MISC if the amount is $600 or more.

Employer's Responsibilities

Correct classification of a worker is the responsibility of an employer. Improper classification by an employer may result in the IRS or another government authority assessing penalties and holding the employer responsible for uncollected taxes. The IRS is now aggressively examining employers who it suspects could be misclassifying workers to avoid the responsibility of withholding and remitting taxes.

The payroll professional should be aware of the rules for classifying workers and make every attempt to obey them. If the professional is in doubt as to how to classify a worker, the worker should be classified as an employee until a complete determination can be made.

Other Classifications of Workers

A worker who is not classified as an employee might not be an independent contractor either. Individuals such as insurance agents, real estate agents, outside salespeople, and direct sellers are classified as statutory employees. Under the statutory employee classification, an employer is responsible for withholding only social security taxes on earnings. A worker can also be considered a temporary agency employee or a leased employee. Figure 2–3 shows the employer's responsibilities for these classifications.

2 PAYROLL ROAD MAP: THE PROCESS OF HIRING EMPLOYEES

We are now a short distance from the starting point on our payroll road map. Our next point on the map begins with a discussion of the hiring process. We have summarized the numerous details of this process into 10 steps. Depending on the business and its size, the steps may become more detailed and specific. Our summary here provides you with a template you can tailor to your own business situation.

Hiring an employee is a process comprised of numerous important steps. Obviously the goal of the process is to find the right employee for the right job. The route required to meet this goal involves proper planning by management, good organizational structure, and a little luck. The process is not scientific but practical; in part, it is governed by federal laws. For the payroll or human resource professional, the process involves *obtaining, documenting,* and *verifying* applicant information.

F I G U R E   2-3

Employer Payroll Tax Responsibilities for Other Classifications of Workers

Worker classification	Examples of this type of worker	Who is the employer of this worker?	Are taxes withheld for this worker?	Who pays FICA taxes?
▪ Leased employee	Professional positions or special assignment employees.	The worker is the employee of the *leasing agency*.	Yes. The agency withholds all appropriate taxes.	The agency matches FICA taxes at 7.65%.
▪ Temporary employee	Clerical and many types of professional occupations.	The worker is the employee of the *temporary agency*.	Yes. The agency withholds all appropriate taxes.	The agency matches FICA taxes at 7.65%.
▪ Statutory employee	Insurance agents, traveling salespeople, and delivery drivers who receive commissions.	The worker is the employee of the company that pays the commissions to the worker.	No. Federal income taxes are withheld. Only FICA taxes are withheld for the employee.	The employer matches FICA taxes at 7.65%.

The final step in the hiring process occurs when an individual is hired. Upon hiring a worker, additional paperwork must be completed to comply with several federal and state laws.

Think of a medium-size or large company with which you are familiar. Most likely, the hiring decisions made for this company involve a formal, established hiring process. Such a business will make use of a personnel form, such as an employment application, when a job applicant makes initial contact with the company. The human resources department will then evaluate the information found on the employment application, verify its accuracy, and document the results of the verification for a manager(s) to review.

Ultimately the decision to hire an employee will most likely rest on the shoulders of one or more decision makers. These managers will rely partially on the documentation and verification of applicant information as well as their own intuition and judgment in deciding whether to hire a particular person.

Now consider for a moment a small business. The hiring decisions for a small business with only a few employees could be made directly by the owner of the business. If this is the case, the hiring process will be direct and might involve an employment application, the owner, and the prospective applicants for the position.

The Steps in the Hiring Process

Whether a business employs 10 or 100,000 workers, there are several steps in which all employers take part to some degree when hiring employees. We have summarized these steps in a generic manner so that they can be adapted to a specific business employment situation. Obviously, larger businesses probably follow all of the steps, while a smaller business could omit several steps in its process. This process can be generically outlined as follows:

- Establish or justify the need for an employee.
- Create or change the job description.
- Search for potential employees.
- Obtain information from applicants.
- Interview selected applicants.
- Verify applicant information.
- Select several "finalists" from those interviewed.
- Interview the finalists for a second time.
- Make a formal offer to the finalist chosen.
- Upon the person's acceptance, hire the individual and complete additional paperwork.

The first step in the hiring process is probably the least visible to employees. A manager or decision maker within the company must **establish the need to hire a person** for a new job position or justify hiring a worker to fill a vacancy for an existing job position.

In today's business world, it is an understatement to say that managers are urged to "do more work with fewer employees." A manager must be able to justify any newly created job position by showing that the money spent paying a worker to do the job will be recovered from increased sales revenue or cost savings by the business.

The same reasoning is applied when a manager wants to fill an existing job vacancy. The manager must answer the question, "Does the business still need an employee to do a particular job?" In many businesses, managers are put under pressure to restructure job duties among existing employees when a job vacancy occurs rather than hire another worker. The company saves money because it does not have to place another new employee on its payroll. This concept is referred to as *downsizing* or *rightsizing.*

Q&A:

Q: I'm starting a new business in which I'll hire two or maybe three employees. Do I have to follow all of these ten steps if the business I'm building is small?

A: Whether you hire one or one hundred employees in a new business venture, it is advisable to give careful thought and consideration to all of the ten steps, even if you consolidate or possibly eliminate several. Remember that hiring employees, a key part of the payroll accounting process, is the same regardless of the initial size of an enterprise.

The next step in the hiring process is **creating or changing a job description.** A job description outlines the nature of the job (full-time, part-time) and defines the qualifications a worker needs in order to perform the job well. The details, duties, and responsibilities of the job are also described. Figure 2–4 shows the job description for an accounting and payroll analyst for U.S. Route 66 Trucking, Inc.

It is important that job descriptions are accurately written and kept current so that a good match can be made between a person hired for a job and the requirements of the job. Anytime an existing job position must be filled, the job description should be reviewed and updated if necessary.

At this point in the hiring process, many medium and large companies will have their managers or decision makers use a formal request form to begin the process of filling a job vacancy. This form is often called a *request for personnel (RFP)* or a *personnel requisition.* This form (not shown here) contains general information about the position such as the title of the job, whether the job is full-time or part-time, the range of pay for the position, the date a worker is needed, and any special qualifications or requirements of the job (such as the ability to lift over 50 pounds). This form will be sent to the human resources department that will use the information in searching for candidates for the position.

The **search for potential employees** to fill a job position will vary depending on the size of the company and the type of job to be filled. A

F I G U R E   2 – 4

U.S. Route 66 Trucking, Inc.
Job Description
Accounting and Payroll Analyst
(Updated: March 1, 200X)

I.   Job information
❏ Full time (40 hours per week)
❏ Non-exempt (hourly) position
❏ Overtime projected after the end of each quarterly time period
❏ Reports to assistant controller, payroll manager, and director of human resources

II.   Minimum qualifications and education
❏ High school diploma, GED, or equivalent educational experience
❏ Good double-entry accounting skills required
❏ Must be detail oriented and have a willingness to be a "team player"
❏ Highly accurate data entry skills required (accuracy preferred over speed)
❏ Must have working knowledge of Excel®
❏ Must have working knowledge of a database program
❏ Any working knowledge of accounting software is very helpful
❏ Any working knowledge of payroll software is very helpful

III.   Job duties and responsibilities
   A.   Accounting duties
      ❏ Prepare bank reconciliations and reconcile them to the general ledger
      ❏ Data input of journal entries into general ledger using software program
      ❏ Assist in preparing working papers for interim financial statements
      ❏ Assist in department work overload situations and special projects
      ❏ Other various duties as assigned and required

   B.   Payroll and human resources department duties
      ❏ Update monthly spreadsheet schedules to calculate medical, dental, life,
         and long-term disability premiums that employees will pay
      ❏ Prepare and mail corporate benefit packages to all new employees
      ❏ Distribute enrollment forms for health and life insurance as required
      ❏ Ensure timely return of all enrollment forms from employees
      ❏ Assist human resources department personnel as required
      ❏ Assist the payroll manager in work overload situations
      ❏ Copying, faxing, typing, and database maintenance as required
      ❏ Other various duties as assigned and required

---

large company usually will first look within the company for any employees who are possibly interested in the job position. If the job cannot be filled by transferring an existing employee to the new job, the company will broaden its search outside the company. A small company will probably begin its search outside the organization to find qualified applicants for a job.

The search can also be conducted through the use of third-party employment agencies. Depending on the nature of the position or the size of the company, using a third-party agency might be a good idea. A company that does not maintain a human resources department or that wishes to remain anonymous in the employee search might rely on an employment agency to conduct the search.

Information must be obtained from any job applicants found through the employer's search efforts. The applicants will be asked to complete a job application and/or submit a résumé. The application form is an important document used in the hiring process. Segment 4 of this chapter discusses employment applications and résumés.

After individuals have completed employment applications or submitted résumés, a decision maker or manager in the human resources department will review the forms and decide on **the candidates who will be asked to interview for the job.** Usually there are several goals connected with interviewing candidates for a job opening. One goal is to clarify the information found on the employment application. Another goal is to obtain general impressions of the candidate as a potential employee of the company.

It is usually at this point in the hiring process that candidates will be separated into "potential employees" and "no-hires." The interviewing stage of the hiring process is not entirely objective, but it also must not discriminate against individuals in the process. Segment 3 of this chapter focuses on federal laws that influence hiring practices of employers.

The information given on the employment application or résumé should be verified by the employer. **Verifying applicant information** can be done in several ways. Many companies will use a standard *reference inquiry form* which asks questions about the applicant. This form will be mailed to the person listed as a reference on the employment application. A human resources manager will review a completed reference inquiry form to determine if the individual's background and prior work experience can be closely matched to the requirements of the job opening.

As an alternative approach, a company might send the people listed as references its own letter that verifies information about the employee. The employer could also call individuals listed as references on the telephone and discuss the candidate with them. Many human resource professionals prefer the telephone approach to get direct, straightforward feedback about the job applicant. No matter what approach is used, the results of the verification should be documented in writing in case there is a question about a person's qualifications or background in the future.

After the verification of information has been completed, the field of candidates will usually be narrowed to those people who appear to fit best with the job position. The employer may choose to **interview several finalists** for the position a second time.

Sometimes the **second interview** is longer in length, and more in-depth questions will be asked of the final candidates for the job position. Perhaps several people may interview a candidate at the same time so that the company can arrive at a mutual decision about the employment potential of each candidate. Interviewing candidates for a second time is not legally required, but many companies find it a valuable decision making tool when hiring employees.

As the hiring process draws to a close, the department manager(s) or decision maker(s) will select an individual believed to have qualities and experience that most closely match the qualifications and requirements of the job position. Upon making the final decision, the individual selected will be offered the job. **The job offer** might be made formally by letter, or the individual could be notified by telephone. The terms of the job offer (such as starting date, working hours, wages or salary, and any employee [fringe] benefit packages) should be outlined for the individual.

When the individual accepts the job offer, the human resources department will **complete paperwork** that is needed to place the employee on the company's payroll. A multicopy form will be prepared and forwarded to the payroll or accounting department that lists the new employee's name, address, job title, hourly rate or salary, and other payroll information. The form is generally referred to as a *hiring notice* (not shown here). One copy of the hiring notice will be kept by the human resources department while the other copy will be filed with the accounting or payroll department.

There are several forms that a newly hired employee must complete. When an employee's benefit package includes medical, life, or long-term disability insurance, the employee must complete the appropriate enrollment forms. These forms will be forwarded to the insurance company by the human resources department. Form W-4 and Form I-9 are two required forms new employees must complete and sign. We will discuss both of these forms in detail in Segments 6 and 7 of this chapter.

Our review of the hiring process divides the process into 10 basic steps leading to hiring an employee. Next we will discuss the federal laws that directly influence the decisions an employer makes in the hiring process.

3 SUMMARY OF LAWS THAT INFLUENCE THE HIRING PROCESS

There are several federal laws that prohibit discriminatory hiring practices. Such laws have been enacted as a response to many long-standing hiring practices that have been found to discriminate against certain individuals for various reasons.

Several major federal laws have been passed since the 1960s that directly impact the hiring practices of employers. Such laws deal specifically with the issue of discrimination in the hiring and promotion of employees. The four laws listed below are examples of the federal government taking action to insure that an applicant for a job position will be evaluated in a fair, equitable manner, without malice or prejudice:

- The Civil Rights Act of 1964.
- The Age Discrimination in Employment Act of 1967.
- The Immigration Reform and Control Act of 1986.
- The Americans with Disabilities Act of 1990.

The Civil Rights Act of 1964 (as amended) is a federal law that deals with discrimination against individuals on the basis of their national origin, sex, race, color, or religious beliefs. The specific section that deals with discrimination in hiring practices is known as *Title VII*. This section prohibits discrimination in employment based on the cultural, physical, speech, or language characteristics of any ethnic or people group of the same national origin. The Civil Rights Act will apply to any company that employs 15 or more workers.

The Age Discrimination in Employment Act of 1967 (as amended) specifically prohibits an employer from discriminating against any applicant between the ages of 40 and 70. One part of this law also restricts an employer from setting a certain retirement age for its employees unless specifically mandated by law (as is the case with a mandatory retirement age for airline pilots).

The Immigration Reform and Control Act of 1986 (IRCA) extended the antidiscrimination rules of the Civil Rights Act to include the *citizenship* of a job applicant. This law helps to protect legal immigrants against job discrimination based on their country of origin or current U. S. residency status. This law applies to any company that employs four or more people. The IRCA also requires newly hired employees to complete and sign the Form I-9 which is discussed in detail in Segment 6 of this chapter.

F I G U R E   2–5

Employers May Not Discriminate Based on the Following Criteria

▪ Age	▪ Marital status	▪ Religious beliefs
▪ Citizenship status	▪ National origin	▪ Gender
▪ Disabilities	▪ Race	▪ Skin color

The Americans with Disabilities Act of 1990 specifically provides protection for the disabled in the area of employment. The section of the act known as *Title I* prohibits discrimination of an employee based on an employee's handicap or disability.

Specifically, an employer may not use any of the following criteria to discriminate against hiring an applicant or limiting an employee from job opportunities within a company. Figure 2–5 recaps the characteristics and criteria.

Employers who claim to be *equal opportunity employers* are stating that their hiring practices are in compliance with the various provisions of the Civil Rights Act of 1964 and any subsequent amendments to it. A government agency, the **Equal Employment Opportunity Commission (EEOC)**, was created to monitor employer compliance with these laws and to investigate violations of the law as they occur. The EEOC is also responsible for enforcement of the Age Discrimination in Employment Act as well as other federal laws.

It is the responsibility of the company to insure that all applicants are treated equally and fairly when they apply for a job. The process of selecting a candidate for a position should be impartial and fair from start to finish.

The employer must also comply with any state fair employment laws which may prohibit discrimination in other areas. The human resource department and payroll professional must keep up with current federal and state laws (and any changes in the law) in this area. These and other employment laws will be discussed in more detail in Chapter 7.

4   THE EMPLOYMENT APPLICATION AND PERSONNEL FILE

As part of the search for qualified candidates for a position, a company may ask applicants to submit a résumé or to fill out an application for employment (or both). This step is essential in evaluating the qualifications of candidates.

A résumé is the creation of the individual looking for work, and it may or may not contain information that the employer requires of the applicant as part of the evaluation process. Most job seekers who prepare a résumé will emphasize their qualifications and skills rather then merely present past work information arranged chronologically. If a résumé does not contain information the employer needs in an application for employment, the candidate may be asked to complete an employment application in addition to submitting the résumé.

Company policy may dictate that *all* applicants for a position complete an application for employment whether they submit a résumé or not. The reason for this is that applications generally require the candidate to sign a statement attesting to the truthfulness of the statements made and authorizing the employer to verify applicant information.

An application for employment is a standardized way of obtaining the necessary information that will help in evaluating a candidate for a job. Although there are no laws that require applications to have a certain appearance, antidiscrimination laws govern the type of questions that can be asked on applications.

Any direct or indirect question that could disclose information relating to an applicant's race, marital status, religious preference, disability, sex, age, or national origin is prohibited. For example, **the following questions and statements should not be asked** on an employment application:

- What is your current age?
- What church do you attend?
- What is your religious preference?
- Where were your grandparents born?
- What is your nationality?
- List any disabilities you may have.

An employment application may ask about a historical event or ask a question in which a range is stated, such as

- Are you at least 18 but less than 72 years of age?

An application may ask for the dates of attendance for high school or college. The request for dates may be made optional on the part of the applicant, thus avoiding any potential misuse of the information to estimate the age of the applicant (in situations where such information might be interpreted as a potential attempt to discriminate based on age).

Figure 2–6 is a typical example of a one-page application form used by U.S. Route 66 Trucking, Inc. for hourly job openings. Personal data such as home residence address, social security number, level of education, work experience, and personal references are standard information requested on an application such as the example in Figure 2–6.

At the bottom of Figure 2–6, note that the applicant must sign the application certifying that the responses to the questions and information given are true, accurate, and complete to the best of the applicant's ability, and that the applicant is granting permission for the employer to make inquiries of any individuals listed as references.

Company policy should specify that a résumé or an application for employment should be retained on file for a stated period of time. Usually this time period is less than one year. During this period, the applicant will be considered for any job openings that the applicant may be qualified to fill. It is important that this policy is followed in the event that a question is raised regarding why a particular individual was hired for a job over another candidate.

The Employee Personnel File

Once an individual is hired for a position, a personnel file should be set up for the employee. The **personnel file** is a permanent record that contains information about the employee and the employee's work history with a company.

The employee's personnel file will contain both *pre-employment* information and *post-hiring* information. Common items that will be kept in a personnel file include the following:

- The employment application and/or résumé.

- Interviewer notes (if any).

- The hiring notice, stating the hourly wage or salary, benefits, working hours, supervisor assignment, and so on.

- Results of any employment physical exams.

- Results of any drug tests.

- Special documentation (such as security clearances, driving records, professional licenses).

- Performance evaluations.

F I G U R E   2– 6

One-page application for employment

APPLICATION FOR EMPLOYMENT	APPLICANT PLEASE NOTE:
U.S. Route 66 Trucking, Inc. Corporate offices and terminal: P.O. Box 66 Adrian, TX 79001	U.S. Route 66 Trucking, Inc. is an *equal opportunity* employer. We consider all applicants for all job positions without regard to race, color, creed, gender, age, national origin, religious beliefs, or any other legally protected status. No question on this application is designed or intended to limit any applicant's consideration for employment with U.S. Route 66 Trucking, Inc.

DMV License #_____ State:___

We appreciate your interest in working for U.S. Route 66 Trucking, Inc. Please print all of your answers. Thank you.

I. Position you are applying for: _____Today's date: _____

   ❏ Full time   ❏ Part time   Are you willing to work weekends? ❏ Yes   ❏ No

Your full name: _____ Social Security no. _____

Street address:_____ Phone no._____

City: _____ State:_____ Zip code:_____ How long have you lived there? _____

Your prior address: _____

City: _____ State:_____ Zip code:_____ How long have you lived there? _____

II. Your employment background: List your last three (3) employers. Any military experience or volunteer positions should be listed as an employer.

(1) Employer name: _____Phone no. _____

Address:_____

City: _____State: _____Zip code: _____Your salary or wages:_____

Your job title: _____Employment dates: From _____ To_____

Your supervisor's name: _____May we contact your supervisor? ❏ Yes ❏ No ❏ Later

(2) Employer name:_ _____Phone no. _____

Address:_____

City: _____State: _____Zip code: _____Your salary or wages:_____

Your job title: _____Employment dates: From _____ To_____

Your supervisor's name: _____May we contact your supervisor? ❏ Yes ❏ No ❏ Later

(3) Employer name: _____Phone no. _____

Address:_____

City: _____State: _____Zip code: _____Your salary or wages:_____

Your job title: _____Employment dates: From _____ To_____

Your supervisor's name: _____May we contact your supervisor? ❏ Yes ❏ No ❏ Later

III. Personal information: Please list high school, college, or other schools you have attended and give three (3) work/school/professional/personal references who know you but who are not related to you.

School(s) at-tended:	Dates: From/to: (optional)	Sub-jects/courses:	GPA/class standing:	Degree/diploma:

Reference name:	Address:	Phone no.:

Please read before signing: By signing this application you, as a job applicant, are certifying that all information you have provided to us is true and correct to the best of your knowledge. Any misrepresentation of information is cause for termination in the event you are hired. You furthermore agree to give us the right to investigate all references and release from any liability all references with whom we might communicate.

_____   _____

The Need for Confidentiality

Almost without exception in all personnel matters involving employees, **confidentiality must be maintained.** This is especially important with employees' personnel files. These files should be safeguarded so that only authorized individuals will have access to the files. Personnel files should be kept in a secure, locked area.

The information contained in personnel files should not be casually discussed by employees at a company-sponsored event or in the employee lunchroom. Any employee who comes into contact with personnel files or payroll accounting information has a corporate and ethical responsibility to insure that such information remains confidential at all times. Failure to maintain confidentiality could result in serious problems for the employees and the company.

5 FORMS SS-4 AND SS-5

Two forms that we wish to mention at this point in connection with the hiring process are the IRS Form SS-4 and the Social Security Administration's Form SS-5. Although these forms are indirectly related to the payroll accounting process, you might on occasion come into contact with them.

The Form SS-4

The Form SS-4 is known as *Application for Employer Identification Number.* (See Figure 2–7.) This form will be completed by a new company to obtain an EIN (employer identification number) from the IRS. Other reasons for completing and submitting this form include hiring employees (for the first time on payroll), changing the type of business, or creating a pension plan. (See question 9 in Figure 2–7.) The EIN (also sometimes called the TIN or taxpayer identification number) is key to filing other payroll federal tax reports and making federal payroll tax deposits. Figure 2–7 illustrates this form.

Once the Form SS-4 application is received and processed by the IRS, the service will begin mailing various payroll tax returns noting the business's name, address, and EIN. The IRS will also place the business on its mailing list to receive various notices and publications.

FIGURE 2-7

Form SS-4
(Rev. April 2000)
Department of the Treasury
Internal Revenue Service

Application for Employer Identification Number

(For use by employers, corporations, partnerships, trusts, estates, churches, government agencies, certain individuals, and others. See instructions.)

▶ Keep a copy for your records.

EIN

OMB No. 1545-0003

1 Name of applicant (legal name) (see instructions)

2 Trade name of business (if different from name on line 1) | **3** Executor, trustee, "care of" name

4a Mailing address (street address) (room, apt., or suite no.) | **5a** Business address (if different from address on lines 4a and 4b)

4b City, state, and ZIP code | **5b** City, state, and ZIP code

6 County and state where principal business is located

7 Name of principal officer, general partner, grantor, owner, or trustor—SSN or ITIN may be required (see instructions) ▶

8a Type of entity (Check only one box.) (see instructions)
Caution: If applicant is a limited liability company, see the instructions for line 8a.

- ☐ Sole proprietor (SSN) _____
- ☐ Partnership   ☐ Personal service corp.
- ☐ REMIC   ☐ National Guard
- ☐ State/local government ☐ Farmers' cooperative
- ☐ Church or church-controlled organization
- ☐ Other nonprofit organization (specify) ▶ _____ (enter GEN if applicable) _____
- ☐ Other (specify) ▶
- ☐ Estate (SSN of decedent) _____
- ☐ Plan administrator (SSN) _____
- ☐ Other corporation (specify) ▶
- ☐ Trust
- ☐ Federal government/military

8b If a corporation, name the state or foreign country (if applicable) where incorporated | State | Foreign country

9 Reason for applying (Check only one box.) (see instructions)
- ☐ Started new business (specify type) ▶ _____
- ☐ Hired employees (Check the box and see line 12.)
- ☐ Created a pension plan (specify type) ▶
- ☐ Banking purpose (specify purpose) ▶ _____
- ☐ Changed type of organization (specify new type) ▶
- ☐ Purchased going business
- ☐ Created a trust (specify type) ▶
- ☐ Other (specify) ▶

10 Date business started or acquired (month, day, year) (see instructions) | **11** Closing month of accounting year (see instructions)

12 First date wages or annuities were paid or will be paid (month, day, year). **Note:** If applicant is a withholding agent, enter date income will first be paid to nonresident alien. (month, day, year) . . . . ▶

13 Highest number of employees expected in the next 12 months. **Note:** If the applicant does not expect to have any employees during the period, enter -0-. (see instructions) . . . . ▶ | Nonagricultural | Agricultural | Household

14 Principal activity (see instructions) ▶

15 Is the principal business activity manufacturing? . . . . ☐ Yes ☐ No
If "Yes," principal product and raw material used ▶

16 To whom are most of the products or services sold? Please check one box. ☐ Business (wholesale)
☐ Public (retail) ☐ Other (specify) ▶   ☐ N/A

17a Has the applicant ever applied for an employer identification number for this or any other business? . . . . . ☐ Yes ☐ No
Note: If "Yes," please complete lines 17b and 17c.

17b If you checked "Yes" on line 17a, give applicant's legal name and trade name shown on prior application, if different from line 1 or 2 above.
Legal name ▶   Trade name ▶

17c Approximate date when and city and state where the application was filed. Enter previous employer identification number if known.
Approximate date when filed (mo., day, year) | City and state where filed | Previous EIN

Under penalties of perjury, I declare that I have examined this application, and to the best of my knowledge and belief, it is true, correct, and complete. | Business telephone number (include area code) ( ) | Fax telephone number (include area code) ( )

Name and title (Please type or print clearly.) ▶

Signature ▶   Date ▶

Note: Do not write below this line. For official use only.

Please leave blank ▶ | Geo. | Ind. | Class | Size | Reason for applying

For Privacy Act and Paperwork Reduction Act Notice, see page 4. | Cat. No. 16055N | Form **SS-4** (Rev. 4-2000)

The Form SS-5

The Form SS-5 (not illustrated) is known as the *Application for a Social Security Card.* The Social Security Administration is responsible for this form, and it can be obtained from a Social Security office. An individual who has not been issued a social security number should complete this form prior to employment.

We will now discuss two forms that are required by federal law to be completed by employees as part of the hiring process: the I-9 and the W-4.

6   THE I-9 FORM

Employers are required to verify that the individual they are hiring for a position is legally eligible to work in the United States. A federal law known as the **Immigration Reform and Control Act of 1986** (discussed in Segment 3 of this chapter) requires that each employee who was hired after November 6, 1986, complete a form known as the **I-9,** or *Employment Eligibility Verification.* (See Figure 2–8.)

The purpose of the **Employment Eligibility Verification** form is to insure that an employee, whether a citizen of the United States or not, is eligible to work in the United States. When the form is properly completed, the employer should be able to establish the employee's identity and eligibility to work in the United States.

Holding employers responsible for verifying that their employees are eligible to work in the United States helps prevent the hiring of aliens who are not legally authorized to work in the United States. Ultimately all workers benefit because employees who are eligible to work will also be protected by federal employment laws regarding minimum wage, overtime, and so on.

Employment Eligibility

A person seeking employment is eligible to work if that person is a U.S. citizen by birth or naturalization. If the person is an alien (that is, a citizen of another country), the person is eligible to work if the individual has filed the appropriate documentation with the *Immigration and Naturalization Service (INS)* or another agency of the U.S. government. The I-9 form serves two purposes from an employment standpoint. It assists in establishing 1) the employee's identity and 2) the employee's legal eligibility to work in the United States.

F I G U R E 2-8

Form I-9, Page One

U.S. Department of Justice
Immigration and Naturalization Service

OMB No. 1115-0136
Employment Eligibility Verification

Please read instructions carefully before completing this form. The instructions must be available during completion of this form. **ANTI-DISCRIMINATION NOTICE.** It is illegal to discriminate against work eligible individuals. Employers **CANNOT** specify which document(s) they will accept from an employee. The refusal to hire an individual because of a future expiration date may also constitute illegal discrimination.

Section 1. Employee Information and Verification. To be completed and signed by employee at the time employment begins

Print Name: Last	First	Middle Initial	Maiden Name

Address *(Street Name and Number)*	Apt. #	Date of Birth *(month/day/year)*

City	State	Zip Code	Social Security #

I am aware that federal law provides for imprisonment and/or fines for false statements or use of false documents in connection with the completion of this form.

I attest, under penalty of perjury, that I am (check one of the following):
☐ A citizen or national of the United States
☐ A Lawful Permanent Resident (Alien # A_____)
☐ An alien authorized to work until ____/____/____
(Alien # or Admission # _____)

Employee's Signature	Date *(month/day/year)*

Preparer and/or Translator Certification. *(To be completed and signed if Section 1 is prepared by a person other than the employee.) I attest, under penalty of perjury, that I have assisted in the completion of this form and that to the best of my knowledge the information is true and correct.*

Preparer's/Translator's Signature	Print Name

Address *(Street Name and Number, City, State, Zip Code)*	Date *(month/day/year)*

Section 2. Employer Review and Verification. To be completed and signed by employer. Examine one document from List A OR examine one document from List B **and** one from List C as listed on the reverse of this form and record the title, number and expiration date, if any, of the document(s)

List A	OR	List B	AND	List C
Document title: _____		_____		_____
Issuing authority: _____		_____		_____
Document #: _____		_____		_____
Expiration Date *(if any):* ___/___/___		___/___/___		___/___/___
Document #: _____				
Expiration Date *(if any):* ___/___/___				

CERTIFICATION - I attest, under penalty of perjury, that I have examined the document(s) presented by the above-named employee, that the above-listed document(s) appear to be genuine and to relate to the employee named, that the employee began employment on *(month/day/year)* ___/___/___ and that to the best of my knowledge the employee is eligible to work in the United States. (State employment agencies may omit the date the employee began employment).

Signature of Employer or Authorized Representative	Print Name	Title

Business or Organization Name	Address *(Street Name and Number, City, State, Zip Code)*	Date *(month/day/year)*

Section 3. Updating and Reverification. To be completed and signed by employer

A. New Name *(if applicable)*	B. Date of rehire *(month/day/year)* *(if applicable)*

C. If employee's previous grant of work authorization has expired, provide the information below for the document that establishes current employment eligibility.

Document Title:_____ Document #:_____ Expiration Date (if any): ___/___/___

I attest, under penalty of perjury, that to the best of my knowledge, this employee is eligible to work in the United States, and if the employee presented document(s), the document(s) I have examined appear to be genuine and to relate to the individual.

Signature of Employer or Authorized Representative	Date *(month/day/year)*

Form I-9 (Rev. 11-21-91) N

The individual must provide the employer with documentation that establishes the individual's identity and eligibility to work. The employer will examine the documentation and make the appropriate notation on the I-9 form. The employer may, at his option, photocopy the documentation and retain the I-9 form.

Figure 2–9, reproduced from Form I-9, shows the types of documentation that can be used by an employer to verify the employee's identity and eligibility. Please note that the I-9 divides the documentation into three lists: *A, B,* and *C.* If the employee submits a document found in *List A* to the employer, *only one document* needs to be submitted for verification. However, if an employee submits documentation found in either *List B* or *C,* the employer will need to examine at least two documents found in these lists. INS rules require that one document must be from List B and the other document from List C.

Any document submitted from List A establishes both the identity and eligibility of the employee to work which is why an employee only needs to submit one document from List A. Documents found in List B only establish the identity of an employee, while documents found in List C only establish the worker's eligibility for employment in the United States. This is why one document from List B and one from List C are required.

The employer cannot tell the employee which specific documents to submit; the choice of documents is up to the employee as long as the employee submits one document from List A or one each from Lists B and C. An employer also cannot refuse to accept a document because it has an expiration date in the near future.

Employer Responsibilities

The employer is responsible for insuring that each employee fills out the form and provides the necessary documentation that establishes work eligibility. The I-9 should be completed by the employee and verified by the employer no later than three days after employment begins. The employer is not required to verify that the documents submitted by an employee are genuine and authentic. The employer is expected to use common sense in examining the documents to verify that they apply to the employee and that they do not appear to be obvious forgeries.

The employer is required to keep Form I-9 and any photocopied documentation. The I-9 form should not be kept in the employee's personnel file, as its presence could be interpreted as providing information that could be

FIGURE 2-9

Form I-9, Page Two

LISTS OF ACCEPTABLE DOCUMENTS

LIST A		LIST B		LIST C
Documents that Establish Both Identity and Employment Eligibility	OR	Documents that Establish Identity	AND	Documents that Establish Employment Eligibility

LIST A — Documents that Establish Both Identity and Employment Eligibility

1. U.S. Passport (unexpired or expired)
2. Certificate of U.S. Citizenship *(INS Form N-560 or N-561)*
3. Certificate of Naturalization *(INS Form N-550 or N-570)*
4. Unexpired foreign passport, with *I-551 stamp* or attached *INS Form I-94* indicating unexpired employment authorization
5. Alien Registration Receipt Card with photograph *(INS Form I-151 or I-551)*
6. Unexpired Temporary Resident Card *(INS Form I-688)*
7. Unexpired Employment Authorization Card *(INS Form I-688A)*
8. Unexpired Reentry Permit *(INS Form I-327)*
9. Unexpired Refugee Travel Document *(INS Form I-571)*
10. Unexpired Employment Authorization Document issued by the INS which contains a photograph *(INS Form I-688B)*

LIST B — Documents that Establish Identity

1. Driver's license or ID card issued by a state or outlying possession of the United States provided it contains a photograph or information such as name, date of birth, sex, height, eye color, and address
2. ID card issued by federal, state, or local government agencies or entities provided it contains a photograph or information such as name, date of birth, sex, height, eye color, and address
3. School ID card with a photograph
4. Voter's registration card
5. U.S. Military card or draft record
6. Military dependent's ID card
7. U.S. Coast Guard Merchant Mariner Card
8. Native American tribal document
9. Driver's license issued by a Canadian government authority

For persons under age 18 who are unable to present a document listed above:

10. School record or report card
11. Clinic, doctor, or hospital record
12. Day-care or nursery school record

LIST C — Documents that Establish Employment Eligibility

1. U.S. social security card issued by the Social Security Administration *(other than a card stating it is not valid for employment)*
2. Certification of Birth Abroad issued by the Department of State *(Form FS-545 or Form DS-1350)*
3. Original or certified copy of a birth certificate issued by a state, county, municipal authority or outlying possession of the United States bearing an official seal
4. Native American tribal document
5. U.S. Citizen ID Card *(INS Form I-197)*
6. ID Card for use of Resident Citizen in the United States *(INS Form I-179)*
7. Unexpired employment authorization document issued by the INS *(other than those listed under List A)*

Illustrations of many of these documents appear in Part 8 of the Handbook for Employers (M-274)

Form I-9 (Rev. 11-21-91) N
FPI-RBK

used in a discriminatory way when evaluating the employee for promotion opportunities. The I-9 should be kept by the employer and should not be sent to the INS or IRS.

7 THE FORM W-4

Employees who are beginning a new job are required to complete an additional form known as the **Form W-4,** *Employee's Withholding Allowance Certificate,* shown in Figure 2–10. The payroll professional will use the information found on the Form W-4 to determine the correct amount of federal income tax to be withheld from each paycheck the employee receives. Chapter 5 discusses how the information from the W-4 form is used in calculating income tax.

Form W-4 Information

The specific information the employee must submit on the form is the *marital status* of the employee and the *number of withholding allowances* the employee is claiming. This information is used exclusively for determining the amount of income tax to be withheld from the employee—the

F I G U R E   2–10

Form W-4

information found on it may not be used to discriminate against the employee in the workplace.

The Form W-4 comes with instructions that will help the employee to determine the number of withholding allowances. As a rule, an employee's withholding allowances should equal the number of dependents the employee claims on his individual tax return plus an allowance for the employee. The amount found by using this rule may change if the employee marries, divorces, or has a child during the year.

In looking at the W-4 form in Figure 2–10, notice that the form requests the employee's name, residence address, social security number, marital status, the number of withholding allowances claimed, and any additional withholding the employee wishes to have deducted. Also there is an area to indicate if the employee is exempt from income tax withholding.

Exemption from Withholding

An employee could be exempt from having federal income tax withheld if, per the instructions found on the W-4, the employee is subject to both of the following conditions:

- The employee had no federal income tax liability last year and received a full refund of any income tax withheld.
- The employee expects the same condition to exist this year—no federal income tax liability *for the entire year.*

If the employee meets both of the above requirements, the employee should write the word *exempt* in the space provided for question 7 on the W-4 form.

Examples of employees who might be exempt from income tax withholding include certain students and retired individuals. Remember that **each employee must examine his or her tax situation to determine if an exempt withholding status is appropriate.** The fact that an employee is a student or retired does not automatically exempt the employee from income tax withholding.

Federal law does not require that the payroll professional assist the employee in completing the form. For example, the payroll accountant is not required to help an employee determine if he qualifies for an "exempt withholding" status. The determination rests entirely with the employee. The payroll accountant's only responsibility is to use the information found on the W-4 to properly calculate the income tax withholding for the employee.

An employee is entitled to revise and change a Form W-4 upon request. As mentioned above, reasons for changing a W-4 would include a change in marital status, birth of a child, or change in the number of withholding allowances to adjust for an over- or underwithholding situation. IRS Publication 919, *Is My Withholding Correct?*, gives detailed instructions for the correct calculation of withholding allowances. It can be obtained by calling the IRS at 1-800-TAX-FORM (1-800-829-3676).

The payroll professional should make every effort to use the new information to calculate withholding the first pay period after the new Form W-4 has been submitted. Form W-4 changes must be reflected in revised payroll withholding no later than 30 days after the new form has been given to the employer.

The employer must retain the completed W-4 form. General practice is to keep the form in the employee's personnel file. Some payroll and human resource professionals prefer not to keep W-4 forms in employee personnel files because they believe that the information contained on the W-4 form could be used in a discriminatory way when considering an employee for promotion. Whether the form is retained in the employee personnel file or in a separate file, the form is not given to the employee or generally sent to the IRS. Exceptions to this procedure are discussed below.

IRS Notification of W-4 Status

Normally, the IRS is not concerned with how an employee fills out a W-4 form. There is an exception to this rule. If an employee claims more than 10 withholding allowances, or if the employee claims an exempt withholding status and earns $200 or more per week, the payroll accountant is required to send a copy of the W-4 to the IRS. The payroll accountant still is obliged to withhold according to the information the employee gives on the W-4 form.

State Versions of the W-4 Form

In most states that require state income tax withholding, the Federal W-4 form can be used as a basis to calculate the amount of state income tax withholding. However, some states require the employee to complete a state withholding form. When this is the case, the employee will complete both federal and state forms that will be used for income tax withholding.

F I G U R E   2–11

Form M-4

FORM M-4
Print full name ... *Paul A. Kawolski*
Print home address ... *80 Garfield Street*

MASSACHUSETTS EMPLOYEE'S WITHHOLDING EXEMPTION CERTIFICATE   Rev. 7/98

Social Security No. *992-16-1510*
City ... *Marblehead* .... State ..... *MA* .... Zip Code ... *01945*

EMPLOYEE:
File this form or Form W-4 with your employer. Otherwise, Massachusetts Income Taxes will be withheld from your wages without exemptions.

EMPLOYER:
Keep this certificate with your records. If the employee is believed to have claimed excessive exemptions, the Massachusetts Department of Revenue should be so advised.

HOW TO CLAIM YOUR WITHHOLDING EXEMPTIONS

1. Your personal exemption. Write the figure "1". If you are age 65 or over or will be before next year, write "2". *2*
2. IF MARRIED and if exemption for spouse is allowed, write the figure "4". If your spouse is age 65 or over or will be before next year and if otherwise qualified, write "5". See Instruction C ....
3. Write the number of your qualified dependents. See Instruction D ......
4. Add the number of exemptions which you have claimed above and write the total.......
5. Additional withholding per pay period under agreement with employer $ _____
   A. ☐ Check if you will file as head of household on your tax return.
   B. ☐ Check if you are blind.   C. ☐ Check if spouse is blind and not subject to withholding.
   D. ☐ Check if you are a full-time student engaged in seasonal, part-time or temporary employment whose estimated annual income will not exceed $8,000.
   EMPLOYER: DO NOT withhold if Box D is checked.

I certify that the number of withholding exemptions claimed on this certificate does not exceed the number to which I am entitled.

(Date) *Dec. 29, 200X* .... (Signed) .... *Paul A. Kawolski*

THIS FORM MAY BE REPRODUCED

States such as Massachusetts, New York, and Alabama require that their own withholding allowance certificates be completed by employees. Figure 2–11 shows the Massachusetts Form M-4, *Employee's Withholding Exemption Certificate.*

Specifically note line 2. For Massachusetts purposes, an additional four withholding allowances are allowed for a spouse who is *not employed.* (If the spouse is employed, no additional withholding allowances can be claimed.) In such cases, the number of the employee's federal and Massachusetts withholding allowances will be different.

8   STATE NEW HIRE REPORTING REQUIREMENTS

With the enactment of a new federal law known as the **Personal Responsibility and Work Opportunity Act of 1996,** states are now required to compile lists of new hires for any company domiciled within their respective state. Such information is used by certain state agencies to help in tracking employees who have not paid previously court ordered child support payments.

This means that the employer must collect certain information on any newly hired worker and forward it to a specific state agency within a 7- to 20-day time period. This time period begins as of the new worker's hire date (different due dates apply if the information is transmitted via elec-

F I G U R E   2–12

Record Retention Requirements

Form number or name	Retention period	Comments
■ Employment application and/or résumé	■ 1 year from date received	■ Employers generally keep applications as a part of any employee's personnel file. "No-hire" applications should be retained for a one-year maximum period according to the FLSA.
■ Form I-9	■ 3 years from hire date or 1 year from termination date	■ Requirement is per the IRCA.
■ Form W-4	■ 4 years to indefinitely	■ Per the Internal Revenue Service, a current Form W-4 must be kept for all active employees. W-4s of terminated employees must be retained for four years.

tronic media). Please note that the reporting time period will vary by state. Information may include (but is not limited to) the information found on the employee's Form W-4; employee's name, address, social security number, and date of hire. Some states may also require additional information such as the worker's date of birth, employer's phone number, worker's medical insurance information (if any), and the employer's state unemployment insurance identification number.

It is important for the payroll professional to know the specific state requirements for his company's state of domicile, as well as other state's rules if the company is a multi-state employer. To obtain more information about specific state requirements, use an established Internet search engine and perform a search using a phrase such as "(Name of state) New Hire Reporting." The search engine should list the web address of the state agency charged with the collection of this "new hire" information.

Please note that there are employer penalties for failure to comply with this law within the specified state reporting time periods. It is to the employer's advantage to comply with this new federal law that is currently administered on the state level.

9 RECORD RETENTION REQUIREMENTS

The employer must follow certain federal laws regarding the length of time that application forms and Forms I-9 and W-4 must be kept. Depending on the form, different laws dictate the record retention period. Figure 2–12 summarizes the record retention period for the forms discussed in Chapter 2.

Figure 2–12 shows the legal minimum requirements for these forms. As a practical matter, a company may wish to keep these forms for a longer period of time in case legal action is taken by a current or former employee.

The method in which the information is stored is entirely at the option of the employer. Original forms can be kept in a filing system, or an employer may want to photograph the form in a microfilm or microfiche format. The information could be transferred to computer disk or CD media. The only legal requirement in this area regards retrieving the information—the employer must be able to recover the information within a reasonable period of time if the employer is audited.

State record retention requirements vary from state to state. Currently the minimum state time period is three years, while the maximum is seven years. The payroll or human resource professional should check with the specific state to determine the current legal period.

10 HUMAN RESOURCES SOFTWARE

In this chapter we have discussed the hiring process and have touched on some of the various job duties of human resources professionals. The personal computer has revolutionized the way businesses operate today, and the human resources function has not been left out of this revolution. We present an overview of several of the programs available for use in human resources and payroll administration.

If you look back at the hiring process, note that one step in the process is that of writing and updating job descriptions. One software company has created a program that will assist the human resource professional to write and customize job descriptions. The software contains a library of some 2,500 job descriptions (which represents approximately 90 percent of all jobs in the United States). The program has menu features allowing the user to select the most appropriate job duties for a particular description. It offers the flexibility of editing and modifying any standard description, or even combining two or more library descriptions.

You might be familiar with software programs that test certain skills of potential employees. Many companies use computerized testing to provide an accurate and objective way of assessing workers' abilities. Several programs are currently available that evaluate data entry skills, speed and accuracy in word processing, spelling and grammar usage, mathematical skills, database program knowledge, and the ability to work with spreadsheet applications.

The task of tracking employee attendance and time off from the job can be a difficult, tedious chore that is a necessary role of human resources. Software is now available that provides a detailed analysis of each employee's attendance record for a company. The software has been programmed to generate attendance reports for each employee, listing days at work and days off for various reasons such as personal or family leave, sick days, and vacation time. The program checks for chronic patterns in an employee's absences (such as Friday or Monday sick days) and will prepare a report listing employees in such situations. The software will also allow the user to design and build a master vacation schedule. The program will check for vacation schedule conflicts among employees. Custom reports can be prepared for management use.

There are many other programs that assist the human resource function. Programs are available that will electronically record and store time worked (or time card) data. Another software program assists the human resource department by providing 160 standard personnel forms that can be used and modified as necessary. There are programs that will help the user to design and update organizational charts. Still other programs allow a manager to design employee surveys using some 200 questions covering many topics of interest to management. The data can be ranked and processed by the program; the results can be printed out as graphs or custom reports for management purposes.

C H A P T E R 3

Laws Affecting Payroll Accounting and Administration

This chapter will provide you with a basic knowledge of some of the major federal laws that affect payroll accounting and administration and how such laws have created the need for payroll professionals in today's business arena. This chapter is not intended to substitute for professional legal advice in the employment law area—specific work situations requiring a legal opinion always should be addressed by an attorney specializing in the area.

1 THE EVOLUTION OF EMPLOYMENT LAW AND PAYROLL ACCOUNTING

Payroll accounting as a profession today can directly trace its beginnings and roots to the enactment of several major federal laws dealing with employment of workers and payroll taxes. Payroll accounting would no doubt be different today in its structure and function if there were no federal or state laws in place that directly affect how the payroll accountant does his job.

The purpose of federal employment law is to set standards that ensure equitable and fair treatment of workers in the areas of earnings, unemployment, and equality in hiring and promotion. Still other federal tax laws govern payroll taxation and withholding. These laws are part of what are commonly known as the *Internal Revenue Code of 1986 (IRC)* and the *Social Security Act of 1935.*

The Beginnings of Payroll Accounting

Prior to the enactment of federal laws, payroll accounting was simply a matter of tracking the hours employees worked, calculating the gross earnings of the employees, and paying the employees. Before the Social Security Act of 1935, the Fair Labor Standards Act of 1938, and the Current Tax Payments Act of 1943, there were no withholdings for social security taxes or federal income taxes and no federal law governing minimum wage. Many companies still paid employees in cash, and there were no federal standards for overtime or working conditions. Payroll accounting as a profession did not exist.

At various times in the history of the United States, the federal government passed legislation that imposed a federal tax on income as a temporary measure to raise revenue during periods of economic crisis. The federal income tax was not withheld from the earnings of employees, but rather individuals paid the tax by the filing of a tax return on an annual basis. The first federal income taxes were imposed in 1861 and again in 1864 during the Civil War. After the war ended, the tax was repealed. Again in 1893, the United States faced a depression and a large national debt, and passed an income tax law that was subsequently declared unconstitutional in 1895.

In 1909, Congress considered another income tax bill, which required amending the U.S. Constitution in order to become law. From 1909 through 1913, various states ratified the Sixteenth Constitutional Amendment which would allow the federal government to tax individuals on their income. Congress' intent to tax income became law on October 3, 1913, and remains in effect today. Figure 3–1 is a timeline showing the development of federal income tax in America.

Initially, employers did not withhold income taxes on the earnings of their employees. Paying federal income tax was an annual event for Americans at the start of each year. This arrangement worked well until World War II when many workers faced large tax bills after the end of each year. Many taxpayers had difficulty in coming up with the money to pay their income taxes once each year; this encouraged Congress to pass the *Current Tax Payments Act of 1943*. The law required employers to withhold federal income taxes each pay period which is known as **pay-as-you-go withholding**. Calculating income tax withholding became another duty of the payroll clerk of the 1940s.

Payroll accounting as a profession grew with the passing of various federal laws. The federal legislation of the 1930s and 1940s increased the

FIGURE 3-1

The Historical Development of Federal Income Tax in the United States

1814	■ First discussion of imposing a federal tax on income by Congress, but no law was passed at this time.
1861	■ First income tax law enacted by the Lincoln administration to help pay for the Civil War.
1864	■ Additional income tax law passed to fund the Civil War.
1871	■ Income tax laws passed during the Civil War were repealed.
1893	■ Congress passed another income tax act during a period of economic depression and crisis in the United States.
1895	■ The law passed in 1893 was declared unconstitutional and was repealed.
1909	■ Congress considered another income tax law. This meant that the Constitution had to be amended for the law to be properly enacted. The process of ratifying the Sixteenth Amendment to the Constitution began on a state-by-state basis.
1913	■ The 36th state ratified the Sixteenth Amendment, and federal income tax again became law on October 3, 1913. The tax was paid annually after individual taxpayers filed a return.
1943	■ The *Current Tax Payments Act* became law, requiring employers to withhold income taxes from employee earnings each pay period. Income tax withholding became a function of the payroll department.

Source: *The Politics and Development of the Federal Income Tax* by John F. Witte, 1985, The University of Wisconsin Press.

duties and responsibilities of payroll clerks. Figure 3–2 shows how federal law increased the duties of the payroll department.

As other legislation that affects the workplace is passed and made law, the duties and responsibilities of the payroll professional continually increase. Thus, the simple matter of paying employees during the earlier part of the twentieth century has developed into a legitimate profession due in part to the regulation of the workplace by federal and state laws.

2 DRAWING A BLUEPRINT FOR EMPLOYMENT LAWS

In order to properly discuss and understand the various federal laws that affect payroll accounting, it is important to know the basic purpose of each law and its application in payroll situations.

F I G U R E   3-2

As Federal Laws Were Enacted, the Duties of the Payroll Accountant Increased

1935   ■ Social security taxes must be calculated and withheld from employees' pay.

   ■ Employers must begin paying federal and state unemployment taxes.

1938   ■ Fair Labor Standards Act requires that employment and payroll records must be maintained by employers.

1943   ■ Federal income tax withholding is required by the Current Tax Payments Act.

The current federal law covers various areas of employment thereby directly impacting payroll accounting. We have defined these general areas in Figure 3–3.

F I G U R E   3-3

Major Areas Covered by Federal Employment Law

■ Wages and earnings	Areas of minimum wage and overtime pay
■ Tax withholding	Withholding laws for social security, Medicare, and federal income taxes
■ Workplace conditions	Laws and standards that create and maintain a safe and healthy work environment
■ Reporting requirements	Rules covering the preparation and filing of payroll tax returns
■ Benefits	Areas of employee pension plans and family medical leave
■ Anti-discrimination	Laws prohibiting discrimination in the areas of gender, age, race, and disabilities

Please note that the general areas impact the duties of the payroll professional as well as the hiring and promotion practices of a company. Human resource personnel must also follow federal laws prior to hiring an employee, and management should comply with the law when promoting employees.

In our discussion of federal law and payroll accounting, it is important to understand that the employer's trade or business activity will determine what specific rules apply in a given job situation. Figure 3–4 shows that federal laws divide employers into three major categories depending on the na-

F I G U R E   3–4

General Categories (and Examples) of Employer Activities for Federal Employment Laws

■ Agricultural activities	Any activity substantially comprised of raising or producing agricultural or horticultural commodities. These activities include produce and fruit farmers. Also included in the definition are the raising and maintaining of dairy, livestock, and fur-bearing animals, nurseries, plantations, truck farms, orchards, ranges, greenhouses, cotton ginning, and turpentine and gum resin production.
■ Nonagricultural activities	Any business whose activities are nonagricultural in nature.
■ Household or domestic activities	Household workers, maids, cooks, chauffeurs.

ture of the employer's business. Different rules and laws apply to the different categories and subcategories.

As an example, employers whose business is agricultural in its nature will follow different employment rules than a company that is not involved in agriculture. Farmers, ranchers, livestock growers, and fruit and vegetable growers are examples of agricultural employers. The same holds true for individuals or families who hire maids, housekeepers, cooks, butlers, chauffeurs, gardeners, or any other workers whose job activities are directly connected with maintaining a private residence. Such employers are considered household or domestic employers. In discussing any law, the payroll accountant must always determine into which category the employer falls and be aware that there are differences in applying these laws to the three categories of employers.

Q&A:

Q: From a payroll administration point of view, what are some of the major differences for the three major activities shown in Figure 3-4?

A: One of the first major differences is that of the application of federal payroll laws. Agricultural and non-agricultural activities have numerous differences when applying federal law to processing a payroll. Another major difference is found in the reporting requirements; an agricultural payroll is reported on different IRS forms than a non-agricultural payroll. Domestic household payroll administration and reporting also vary somewhat from both agricultural and non-agricultural payroll administration and reporting.

By far the majority of employers in the United States today are non-agricultural businesses. Therefore, the focus of this book is on the payroll procedures and rules for non-agricultural employment.

3 THE SOCIAL SECURITY ACT OF 1935

A major aspect of the Roosevelt administration's New Deal was the Social Security Act of 1935 which was the first federal law that had a direct impact on payroll preparation. This law established two major programs known as FICA (Federal Insurance Contributions Act) and FUTA (Federal Unemployment Tax Act) that would provide benefits to workers. Figure 3–5 illustrates the major parts of the Social Security Act of 1935.

Social Security Insurance

The first program, commonly known as *social security,* provides insurance benefits to workers or their dependents to help them financially as follows:

- In their retirement years *(old age insurance).*
- In the event that they become disabled prior to their retirement *(disability insurance).*
- In the case of death, benefits are paid to the surviving dependents and spouse of a deceased worker *(survivor's insurance).*

FIGURE 3–5

Major Parts of the Social Security Act of 1935

Federal Insurance Contributions Act (FICA)	■ Established social security insurance program 　■ Old age 　■ Survivor's 　■ Disability
Federal Unemployment Tax Act (FUTA)	■ Created federal unemployment insurance program ■ Created state unemployment insurance programs 　■ Benefits are provided to unemployed workers under each state program

These three insurance programs are technically referred to as *OASDI (old age, survivor's, and disability insurance)*. Most people prefer to use the more common terms *social security* or *FICA taxes*.

The specific law that provides this insurance is known as the **Federal Insurance Contributions Act (FICA)**. Under FICA, employees must make contributions into the fund up to certain earning limits each year. These contributions made by an employee must be matched by the employer on a dollar-for-dollar basis.

The Social Security Act was passed in 1935, and, according to the law, employees and employers were required to pay into this fund beginning in 1937. The original rate for social security tax was 1 percent of the first $3,000 each employee made in a calendar year. The maximum tax an employee would pay in 1937 amounted to $30. This 1 percent amount was matched by the worker's employer dollar for dollar, so the maximum contribution that was paid jointly by employee and employer was $60.

The rates and earnings limit amounts have risen more than nine times since 1937. The 2001 rate for social security tax is 6.2 percent. The 2001 earnings limit maximum is $80,400, upon which this tax is paid.

In the 1960s, an additional tax was approved to provide funds for the hospitalization costs of eligible individuals. This tax, which was passed into law in 1965, is known as *Medicare* or *hospital insurance* (abbreviated as *HI*). From 1965 to 1990, the earnings limit maximum for Medicare tax was the same dollar amount as the earnings limit maximum for social security taxes. As of January 1, 1991, the Medicare tax had to be shown and accounted for separately from social security tax (1.45%) due to the fact the Medicare earnings limit exceeded the social security earnings limit.

As of this writing, there is no earnings limit maximum for Medicare tax purposes. The Medicare tax will be paid on all earnings, as is the case with federal and state income taxes. Remember that the amount paid by an employee must be matched by the employer during each calendar year.

The Social Security Act also established a federal unemployment program known as the **Federal Unemployment Tax Act (FUTA).** This law requires each state to establish a *State Unemployment Tax Act (SUTA)* to provide benefits to workers who become involuntarily unemployed due to lack of work. Money to fund benefits are paid as a tax by employers. Under FUTA, an employer pays a tax to fund the federal program.

The federal tax is used for administrative purposes to ensure that each state is in compliance with federal requirements. The employer must also pay an unemployment tax to each state where employees work; this provides money for state operating funds. Each state fund is designed to provide unemployment benefits to workers who are involuntarily unemployed. Because the state funds provide the majority of unemployment benefits, the amount of tax paid into a state fund is greater than the amount paid into the federal fund.

The 2001 tax rate an employer pays on employee earnings for federal unemployment purposes is 6.2 percent of the first $7,000 each employee earns in a calendar year. The rate of 6.2 percent is offset by what is commonly known as a *normal credit* of 5.4 percent. The net effect is an effective FUTA rate of 8/10 of 1 percent (.008 expressed as a decimal). This credit is given to employers who meet two FUTA requirements. The first requirement is that the employer must pay into one or more state unemployment funds. The second is that the employer must be current with all payments into the state fund(s).

Q&A:

Q: What will be the total federal unemployment tax paid for an employee who earns at least $7,000 during a calendar year?

A: The total the employer will owe for any employee who earns at least $7,000 in a calendar year is $56.00. This amount is arrived at by multiplying the maximum earnings limit amount by the FUTA percentage as follows: $7,000 × .008 = $56.00. Obviously the amount will be less if the employee has earned less than the $7,000 maximum during a calendar year.

The percentage rate of unemployment tax an employer pays into a state fund is based on several factors. Among these factors is the length of time the employer has been in business, the dollar amount of tax paid into the fund, and the benefits that have been collected by former employees from the employer's account. These factors are commonly called an *experience* or *merit rating*. From a payroll accounting standpoint, the rate of state unemployment tax an employer pays could increase or decrease over time.

The earnings limit maximums for state unemployment taxes vary from state to state. The lower limit is the first $7,000 an employee earns in a calendar year. The upper state earnings limit was $28,400 in 2001. Be sure to check with the specific state in question before calculating a state's unemployment tax. For a listing of state unemployment agencies and their Web addresses, please see Appendix 3.

In the majority of states, unemployment taxes are paid by only the employer. A handful of states currently require employees to contribute to state unemployment or disability insurance funds. This situation could change in the future as employers find themselves paying more in total employment taxes and more workers become involuntarily unemployed.

Q&A

Q: Do employees ever have to pay their own federal unemployment taxes?

A: No, only the employer pays federal unemployment taxes.

As we have seen, the Social Security Act of 1935 brought about a significant change in payroll accounting due to its taxation and withholding requirements. A mere three years later, in 1938, another federal law, the Fair Labor Standards Act, would have a far-reaching impact on the American worker and on payroll accounting and administration.

4   THE FAIR LABOR STANDARDS ACT

In 1938, Congress passed legislation that would change the way America worked. The law, known as the **Fair Labor Standards Act (FLSA),** had then, as it does today, a direct effect on how employees are hired, paid, and promoted. This law is also referred to as the *Federal Wage and Hour Law* because it sets minimum standards that the vast majority of businesses must observe and follow.

FLSA is a complex and lengthy law that has been amended and changed in the last half-century. The law can be divided into five major parts or provisions that govern payroll accounting and administration. These provisions or standards deal with the following:

- Minimum wage.
- Overtime earnings.
- Equal pay.
- Employment of young people.
- Keeping payroll and personnel records.

Employers Subject to the Fair Labor Standards Act

The intent of Congress in passing this law was to ensure that the great majority of businesses would have to comply with the provisions of the law. The way to ensure compliance with the law was to create and apply a simple test to the business activity of an employer. The test involves the employer's *interstate commerce activities.*

For FLSA test purposes, interstate commerce is defined in a broad sense. **Interstate commerce** is any business activity, such as buying, selling, or communicating that occurs between one business and another in different states. For example, a business whose employees make long-distance phone calls to a business in another state is considered to be engaged in interstate commerce for purposes of the Fair Labor Standards Act.

The original FLSA interstate commerce test was applied to the activities of individual employees of a business. This test, known as the *individual test,* states that if employees either were directly engaged in *interstate commerce* or produced goods that were shipped across state lines, the employer was subject to FLSA.

Some types of businesses, such as certain retail stores, initially did not qualify under this test. The law was later amended to include employers who were not subject to FLSA under the individual test. This second measure is called the *enterprise test.* Under the enterprise test, some businesses that would otherwise not qualify are still required to obey FLSA. A business must comply with FLSA if two conditions are met:

- The business exceeds an annual dollar amount of gross sales.
- Two or more employees within the business are engaged in interstate commerce activities.

Before April 1, 1990, a retail business would qualify under the enterprise test if it had sales of $362,500. A nonretail business would qualify with sales of $250,000 or more in a year. After April 1, 1990, these limits were raised to $500,000 for both retail and nonretail businesses. The earlier 1990 rules still apply to any business in operation prior to April 1, 1990.

Still other businesses automatically qualify based on their business activities. Hospitals, nursing homes, schools, institutions that care for the aged, sick, disabled or mentally ill, and public agencies fall into this category no matter what their annual gross sales volume.

One type of employer that is granted an exception to FLSA is a family business. A family business that only employs immediate family members is not subject to FLSA for those individuals. However, if the business also employs individuals who are not immediate family members, it could lose its exemption and be treated as any other business.

By applying the individual and enterprise tests, most employers find they must comply with the various parts of FLSA. The major parts of the law are discussed below.

Q&A

Q: I'm not certain if my small business would be covered by FLSA. Do I need to follow FLSA rules regarding paying workers?

A: It would be advisable to follow FLSA and its regulations until you can obtain a legal opinion from a qualified employment law attorney regarding the business' status.

Minimum Wage Requirements

The Fair Labor Standards Act established a federal minimum wage of 25 cents per hour in 1938. This minimum has increased over the years to its January 2001 rate of $5.15 per hour. Figure 3–6 shows the increases in minimum wage over the last 50 years. The minimum wage is a controversial issue with both businesses and lawmakers because many believe that increases in the minimum wage could trigger price increases and inflation.

Some states (e.g., California) might impose a higher minimum wage than FLSA does. In those states, an employer must comply with the state law. A state employment law can legally increase a minimum set by federal law—it cannot, however, lower a federal standard. For example, as of January 1, 2001, the minimum wage in the state of California was increased to $6.25 per hour while the federal minimum as of the same date remains at $5.15 per hour. In Alaska, the state minimum wage is based on the federal minimum wage and is always $.50 per hour greater than the federal minimum wage.

F I G U R E   3–6

The Rise in the Federal Minimum Wage from 1938 to 2001

▪ 1938	$ .25	▪ 1974	$2.00
▪ 1940	$ .30	▪ 1980	$3.10
▪ 1950	$ .75	▪ 1981	$3.35
▪ 1956	$1.00	▪ 1990	$3.80
▪ 1963	$1.25	▪ 1991	$4.25
▪ 1967	$1.40	▪ 1997	$5.15

Source: *USA Today,* August 31, 1993. Updated January 2001.

In 1989, federal lawmakers passed a *training wage* for young people under the age of 20. The training wage was 85 percent of the existing federal minimum wage for those between the ages of 16 and 20 who are employed for the first time in a job. If an employee met the qualifications, the employee would be paid this training wage for the first 90 days of employment on his first or second job. This law was enacted to encourage employers to hire youth who did not possess extensive job skills. This provision of FLSA expired on March 31, 1993.

New legislation passed in July 1996 (The Small Business Job Protection Act) now allows employers to pay a *youth opportunity wage* of $4.25 per hour for the first 90 days of employment. In order to pay the training wage, other specific conditions such as the following must be met:

- The employee is aged 19 or younger;
- The employee is in his initial 90 days of employment with the employer;
- The youth opportunity wage employee is not being utilized by the employer to "displace" any other existing employee who is paid more per hour.

Employees who receive tips as part of their regular income (e.g., waiters, waitresses) may receive less than the current minimum wage if their tips on average equal the current minimum. See Section C, Chapter 9, "Tips and Taxes" for a detailed discussion of how this works.

Another major provision of FLSA deals with paying employees a higher rate for extra hours worked each week. This higher rate of pay is called *premium* or *overtime pay.* The standard rule under FLSA states that an employee must be paid at a rate of 1.5 times the employee's regular rate of pay for any hours worked in excess of 40 in a workweek. A key part of determining if an employee will receive overtime pay lies in the definition of the term *workweek.*

The Fair Labor Standards Act Workweek

A **workweek** has a specific definition under FLSA. A workweek can be defined as seven 24-hour consecutive days (or 168 consecutive hours) that can begin at any time on any day in a week. This period of time is used to measure the number of hours an employee works. If the employee works over 40 hours during this 168 consecutive-hour period, the employee is entitled to overtime pay under FLSA.

Employers are not allowed to arbitrarily switch workweeks in order to avoid paying overtime earnings. Employers, however, may establish different workweeks for different groups of employees or divisions of a business.

FLSA grants an exception to an employer who employs workers in any of four areas:

- Executive.
- Administrative.
- Professional occupations.
- Salespeople.

These terms are defined specifically under the law so that an employer cannot merely classify an employee into one of these groups to avoid paying overtime earnings. An employee can correctly be grouped into one of the above categories based on the earnings of the employee and the job duties and responsibilities of the employee. Figure 3–7 outlines the earnings and job responsibilities for each of these four groups of workers.

FLSA established the concept of *equal pay for equal work,* which was a move forward in eliminating discrimination using earnings as a factor. The law states that an employer must be able to justify any differences in the earnings of two or more employees who perform the same job. The law allows for differences in the earnings of employees based on seniority with the company or based on the employee's performance on the job. The law also allows a company to comply with the specifics of labor union agreements regarding employee earnings.

FLSA has specific restrictions regarding employment of young people under the age of 18. The restrictions are designed to prevent the abuse of young people who are going to school and working at the same time. Specific rules apply depending on the young person's age. Figure 3–8 summarizes federal rules. Please note that many state labor laws regarding child labor are more restrictive than the federal statutes. It is advisable to check the state and local laws in your area before offering employment to a minor.

FLSA established record-keeping requirements for employers. Information that must be kept on each employee includes name and address, rate of pay, hours worked, and cumulative totals.

Employers generally obtain the necessary information that must be maintained under FLSA from the following records and documents:

- Personnel applications and résumés.

F I G U R E 3–7

Types of Job Occupations Exempt from Overtime Under FLSA

Job classification	Job description or occupation, duties and responsibilities
Executive	• Manages a department or some part of a company • Can hire and terminate workers • Has various decision-making responsibilities • Directly supervises two or more employees • Earnings must be at least $155 per week • Any time spent working in a non-executive capacity must be no more than 20 percent of the total time spent on the job (40 percent for retailers)
Administrative	• School administrators such as principals and department heads • Executive secretaries and administrative assistants • Retail managers and buyers • Various staff employees in a company
Professional occupations	• News announcers and news editors • Computer professionals such as software engineers, systems analysts, programmers, business analysts • Teachers • Nurses • Lawyers
Salespeople	• Outside salespeople • Auto and truck salespeople working in dealerships

- Time card or time sheet data.
- Records of employees' pay.

FLSA and other federal laws require that information about an employee be kept for various periods of time. Currently, the shortest length of time is two years, and the longest is five. As a practical matter, some professionals suggest that employers maintain such information for an indefinite period of time (beyond five years), in the event of any legal action that could be taken by a former employee against the employer. See Figure 3–9 for a general list and time periods.

General Rules for Employing Young People Under the Age of 18

If the young person is under the age of 14	▪ Job occupations are restricted. Occupations allowed are: ▪ Newspaper delivery ▪ Various jobs when employed by parent ▪ Some agricultural jobs
If the young person is 14 or 15 years old	▪ May work before or after school hours in various non-farm, non-manufacturing, non-mining, and non-hazardous jobs ▪ May work from 7:00 A.M. until 7:00 P.M. during the school year. Hours are extended to 9:00 P.M. from June 1 through Labor Day. ▪ Working hours are restricted during the school year: ▪ 3 hours maximum after school while attending school ▪ 18 hours per week maximum ▪ Working hours outside of the school year: ▪ 8 hours per day maximum ▪ 40 hours per week maximum
If the young person is 16 or 17 years old	▪ Job duties must be of a non-farm and a non-hazardous nature. Examples of hazardous duties are: ▪ Manufacturing jobs ▪ Operating cutting equipment ▪ Operating heavy equipment

FLSA and other federal laws are not specific about *how* such information must be maintained. An employer can use any storage media (e.g., computer disk, CD-ROM, or microfiche) for keeping the information.

There is a requirement that the employer must be able to retrieve and view the information from the storage format it selects. If the information has been stored in a format that is now obsolete, it must also maintain equipment capable of extracting the information in that format. The employer must also provide copies or a transcript of the information it has stored if requested.

5   OTHER LAWS THAT AFFECT PAYROLL ACTIVITIES

Other federal laws impact the hiring and promoting of workers in a business. Such laws will affect the hiring and payroll procedures of the employer. These major laws are shown in Figure 3–10.

FIGURE 3–9

Time Periods for Retaining Information Related to Payroll

Minimum retention period in years	Applies to	Examples of records that should be retained
2 years	Certain employer payroll documents	Time cards or sheets, work schedules for teams or departments, tables or documents showing wage rates, etc.
3 years	Immigration Reform and Control Act and the Fair Labor Standards Act	I-9 forms and various payroll records (payroll registers, employee earnings records, etc).
3 Years	Family Medical Leave Act	Employee names, addresses, leave dates, compensation, notices to employee, etc.
4 years	Internal Revenue Service, Social Security Administration, and Federal Unemployment Tax Act	W-2s, W-3s, W-4s, 940s, 940-EZs, 941s, checks, employee information (found on an application), various tax returns and tax deposit information (copies).
5 years	Occupational and Health Safety Administration	Documents such as accident reports, on-the-job mishaps, and records of employee illnesses.

The Equal Pay Act

This law was passed in 1963 and helps support and expand the equal pay for equal work provision of the Fair Labor Standards Act. Specifically, the law prevents discrimination in the area of earnings based on the gender of the employee. This means that two employees, one female and the other male, performing the same job tasks should be paid the same rate of pay.

Even though this law was implemented in 1963, a recent news service survey indicated that women earn approximately 72 percent of what men earn in the workplace. Complete equality in this area is yet to come; how-

F I G U R E   3–1 0

Other Federal Laws That Affect Workers
and Payroll Accounting

1963	The Equal Pay Act (as amended)
1964	The Civil Rights Act, Title VII (as amended)
1967	Age Discrimination in Employment Act (as amended)
1970	The Occupational Safety and Health Act
1974	Employee Retirement Income Security Act
1986	Immigration Reform and Control Act
1987	Employee Polygraph Protection Act
1990	Americans with Disabilities Act
1993	Family and Medical Leave Act

ever, passage of this law has brought about some positive changes in this area of employment.

The Civil Rights Act (Title VII)

This 1964 law provided major reform in the area of discrimination in the workplace. It specifically prohibits discrimination in the workplace based on the following:

- Race.
- National or ethnic origin.
- Gender.
- Religious beliefs.

Employers may not discriminate in hiring, promoting, earnings, fringe benefits, job training, or other areas of employment based on any of the above characteristics or beliefs of its employees.

Most employers are subject to the rules of the Civil Rights Act. Any employer who is engaged in interstate commerce and employs 15 or more workers for a period of 20 or more weeks in the current or prior year must follow the Civil Rights Act.

The **Equal Employment Opportunity Commission (EEOC)** is the federal agency charged with monitoring the Civil Rights Act. The EEOC is also responsible for enforcing the Equal Pay Act of 1963.

Age Discrimination in Employment Act

This 1967 law prohibits discrimination against women and men who are 40 years of age or older. Specifically, the law prohibits discrimination on the basis of age in hiring, promoting, earnings, or any other area of employing workers. The law applies to the majority of employers as well as the federal, state, and local governments and labor union organizations. Another key element of this law prohibits the mandatory retirement of employees at a certain age. The EEOC is responsible for enforcement of this law.

The Occupational Safety and Health Act

This 1970 federal law has had a major impact on U.S. industry. The intent of this law is to protect workers by promoting job safety and safe working conditions. Employers are required to keep their places of employment free from any hazards that could cause (or are causing) workers harm, injury, or death. Employees likewise must be responsible for following health and safety standards and rules, and they are responsible for their own conduct on the job.

The act is enforced by the Occupational Safety and Health Administration (OSHA), an agency of the U.S. **Department of Labor**. OSHA employs inspectors who vigorously enforce the rules of this law. Although this law does not directly relate to the hiring of employees, the payroll professional should be aware of its existence and the impact it has on employees and businesses.

Employee Retirement Income Security Act

This act (known as *ERISA*), passed in 1974, was the first federal law designed to regulate employee pension plans. Prior to enactment of this law, some employees with many years of service would lose benefits due to vesting problems, while other plans lacked enough funding to provide benefits to employees who retired. ERISA was passed by Congress to help prevent these and other similar problems.

ERISA specifically (1) provides rules for employee participation in pension plans and vesting requirements, (2) gives guidelines for managing the plan and its assets as well as disclosure of plan information to employees and other interested parties, and (3) provides insurance coverage for certain types of pension plans. This act is enforced by the U.S. Department of Labor.

Immigration Reform and Control Act

This 1986 law (known as IRCA) is designed to help prevent illegal immigration into the United States by requiring employers to verify an individual's eligibility to work, based on citizenship or legal-alien status. The IRCA is enforced by the **Immigration and Naturalization Service (INS).**

Employers are required to have any employee hired after November 6, 1986, complete a Form I-9 (Employment Eligibility Verification Form). The employee must produce identification that verifies both identity and authorization to work in the United States. (Refer to our discussion of this form in Chapter 2.)

Employee Polygraph Protection Act

This 1987 law generally prohibits the use of polygraph (lie detector) tests before hiring and during the course of a worker's employment. Employers whose gross receipts are $500,000 or more in a year or who are engaged in interstate commerce with other businesses are subject to this law. Companies are barred from (1) requiring or requesting their workers to submit to lie detector tests, and (2) terminating, discriminating against, or penalizing any employee who refuses to submit to such a test.

Certain exceptions apply to security services and companies in the pharmaceutical industry. These companies may give polygraph tests under strict rules and guidelines. Employees retain the right to receive a written notice before testing and to refuse or discontinue a test.

Americans with Disabilities Act

This act was signed into law in 1990. It provides protection to job applicants and employees from discrimination based on a disability. The law covers hiring, promoting, compensation, fringe benefits, job training, and other areas of employment. Employers who are subject to this law must also provide reasonable accommodations (e.g., ramps, walkways, or special equipment) to help workers with disabilities to perform their job duties.

Q&A

Q: Should the employer inform employees about these laws?

A: Yes. Employers generally communicate information about these laws by using posters that summarize the points of employment law. Such posters should be posted in a common area (such as a lunch room or by a time clock).

This law has proven to be controversial because it originally did not clearly define a disability. The scope of this act will become more clearly defined as more cases involving worker disabilities are brought to court.

Family and Medical Leave Act of 1993

This law (abbreviated as *FMLA*) requires certain employers to provide up to 12 weeks of unpaid leave to eligible employees for some family and medical situations. Specifically, an employee can be covered by this law if he has worked for an employer for at least one year and has worked 1,250 hours within the last 12-month period. The employee must be one of at least 50 employees within 75 miles of each other—this rule is designed to prevent employer staffing problems in certain geographic areas.

When the employee is covered by FMLA, the employee can be granted unpaid leave due to the birth or adoption of a child; to care for a spouse or child who has a serious health condition; and for an employee's own serious health condition that prohibits the employee from working.

Employers are prohibited from terminating or discriminating against any employee who takes leave under FMLA, or from interfering with any rights granted under this law. The employer must also maintain the employee's health insurance under a group plan and restore the employee to his original position in a company (or an equivalent position) when the employee returns to work.

Federal Laws Dealing with Government Contracts and Contractors

Noted here are three major federal laws that govern certain payroll matters if the employer is a contractor (or in some cases sub-contractor) for the federal government. The Davis-Bacon Act of 1931 applies to federally funded construction projects. A contractor or sub-contractor must comply with the rules set forth under this Act if a contractor has been awarded a contract in the amount of at least $2,000. The Walsh-Healy Public Contracts Act of 1936 applies to companies who manufacture and/or furnish materials, supplies, or equipment. This Act applies when the company has a contract with the federal government greater than $10,000. The McNamara-O'Hara Service Contracts Act of 1965 applies to companies with federal contracts of $2,500 or more who provide services to the federal government.

Generally, if a company is regulated by one or more of the above three laws, it must comply with several payroll regulations. Such regulations cover minimum wage and fringe benefits, overtime, and maintaining sanitary and safe working environments. The regulations also prohibit the employment of minors (under 16 years of age), prison laborers, and any "kickbacks" or rebates from employees to the employer.

The payroll professional should make it a priority to stay current with the changes in federal and state employment laws. As shown in Figure 3–10, it is expected with the passing of time that more acts of this type will be written and made law by members of Congress.

Tracking Working Time and Calculating Earnings

CHAPTER 4
Calculating Gross Pay

In Section B on our road map, we stop first to do some arithmetic and calculate the wages and salaries of employees. Specifically in this chapter, we discuss how to calculate the gross earnings for employees based on the hours worked or time spent on a job. Other topics covered are the ways that employers keep track of employee working hours, different ways of compensating employees, and how overtime earnings are computed.

1 ACTIVITIES FOR WHICH EMPLOYEES ARE PAID

If most people were asked what their employer paid them to do, they would probably respond, "For doing my job!" The question seems simple enough, but when calculating regular earnings and overtime pay, the payroll professional needs to specifically define the duties for which employees can be compensated.

For most people, the time spent on a job each day occupies the better part of their waking hours. Activities that focus around the actual time spent on the job consume time as well. Consider the fact that an employee who works during the day has to get up, shower, dress, eat breakfast, and commute to work before the working day begins. These activities are known as **before-the-job** or **prejob activities.**

Likewise, activities that take place after work ends, such as the commute home or playing on a company-sponsored softball team, are generally

73

not compensated by employers. Payroll professionals refer to such activities as **after-the-job** or **postjob activities.**

On-the-Job Activities

The payroll professional needs to define what constitutes a given employee's job duties in order to properly calculate the earnings for the employee. The employee will be paid for what can be called *on-the-job activities*. These are activities that have been identified in an employee's job description.

The payroll professional must distinguish between on-the-job activities and those activities that occur both before and after the employee's work activities. The professional must make this distinction so that the employee will be paid only for on-the-job activities and any job-related duties that are required of the employee.

An employer could have to pay an hourly employee for certain activities performed prior to or after the usual on-the-job activities. Consider the following example of a work situation in a doctor's office.

E X A M P L E 1

Jessica is a receptionist for a doctor's office. She is paid on an hourly basis, and her usual working hours are 8 A.M. to 4 P.M., Monday through Friday. Her immediate supervisor, Dr. Jones, gives her $20 on Thursday evening and asks her to stop by the doughnut shop Friday morning on her way to work to buy doughnuts for the office. Going to the doughnut shop requires an extra 20 minutes of travel time.

Solution to Example 1

Jessica's employer might have to pay her for the extra time spent in buying doughnuts because her boss told her to do so; therefore, the activity is directly related to her job duties for Friday. As a rule, an hourly employee will be compensated for any before- or after-the-job activities that are required as part of performing the usual on-the-job duties or per the request of an immediate supervisor.

E X A M P L E 2

Jessica is required to help with a seminar that Dr. Jones is giving on a Tuesday evening at a local health clinic. She is asked to distribute programs to guests and help them with finding seats. She must also make coffee and serve refreshments during an intermission period.

Solution to Example 2

Dr. Jones must pay Jessica for the time spent in planning and attending the seminar which is held after her normal working hours and at a different location than the doctor's office.

The following test can be applied to determine if a worker's time should be considered working time:

- Does the employer have enough control over the activities and movement of the worker to prevent the worker from engaging in personal or some other non–job-related activities?

If the answer to the question is yes, the employer should pay the employee for his time. Consider the examples of an emergency room doctor at a hospital and a woman who works at an answering service.

E X A M P L E 3

An emergency room doctor is required to stay at a hospital after her normal shift is over at the request of the chief of staff. The doctor could have a makeshift apartment within the hospital because the doctor is the on-call physician for emergencies.

Solution to Example 3

The hours the doctor spends at the hospital must be paid due to the amount of control and restriction placed on the movement of the doctor.

E X A M P L E   4

Donna works as an operator at a local answering service. One weekend per month she is considered to be "on-call," meaning that she must carry a pager and call the answering service if she is paged. In the event that an operator cannot work during the weekend, Donna has agreed to go to the answering service and substitute for the absent operator. Donna's only requirement in being on-call is that she calls in when paged, and comes in and works as soon as she can.

Solution to Example 4

Donna does not have to be compensated for the entire weekend she is on-call as she has significant freedom of movement and her employer has little control over her activities. She would, of course, be paid for any hours she actually works at the answering service during the weekend.

Please note that Examples 1, 2, and 4 have dealt with employees who are paid by the hour. Employees who are paid a salary may or may not be compensated for additional working time spent either before or after normal working hours. We will discuss the issue of salaried and hourly employees in Segment 5 of this chapter.

Modern Work Schedules

Due to the changing structure of families and modern lifestyles, many employers are making efforts to accommodate employees with flexible work schedules, known as **flextime.** The concept of flextime allows a worker to come in at any time within a range of hours as long as the worker is present and working during a specific time period called a *core time period.* The worker will then work until a given number of hours have been put in on the job.

E X A M P L E   5

At U.S. Route 66 Trucking, Inc. the data processing department has adopted a flextime schedule. Employees are required to be at work no later than 9 A.M., and cannot leave until 3 P.M. If an employee wants to begin work at 7 A.M., the employee could leave at 4 P.M. if the employee takes a one-hour lunch. An employee starting work at 9 A.M. would work until 5:30 or 6 P.M. depending on if the employee takes 30 minutes or one hour for lunch.

Solution to Example 5

Flextime is quite popular in occupations that do not depend on a rigid schedule. Accountants, programmers, and administrative personnel in many companies can now take advantage of flextime.

Many of today's workers choose to work part-time while attending school or raising a family. Employers who recognize this have developed **job-sharing** arrangements for certain positions that allow two quality employees to share one full-time position. Many employers who have adopted such an arrangement will pay benefits to the part-time workers as if they were full-time employees. This arrangement can benefit both employees and the employer; employees would be more productive on the job, and the employer would receive a higher quality of work from these employees.

Some companies have opted to provide their employees with more leisure time by having them work four, 10-hour days. This arrangement will give employees three days off every week.

Still other employees could have the option of choosing to do their work at home, using the technology of PC computers and the Internet. Programmers, writers, and salespeople are examples of employees who could be able to work at home, staying in touch at all times using a computer and modem. The obvious advantage to such an arrangement is that the employee can put in a full day working without ever having to start the car and commute to and from the office.

With employers today being under continual pressure to scale back or eliminate employee benefits, offering unique work schedules to employees is one benefit plan that will possibly increase in the future. The advantage to the employer is that such a move will cost little to implement and manage. The advantage to the employee is that the job can be made to fit into a hectic lifestyle, making the balancing act of life's priorities somewhat easier to handle.

Regardless of the type of work schedule the employer adopts for its employees, the employer still must track the working hours of its employees. The next section discusses the various ways employers track time.

2 TRACKING WORK HOURS

In order to properly calculate the earnings for employees, the payroll accountant must know the amount of time that employees spend working. Employers have traditionally used any of several methods to keep track of the time spent on the job.

Most people are familiar with time clocks. These devices record the time on a card when an employee punches in or out, producing a written record of time spent working. Mechanical time clocks have been a part of American industry for decades, and many companies still use them as the principal means of tracking employee working hours.

Older mechanical time clocks may record the hours an employee works using hours and minutes with the A.M. or P.M. designation. This is known as the 12-hour time system. Later-model mechanical time clocks record the hours worked in hundredths of an hour instead of minutes and use the 24-hour (military) time system designation rather than 12-hour system designations.

Whether a time clock uses the 12- or 24-hour system designations, the notation for the hours between 12 midnight and 12 noon will be the same. However, 1 P.M. will be noted in military time as 13:00 (1300 hours). Figure 4-1 shows the differences in time notation for 24-hour (or military) time clocks.

Figure 4-2 shows the time card for Pascual Lorenzo for the week ending March 8. Mr. Lorenzo works in a small manufacturing company. Please note that the time clock at this company records hours in military time, using hundredths of an hour. In looking at Figure 4–2, note the numbers written in on the left side of Mr. Lorenzo's time card. These numbers represent the various manufacturing jobs on which Pascual worked during the week and are used to assign the cost of Mr. Lorenzo's earnings to those jobs the company had in process during that week.

F I G U R E   4–1

Converting from the 12-hour to the 24-hour Time System

P.M. time	24-hour time	P.M. time	24-hour time
1:00	13:00	7:00	19:00
2:00	14:00	8:00	20:00
3:00	15:00	9:00	21:00
4:00	16:00	10:00	22:00
5:00	17:00	11:00	23:00
6:00	18:00	12:00 midnight	00:00

F I G U R E   4-2

Time Card

CLOCK # 1070 DEPT   51-AC

PASCUAL LORENZO

FOR PERIOD ENDING 03/08

EXTRA TIME				REGULAR TIME
6 0 1	WEDNESDAY	IN	A.M	6 65 ᴣᴿ 3
		OUT	NOON	
		IN		8 15 50 ᴣᴿ 3
		OUT	P.M	
6 2 8	THURSDAY	IN	A.M	6 62 ᴣᴿ 4
		OUT	NOON	
		IN		8 15 50 ᴣᴿ 4
		OUT	P.M	
4 3 9	FRIDAY	IN	A.M	6 64 ᴣᴿ 5
		OUT	NOON	
		IN		8 15 50 ᴣᴿ 5
		OUT	P.M	
4 3 9	SATURDAY	IN	A.M	6 58 ᴣᴿ 6
		OUT	NOON	
		IN		8 15 50 ᴣᴿ 6
		OUT	P.M	
	SUNDAY	IN	A.M	
		OUT	NOON	
		IN		
		OUT	P.M	
4 3 9	MONDAY	IN	A.M.	6 62 ᴣᴿ 0
		OUT	NOON	
		IN		8 15 50 ᴣᴿ 0
		OUT	P.M	
4 3 9	TUESDAY	IN	A.M	6 64 ᴣᴿ 9
		OUT	NOON	8
		IN		
		OUT	P.M	15 50 ᴣᴿ 0
TOTAL				TOTAL

THIS SIDE OUT

Modern time clocks can record employee time electronically and write the data to tape or floppy disk. A computer can then read the tape or disk and produce a report by employee ID number, department, and name that lists the time spent on the job by day, date, and week. These time clocks use the employee's ID badge or an ID number entered on a keypad instead of the traditional time card. If an ID badge is used, it has an encoded magnetic strip that can be inserted into an electronic card reader to record the hours worked.

E X A M P L E 6

The following information has been taken from a time card for Jeff Warren, a maintenance technician for U.S. Route 66 Trucking, Inc. Jeff works from 3 P.M. to 11 P.M. Monday through Friday. The payroll accountant needs to figure the total number of hours Jeff worked on Monday, September 21. The time clock tracks time in hundredths of an hour. The time card information is as follows:

IN	13:01
OUT	17:00
IN	18:05
OUT	21:92

Steps to Solve Example 6

The payroll accountant can calculate the two periods of time separately and then add the results together to arrive at the total hours worked for Monday:

1. When the time has been recorded using the colon (:), replace it with a decimal point (.).

2. Subtract the "IN" hour number from the "OUT" hour number for each period of time worked.

3. Add the results of the two time periods together. This becomes the total hours worked for the day.

Solution to Example 6

1.

17.00	**OUT**
−13.01	**IN**
3.99	total hours worked before lunch

21.92	**OUT**
−18.05	**IN**
3.87	total hours worked after lunch

2.

3.99	hours worked before lunch
+ 3.87	hours worked after lunch
7.86	total hours worked for Monday

Most time clocks will record time in hundredths of an hour. This feature allows the payroll accountant to calculate earnings easily as the total time spent working can be multiplied by the rate of pay to arrive at gross earnings.

Some time clocks record time in actual minutes instead of hundredths of an hour. When this type of time clock is used, the payroll accountant must convert the minutes worked to a decimal equivalent number. This task is actually a math problem of converting a proper fraction to a decimal equivalent number. The formula to convert hours to a decimal number is simple to use:

$$\frac{\text{Minutes worked}}{60} = \frac{\text{Hundredths of an hour}}{100}$$

Keep in mind that the hours that have been worked are not converted. Only the minutes, or fractions of an hour worked are converted.

E X A M P L E 7

Jim Johnson is the payroll accountant for U.S. Route 66 Trucking, Inc. The truck line uses an older-model time clock (that tracks time on the basis of hours and minutes) in the maintenance department. Jim is figuring the time spent for Sam Snider and finds that Sam worked four hours and 43 minutes before lunch on Friday.

Steps to Solve Example 7

Jim will need to convert the minutes worked to a decimal equivalent number, as follows:

1. The number of minutes becomes the numerator of a fraction; 60 will always be the denominator for the fraction.
2. Divide the numerator by the denominator. This becomes the decimal equivalent number.
3. Round the number to the nearest *hundredths* (0.00) place. If the digit to the right of the hundredths place is 5 or more, increase the hundredths place by 1. If it is less than 5, do not change the hundredths place.
4. The decimal equivalent number should be added to the number of hours worked.

Solution to Example 7

1. Jim uses 43 as the numerator to create the following fraction:

$$\frac{43}{60}$$

2. When dividing the fraction, the result is **.716666**
3. Round the decimal equivalent number to .72 and drop all digits to the right of the hundredths place.
4. Therefore, we find that Sam Snider worked 4.72 hours on Friday morning.

The hours worked each day should be calculated first and then summed for a weekly total. This way the payroll professional has an accurate record of the hours worked *each* day as well as each week. When we discuss calculating gross pay in Segment 4 of this chapter, you will see the advantage of converting the time employees work from minutes to a decimal equivalent number. For your convenience, a chart that converts minutes into their decimal equivalent numbers can be found in Appendix 1.

Using Time Sheets

A company does not have to use a time clock and time cards. In such cases hourly employees record their time worked on a **time sheet.** Employees may simply write in their time using hours and minutes without noting A.M., P.M., or decimal equivalent numbers in place of minutes. The time sheet, after being approved by an immediate supervisor, will then be forwarded to the payroll department for processing.

The payroll accountant can use two charts for time conversion. One chart converts minutes into decimal equivalent numbers and the other converts A.M./P.M. hours into the 24-hour time equivalent. Appendix 1 contains both charts for your use in calculating the hours worked on time sheets or time cards.

Rounding Employee Time

In this section we have calculated employee working hours to the nearest hundredth of an hour. Some employers do not calculate the exact number of hours their employees work but rather use a rounding method in computing working hours. Two rounding methods are frequently used: rounding to the nearest five minutes (or .0833 of an hour) or rounding to the nearest 15 minutes (.25 or the nearest quarter of an hour).

Using a rounding method is appropriate as long as it is consistently used. An employer cannot choose to round for one pay period and then calculate the exact working hours for the next pay period.

Look back at the time card for Pascual Lorenzo in Figure 4–2. The payroll accountant has rounded the time worked each day. Notice that the payroll accountant has written the total working hours for each day to the immediate left of the time clock notation. In this example Pascual was credited with working eight hours each day for a total of 48 hours for the week. The company Mr. Lorenzo works for does not require its employees to clock out and back in for lunch—one hour is automatically deducted each day.

There are no federal guidelines regarding how a company must keep track of the working hours of its employees. Federal law does require that employee hours be tracked for employees who are paid hourly. Any documents that show the hours worked must be retained for a minimum period of time which currently is two years. The method used to track employee hours is entirely at the option of the employer.

3 PAY PERIODS AND WORKWEEKS

In order for the payroll professional to properly calculate earnings for employees, the time spent working must be divided into segments of time known as pay periods. A **pay period** is a recurring period of time with specific starting and ending dates that will be used to record the hours worked by employees. Pay periods generally determine how often employees are paid and allow a company to regulate and plan its payroll.

The shortest pay period for payroll accounting purposes is one day; the longest is one year. Pay periods generally are divided into the lengths of time shown in Figure 4–3.

A pay period can start on any day of the week. If a biweekly pay period began on a Sunday, it would end 14 days later on a Saturday. For measurement purposes, most pay periods start at midnight and end after the appropriate number of days at midnight. This allows companies that employ workers on night shifts to easily track their time spent working.

When dealing with pay periods, note that a biweekly pay period will always be 14 days (two weeks) in length. Many dictionaries define *biweekly* as either twice a week or once every two weeks. However, for payroll purposes a biweekly payroll will never occur twice in one week.

Defining a Workweek

For payroll accounting purposes, a **workweek** is a fixed, recurring period of time that can start on any day but must end 168 consecutive hours (or

F I G U R E   4–3

Pay Periods Used to Calculate Gross Pay

Pay period	Length of time	Number of periods annually	Use in payroll accounting
Daily	24 hours or less (one day)	365	Used by temporary agencies
Weekly	7 days	52	Hourly workers
Biweekly	14 days	26	Hourly or salaried workers
Semimonthly	one-half of a month	24	Hourly or salaried workers
Monthly	28, 29, 30, or 31 days	12	Salaried or management employees
Quarterly	3 months	4	Infrequently
Annual	12 months	1	Infrequently

seven consecutive days) after it begins. A workweek has this specific definition because the workweek is used to determine how many hours of overtime an hourly employee must be paid. We will discuss overtime in Segments 4 and 5 of this chapter.

A workweek may be the same period of time as a weekly pay period. However, there would be two workweeks in one biweekly pay period and slightly over two in a semimonthly pay period.

Look back at the example of the time card in Figure 4–2. You can see that the printed time card begins the pay period on Wednesday of the week, ending it on the following Tuesday. For this particular company, the pay period and workweek are the same period of time—having the time clock and time cards set up to correspond with the workweek and pay period simplifies matters for the payroll accountant in figuring hours worked.

People new to payroll accounting could confuse the concept of a workweek with a pay period. It is important to understand the difference between the two concepts when working in payroll accounting. As was mentioned above, the workweek determines *if* an hourly employee will receive overtime pay; the pay period determines *when* the employee will be paid.

Q&A

Q: Does a flextime schedule in any way affect the workweek for an employee?

A: No. Recall that the workweek is a 168-hour period of time. Any flextime schedule should be designed to fit within the 168 consecutive hours that make up a workweek.

4   CALCULATING GROSS PAY FOR HOURLY EMPLOYEES

Calculating the earnings for an hourly employee is usually not difficult. In fact, it can be as simple as taking the total hours worked and multiplying the number by the rate of pay per hour. If any difficulty is encountered by the payroll professional, it will generally be in one of two areas: arriving at the total number of hours worked or calculating the appropriate rate of pay. For purposes of our discussion, we will begin with basic calculations and work our way into more complex situations.

E X A M P L E 8

Jessica, who is the receptionist for Dr. Jones's office, earns an hourly wage of $9.50 per hour. She is paid weekly. If she works the following hours for Monday through Friday (for the pay period ending on August 22), how much will her total earnings be for the week?

Monday	Tuesday	Wednesday	Thursday	Friday
7.98	7.90	7.85	8.00	7.75

Steps to Solving Example 8

1. Calculate the total hours worked for the pay period. If the hours are not recorded in hundredths of an hour, first convert the minutes worked to hundredths of an hour.

2. Using the hourly rate of pay, multiply the total hours worked by the rate of pay.

Solution to Example 8

1.
   | 7.98 | Monday |

   7.98   Monday
   7.90   Tuesday
   7.85   Wednesday
   8.00   Thursday
   +7.75   Friday
   39.48   total hours worked
           for the week (in hundredths of an hour)

2.
   39.48   total hours worked
   × $9.50 hourly rate of pay per hour
   $375.06 total earnings for pay period

Example 8 is simple in that Jessica did not work any overtime hours. Overtime will be addressed in the next section of this chapter.

The total earnings that Jessica has made for the August 22 pay period is referred to as gross earnings. The term **gross earnings** means the total of all regular and overtime earnings of an employee for a given pay period. *Gross* earnings is also called *gross pay*. Gross refers to the amount earned before the deductions for taxes withheld or any other deductions have been applied. **Net earnings** then refers to the amount of money the employee will receive after taxes have been withheld and any other deductions have been withheld from gross earnings. Many refer to net earnings as *take-home pay*.

5 CALCULATING OVERTIME FOR HOURLY EMPLOYEES

All of the examples in this chapter have dealt with employees who have worked 40 hours per week or less. We will now discuss the concept of overtime pay as it applies to hourly employees.

Premium pay, more commonly known as **overtime pay**, is paid to employees who work in excess of 40 hours in one workweek. Overtime pay is calculated on any hours worked in excess of 40 as measured by a workweek, and it is paid at a rate that is 1.5 times the regular hourly rate of the employee. This is the *minimum rate* of pay for overtime hours worked.

A company may elect to pay overtime at a rate that exceeds 1.5 times the regular rate of pay. Some employers have adopted this policy if an employee works in excess of 40 hours in a workweek and they must work on a Saturday or a Sunday. This is not a requirement of federal law; such a policy is entirely at the option of the employer. The employer could be required to pay a higher rate of overtime if the company has entered a labor union that requires the employer to do so.

Employee Classification

We stated previously that certain employees who are salaried may not be eligible to receive overtime pay. Whether an employee is legally entitled to receive overtime pay depends on how the employee is classified by the Fair Labor Standards Act (FLSA). Employee classification is addressed in Chapter 3. Please refer back to Section 4 in Chapter 3 for a more in-depth discussion of this topic.

Classifying an employee can be more complicated than it seems from looking at Figure 4–4. If an employee's job duties meet specific criteria, the employee can legally be classified as exempt from overtime. Many employees who are managers, executives, and computer programmers as well as certain administrative workers are exempt because of their specific job duties.

Another way an employee could be exempt from overtime earnings is based on the occupation itself. School teachers, taxi drivers, and news broadcasters are exempt from overtime due to their occupation. This and other points of the Fair Labor Standards Act are covered in Section A, Chapter 3.

FIGURE 4–4

Classifying Employees for Overtime Purposes

Legal classification	Overtime paid?	Examples of workers
Exempt	No	Teachers, lawyers, computer programmers, business analysts, some managers
Non-exempt	Yes	Hourly workers

Overtime Pay and the Workweek

Notice that the rule for overtime applies to any hours worked in excess of 40 hours in a workweek. Remember that a workweek is a 168–consecutive-hour period of time or seven consecutive days.

Many believe that overtime need not be paid for a biweekly pay period until an employee works in excess of 80 hours for the pay period. This belief is incorrect; the rule for overtime applies to workweeks, not pay periods. Therefore, if an employee is paid biweekly and works 45 hours in the first week of the pay period and 38 hours in the second week, the employee is entitled to 5 hours of overtime for the pay period. The reason for the 5 hours of overtime is that the employee worked over 40 hours during the first week of the biweekly pay period, irrespective of how many hours are worked during the second week of the pay period.

Overtime is not calculated until at least 40 hours have been worked in the workweek. If an employee works 10 hours on a Monday, 8 hours on Tuesday through Thursday, and only 6 hours on Friday, no overtime hours have been worked. (The total hours worked for the week is 40 hours.) An employer may elect to pay employees for any additional hours worked in excess of eight on a daily basis. This policy is not required by federal law; it is solely the employer's option to pay overtime in this situation.

Rounding Overtime Rates

When an hourly rate of pay is multiplied by 1.5, the overtime rate of pay may result in a three-decimal place amount. Let's use an hourly rate of $6.15. If we multiply this to obtain the overtime rate, our calculation would be:

$$\begin{array}{ll} \$\ 6.15 & \text{hourly rate of pay} \\ \underline{\times 1.50} & \text{standard overtime rate} \\ \underline{\$\ 9.225} & \text{overtime rate of pay} \end{array}$$

The rounding method used for overtime rates of pay is entirely at the option of the employer. As a practical matter, rounding the overtime rate in our example to $9.23 would mean that an employee would be paid one additional cent for every two hours of overtime worked, which many would consider an insignificant amount. However, if a company employs a large number of people, rounding the overtime rate upward for any employee who works overtime would result in additional wage expense that would be noticeable to management.

Most companies will choose to carry the overtime rate out to three or more decimal places. This assures more accuracy in computing the overtime earnings of employees. If the gross earnings of an employee compute to three decimal places, the amount can then be rounded up to the next cent. This way, the additional wage expense due to rounding is kept to a minimum.

E X A M P L E 9

Jessica, the receptionist at Dr. Jones's office, worked in excess of 40 hours for the week ending on August 29. On Tuesday evening, she assisted Dr. Jones with her seminar at the local clinic, spending an additional 3 hours of time, and on Friday she went to the doughnut shop before work, which took an additional 20 minutes.

Given the following daily total of the hours Jessica worked for the week (expressed in hundredths), calculate the gross earnings for Jessica for the week ending on August 29. Jessica's regular rate of pay is $9.50 per hour. Note that the additional time she worked on Tuesday night and Friday morning is included in the daily totals.

Monday	Tuesday	Wednesday	Thursday	Friday
7.75	10.75	8.10	7.95	8.33

Steps to Solve Example 9

1. Calculate the total number of hours worked for the week.
2. Find the subtotals of the total regular hours and the total overtime hours worked.
3. Multiply the total regular hours by the regular rate of pay to arrive at the total regular earnings for the week.
4. Multiply the total overtime hours by the regular rate of pay times 1.5. The result is the total overtime earnings for the week.

5. Add the total regular earnings with the total overtime earnings to arrive at the gross earnings for the week.

Solution to Example 9

1.
7.75	Monday
10.75	Tuesday
8.10	Wednesday
7.95	Thursday
+ 8.33	Friday
42.88	total hours worked for the week

2. Subtotaling these hours, we find that

40.00	total regular hours worked
2.88	total overtime hours worked

3.
40.00	total regular hours worked
× $9.50	Jessica's regular rate of pay
$ 380.00	total regular earnings for pay period

4.
2.88	total overtime hours worked
× $14.25	overtime rate of pay ($9.50 × 1.5)
$ 41.04	total overtime earnings for pay period

5.
$380.00	total regular earnings
+ 41.04	total overtime earnings
$ 421.04	total gross earnings for pay period

Employers may offer employees the option of "banking" overtime hours worked and taking the earnings as paid time off at a later date rather than being paid overtime each pay period. This arrangement is commonly called **compensation time (or comp time).** Comp time gives the employee more time off rather than more money. This has become popular in professions such as law and accounting where employees are required to work a considerable number of overtime hours during a short period of time.

6 WAGES, SALARIES, AND COMMISSIONS

People use the terms *wages* and *salaries* interchangeably. In payroll accounting the two terms have different definitions. **Wages** refer to the earnings of employees who are generally paid on an hourly basis. The term **salary** refers to earnings paid on a weekly, biweekly, semimonthly, or monthly basis.

Salaried Employees and Overtime

Some people believe that the definition of salary automatically means that a salaried employee will not be paid overtime for additional hours worked in a workweek. Whether or not a salaried employee will receive overtime compensation depends on if the employee is classified as *exempt* or *nonexempt* according to federal law as we pointed out in Segment 5 of this chapter.

Converting Salaries to Hourly Rates

If a salaried employee is paid overtime earnings, how should the amount be computed? The payroll professional must be able to take the amount paid as a salary and convert it to an hourly rate which can then be increased to the overtime rate of pay. The number of working hours in a year must be known before the payroll professional can use the conversion process. The formula to find the total regular hours worked in a year can be found as follows:

40	total regular hours in a workweek
× 52	number of weeks in a calendar year
2,080	total working hours in a year

The 2,080-hour figure is based on a 40-hour workweek and includes holidays and vacation time taken by employees. If the company uses a 37.5- or a 35-hour workweek, the total hours worked for the year will be a smaller amount based on fewer hours in the workweek.

E X A M P L E   10

Julie Davis is an administrative assistant for U.S. Route 66 Trucking, Inc. She is paid a monthly salary of $2,000 plus overtime for any hours worked in excess of 40 per week.

For the month ending on July 31, Julie worked a total of 15 overtime hours. How much will her gross earnings be for the pay period ending on July 31?

Steps to Solve Example 10

1. Convert the monthly salary to a yearly total by multiplying by 12 months.

2. Take the yearly salary and divide by the total number of working hours in a year. This will result in an hourly rate of pay.

3. Multiply the hourly rate found in step 2 by 1.5 to arrive at the overtime rate of pay.

4. Multiply the overtime rate of pay by the number of overtime hours worked to find the total overtime earnings for the pay period.

5. Add the overtime earnings to the monthly salary to obtain the gross earnings for the pay period.

Solution to Example 10

1. $ 2,000   monthly salary
        × 12   number of months in the year
        $ 24,000   annual salary

2. $\dfrac{\$24,000\ \text{annual salary}}{2,080\ \text{hours}} = \$11.54$ per hour (rounded the nearest cent)

3. $ 11.54   hourly rate of pay
        × 1.50   overtime rate
        $ 17.31   overtime rate of pay

4. $ 17.31   overtime rate of pay
        × 15   total overtime hours for July
        $ 259.65   total overtime earnings for July

5. $ 2,000.00   salary for July
        + 259.65   overtime earning for July
        $ 2,259.65   Julie's gross earnings for July

Commissions

The amount earned by a salesperson is referred to as a commission. A **commission** is income that is received by an individual who transacts business on behalf of a company. A business transaction that is successfully concluded results in (1) the company making a sale and (2) a commission for the salesperson who will then be paid a certain percentage of the sales price.

Commission income is considered to be the same as wages or salaries from a payroll accounting standpoint. Commissions will be computed based on a given time period and paid on specified dates. Usually, salespeople are not paid overtime and may be classified as exempt employees. Successful salespeople's commission income could handsomely compensate them for any additional hours spent in closing sales each pay period. We will discuss calculating commissions in the next section of this chapter.

Draws

Draws are often given to salespeople who work only for commissions. A **draw** is *an advance* given to a salesperson that will be collected when future sales transactions are closed by the salesperson. A draw is a practical way of helping salespeople to live while sale transactions are in the process of being completed.

Draws will be subtracted from a salesperson's commissions *after* any applicable taxes and deductions have been withheld from the commissions. The draw is therefore subject to all payroll withholding taxes. Generally, draws are paid back to a company in this way.

Bonuses

Companies may offer bonuses to employees based on performance or meeting a specific goal by a certain deadline. Examples of goals earning bonuses include achieving a certain dollar amount in sales, finishing a project ahead of schedule, and signing up a large new client with the firm. A **bonus**, then, is income received by an employee as an incentive for performance or achievement of specific goals.

A bonus will be treated in the same way as commissions or salaries are for payroll accounting purposes. The bonus amount will be added to the employee's salary to arrive at the gross earnings for a pay period, and the appropriate taxes and deductions will be withheld to arrive at the net pay for the employee.

7 CALCULATING OTHER TYPES OF EARNINGS

As we discussed in the last section, to calculate commissions for a salesperson the payroll accountant must first figure the commissions that have been earned based on the sales made for the pay period. Then any payroll taxes and other deductions will be subtracted from the amount of commission income to arrive at a net amount. The draws will then be subtracted to arrive at the salesperson's net or take-home pay.

E X A M P L E   11

David Watkins is a salesperson for a retail furniture store. His commissions are figured on a monthly basis which is also the length of the pay period. On the fifteenth of each month, David is given a $600 draw against his commissions for the month. For the month ending on October 31, David's retail sales are $78,569.31. His commission rate is 3 percent of his sales. What is the dollar amount of his gross earnings for the month?

Step to Solve Example 11

Calculate the dollar amount of the commissions for the pay period. This amount becomes the gross earnings of the employee.

Solution to Example 11

$ 78,569.31	Sales made for the pay period
× .03	Rate of the commission on sales
$ 2,357.08	Gross earnings for the month (rounded to the nearest cent)

Please note that the $2,357.08 is gross pay subject to payroll tax withholding and any other deductions. This net amount will be further reduced by the repayment of his draw.

Calculating a Bonus

To include a bonus for an employee, the payroll professional must know the dollar amount of the bonus or be able to calculate the dollar amount based on information supplied by management. When the dollar amount of the bonus has been determined, the amount is added to the gross earnings of the employee for the pay period.

E X A M P L E   12

The vice president of the retail furniture store where David Watkins works gives a bonus to any salesperson whose monthly sales exceed $60,000. The bonus is 3 percent of the sales over the $60,000 threshold amount. Because David Watkins' sales for the month of October exceeded $60,000, he will receive the bonus amount in addition to his commissions for the month.

Steps to Solve Example 12

1. Calculate the amount of the bonus based on the guidelines from management.

2. After calculating the bonus, add this amount to the total earnings of the employee for the pay period to arrive at gross earnings for the employee.

Solution to Example 12

For this example, we need to find the amount of the sales that are subject to the bonus percentage as follows:

1.	$ 78,569.31	David's total sales for October
	− 60,000.00	threshold amount of sales for bonus
	$ 18,569.31	sales subject to the bonus percentage
	$ 18,569.31	bonus sales
	× .03	bonus percentage
	$ 557.08	bonus for October
2.	$ 2,357.08	total commissions for the month.
	+ 557.08	bonus amount for October
	$ 2,914.16	gross earnings for the month

Commissions and bonuses are technically referred to as **supplemental wages.** Such earnings may be taxed at a different rate than regular hourly earnings. Please see Section C, Chapter 7 for more information.

Profit-Sharing Plans

The idea behind a profit-sharing plan for employees is similar to that of a bonus in that the company wants to reward employees who perform their jobs efficiently as evidenced by the profit a company makes.

There are many ways to calculate a distribution of income that will be received from a profit-sharing plan. Each company will design its own plan with specific rules and guidelines. A company usually will distribute the amounts from a profit-sharing plan directly into a retirement plan for its employees.

The guidelines for calculating income from a profit-sharing plan will be given to the payroll accountant by senior management. The payroll accountant will then calculate the amount of income employees will receive based on the outline of the plan. Profit-sharing plans usually make distributions to employees either semi-annually or annually.

E X A M P L E 13

The employees of U.S. Route 66 Trucking, Inc. will receive a semiannual profit-sharing distribution for the pay period ending on July 31. The distributions will be placed into an employee retirement fund, based on the following plan:

1. Three percent of the net income (this amount may vary year-to-year at management's discretion)

2. The employee's gross year-to-date earnings as of May 31 will be divided by the total gross year-to-date earnings for all employees as of May 31.

3. The percentage found in Step 2 will be multiplied by the total profit-sharing distribution to arrive at the individual's proportionate share of the distribution. (To insure the most accurate distribution amounts, this percentage will not be rounded but carried out to several decimal places.)

For example, in the case of Sam Snider who is working in the maintenance department at U.S. Route 66 Trucking, Inc., the payroll accountant will first find his year-to-date earnings as of May 31, and the total year-to-date for all employees as of May 31.

$ 10,760.45	Sam's May 31 year-to-date earnings
$1,254,781.92	All employees' May 31 year-to-date earnings
$2,100,562.12	U.S. Route 66 Trucking's net income as of May 31

Steps to Solve Example 13

1. Determine the amount of the profit-sharing distribution to be given to all employees.

2. Calculate each employee's share of the distribution based on the individual employee's year-to-date earnings divided by total year-to-date earnings of the company. Carry this percentage out to several decimal places.

3. Multiply the amount in Step 1 by the percentage found in Step 2 to arrive at the individual employee's portion. Round to the nearest cent.

4. The amount of the profit-sharing distribution will be placed into the employee's retirement fund or distributed to the employee in another way.

Solution for Example 13

1. $ 2,100,562.12   U.S. Route 66 Trucking's net income as of May 31
         × .03   percent of the distribution
    $ 63,016.86   total distribution amount

2. $\dfrac{\$10,760.45}{\$1,254,781.92}$ = .00857550 Sam's percentage share.

3. $ 63,016.86   total distribution amount
        ×.00857550   Sam's percentage of the distribution
    $ 540.40   Sam's profit-sharing amount

The additional $540.40 will be placed into Sam Snider's retirement fund account.

Depending on the design of the profit-sharing plan, a company may give the employee shares of its stock in lieu of a cash payment into the plan. Usually, the company determines the price of a share of its stock using the fair market value of its stock at one or more dates of valuation during a year. These dates are days that have been determined in advance for stock valuation purposes. When several valuation dates are used, a weighted-average price for a share of stock is computed. This price is then divided by the dollar amount of the profit-sharing distribution to determine the number of shares to be added to the employee's account.

Calculating Earnings Based on a Piece-Rate Plan

We have discussed calculating employee earnings using an established rate of pay per hour or salaried amount, or an established percentage that will be multiplied by a variable amount to arrive at gross earnings as is the case with commission income. In some production situations, a company could pay its employees based on what is known as a piece-rate method.

The idea behind the piece-rate method is to reward employees based on their production. From the employee's point of view, the more that is produced, the more that is earned. Using the **piece-rate method,** employees will be compensated for every unit or piece produced during working hours. Employees will not be paid an hourly rate. The piece-rate method is best suited to companies that manufacture products.

E X A M P L E 14

Martha Jones works for a company as an assembly specialist. She is paid 9 cents for each unit she assembles that passes a quality control inspection. During the week ending on November 14, she worked 40 hours and produced 3,310 units that were acceptable and without any flaws. What is the dollar amount of her gross earnings for the week?

Steps to Solve Example 14

Calculate the total production for the week by the amount per unit produced.

Solution to Example 14

3,310	acceptable units for the week
× .09	amount paid per unit produced
$ 297.90	Martha's gross earnings for the week ending November 14

When a company uses a piece-rate method, it must still keep track of the time employees spend working. There are two reasons for this. First, employees who work in excess of 40 hours per workweek are entitled to overtime. Second, if an employee's calculated wage is less than what the employee would be paid on an hourly basis using federal minimum wage, the employee will be paid minimum wage for the hours worked.

Once the gross earnings have been calculated under the piece-rate method, the payroll accountant must check to see that the piece rate, if converted to an hourly amount, equals or exceeds the minimum wage.

E X A M P L E 15

Taking Martha's gross earnings for the week of November 14, the payroll accountant will make a calculation for the number of hours worked times the minimum wage per hour. Using the current minimum wage rate of $5.15 per hour, this dollar amount is computed as follows:

$ 5.15	Minimum wage per hour
× 40	Number of hours Martha worked
$ 206.00	Earnings for week at minimum wage

The accountant will then compare the minimum-wage earnings to Martha's actual earnings for the week. Martha will receive the greater of the earnings computed under the piece-rate method or the earnings computed using minimum wage. The piece-rate method calculation is greater than the minimum-wage computation, so Martha will receive $297.90 for the week of November 14.

Overtime and the Piece-Rate Method

We said that employees who work over 40 hours in the workweek are eligible to be paid overtime under the piece-rate method. There are several ways that overtime earnings can be computed under the piece-rate method. One method is illustrated in Example 16. To compute piece-rate overtime using this method, we first must calculate the amount paid for the units produced during the workweek and then convert this dollar amount to an hourly overtime rate. There are several steps involved in making this calculation, as follows.

E X A M P L E 16

Assume that for the week ending on November 21, Martha Jones works 43 hours and produces 3,485 acceptable units. Martha will be paid 9 cents per unit. Because Martha has worked in excess of 40 hours for the workweek she will also be paid overtime. The overtime earnings will be based on an hourly rate of pay which is computed using the piece-rate earnings for the week.

Steps to Solve Example 16

1. Calculate the piece-rate earnings for the workweek.

2. Verify that the piece-rate earnings are greater than the hours worked at the minimum wage rate.

3. Since overtime hours have been worked, divide the total piece-rate earnings by the total hours worked for the week. This will give an hourly rate of pay, based on the piece-rate computation. Remember not to round the overtime rate at this point.

4. Multiply the hourly rate of pay times 40 hours to arrive at the total regular earnings for the week. Round to the nearest cent.

5. Multiply the hourly rate of pay times 1.5 to arrive at the hourly over-time rate.

6. Multiply the hourly overtime rate of pay times the overtime hours worked to obtain the total overtime earnings for the week. Round to the nearest cent.

7. Add the total regular and overtime amounts together to obtain the gross earnings for the week.

Solution to Example 16

1.
3,485	acceptable units produced
× .09	price per unit produced
$ 313.65	total piece-rate earnings for week

2.
$ 313.65	piece rate earnings are greater than minimum wage earnings of $221.45 (43 hours × $5.15)

3.
$$\frac{\$313.65 \text{ Piece-rate earnings}}{43 \text{ hours worked for the week}} = \$7.2942 \text{ per hour (rounded)}$$

4.
40	total regular hours worked for week
× 7.2942	hourly rate using piece-rate method
$ 291.77	total regular earnings (rounded)

5.
$ 7.2942	regular hourly rate
× 1.50	standard overtime rate
$ 10.941	overtime rate using piece-rate method (rounded)

6.
$ 10.941	hourly overtime rate
× 3	total overtime hours for week
$ 32.82	total overtime earnings for week (rounded)

7.
$ 291.77	total regular earnings for week
+32.82	total overtime earnings for week
$ 324.59	Martha's gross earnings for week

If the payroll accountant had not made the overtime calculation for Martha Jones, she would have been paid only $313.65. Overtime earnings of $10.94 for the additional three hours worked would have been lost ($324.59 – $313.65). This amount can also be verified by finding the difference between the regular and overtime rate of pay, then multiplying this amount by the overtime hours for the week ($10.941 – $7.2942 = $3.6468 × 3 hours = $10.94).

Please be aware that the weekly rate of pay (and possible overtime rate of pay) for Martha Jones will vary based on her productivity each week. Obviously, she may produce fewer or greater than the 3,485 units used in Example 16. This is the reason that the payroll person must repeat these steps each week.

CHAPTER 5

The Earned Income Credit

Our next stop in our payroll journey focuses on the earned income credit. Certain individuals could be eligible to receive this refundable credit as an advance with each paycheck they receive during a year. We include our discussion at this point in Section B of our road map as the credit that is *received* by certain eligible employees, *not paid* by them.

1 ELEMENTS OF THE EARNED INCOME CREDIT

Employees who work and support one or more children may claim a credit on their individual tax returns known as the *earned income credit* (**EIC**). Low-income workers without children may also be eligible for the earned income credit. Congress has granted this credit to eligible working taxpayers to help them with the costs associated with maintaining a home either for themselves or for one or more *qualifying* children.

The idea behind allowing qualified individuals to take this credit is to give low-income wage earners without children and working parents who earn less than a certain annual dollar amount a credit against their individual tax liabilities. If an individual's tax liability for the year is zero, the individual will still receive the EIC. The EIC is known then as a *fully refundable credit*. The actual amount of the credit is computed as part of filing a Form 1040 or 1040A after the end of each calendar year.

Earned income credit is by definition a credit, and so it is not considered income to anyone who receives it. EIC is not subject to income, social security, Medicare tax withholding.

Who Is Eligible for Earned Income Credit

This credit may be given to any worker in the following situations—note that the requirements to receive the EIC change yearly, so be sure to check for the year in which you want to calculate advance EIC for an employee. Please note that the amounts found below are current for the 2001 calendar year. These amounts will change each year due to economic and cost-of-living adjustment data (COLA). For years after 2001, please consult the instructions found on IRS Form W-5 for current year amounts and limits:

- The employee has earned less than $28,281 in wages during 2001 and has what the Internal Revenue Service (IRS) calls a "qualifying child."
- The employee has earned less than $32,121 in wages during 2001 and has two or more qualifying children.
- The employee has less than $2,450 in investment income (i.e., taxable interest, ordinary dividends, etc.) for 2001 calendar year, or the employee plans to file a Form 2555 or 2555-EZ (a form relating to foreign earned income) for 2001 tax purposes.

A qualifying child, for purposes of the earned income credit, is defined by the IRS according to three tests: relationship, residency, and age. In order for any employee to receive advance EIC payments, all three tests must be met. Figure 5–1 outlines the criteria for each test.

Please note that the employee cannot be a qualifying child of someone else who is taking the credit.

EIC and Payroll Accounting

The IRS allows an eligible employee who has one or more qualifying children the option of taking the credit after the end of each calendar year when filing a **Schedule EIC** as part of Form 1040 or 1040A, or the credit can be advanced by the taxpayer's employer on a pay period basis after the employee files a Form W-5 with the employer. The current Form W-5 is illustrated in Figure 5–2.

F I G U R E   5-1

Who Is a Qualifying Child for EIC Purposes?

Test	Criteria for the test
Relationship	To pass this test, the child must be one of the following:
	■ The employee's son, daughter, or adopted child.
	■ A stepson or stepdaughter.
	■ An eligible foster child.
Residency	To pass this test, the employee and the child must satisfy both of the following:
	■ Live in the same house or residence for more than six months of the year.
	■ The house or residence must be in the United States or Washington, D. C.
Age	To pass this test, the child must be one of the following:
	■ Under 19 years old at the end of the year.
	■ A full-time student under 24 years old at the end of the year.
	■ Permanently and totally disabled during the year, regardless of age.

F I G U R E   5-2

Form W-5

Form **W-5**

Earned Income Credit Advance Payment Certificate

OMB No. 1545-1342

▶ Use the current year's certificate only.
▶ Give this certificate to your employer.
▶ This certificate expires on December 31, 200X.

Department of the Treasury
Internal Revenue Service

200X

Print or type your full name

Donald Johnson

Your social security number

991 45 6789

Note: If you get advance payments of the earned income credit for 200X, you **must** file a 200X Federal income tax return. To get advance payments, you **must** have a qualifying child and your filing status must be any status **except** married filing a separate return.

		Yes	No
1	I expect to be able to claim the earned income credit for 200X, I do not have another Form W-5 in effect with any other current employer, and I choose to get advance EIC payments	X	
2	Do you expect to have a qualifying child?	X	
3	Are you married?		X
4	If you are married, does your spouse have a Form W-5 in effect for 200X with any employer?		

Under penalties of perjury, I declare that the information I have furnished above is, to the best of my knowledge, true, correct, and complete.

Signature ▶ *Donald Johnson*   Date ▶ *December 15, 200X*

Cat. No. 10227P

Note that only employees with one or more qualifying children are entitled to advance EIC on their paychecks. Low-income wage earners who do not have any children cannot receive EIC in advance. The only way low-income taxpayers without children can receive the credit is to file a Form 1040 or 1040A after the end of the year.

Generally, advance EIC payments are added to an employee's take-home or net pay each pay period. If the advance EIC payment is more than the employee's total federal tax liability for a pay period (i.e., federal income, social security, and Medicare taxes) *and* the employer's federal tax liability for the employee (social security and Medicare taxes), there are special rules that can be applied regarding the EIC payment that are not discussed here.

Q&A

Q: Is any low-income worker eligible for advance EIC?

A: No, the employee must have one or more qualifying children and meet certain income guidelines in order to be eligible for EIC.

When EIC is advanced to an employee with each paycheck he receives, the employee must still file a Schedule EIC along with a Form 1040 or 1040A after the end of the year. Keep in mind, however, that it is not the responsibility of the payroll professional to ensure or guarantee that the employee files an individual tax return when EIC has been advanced to the employee.

Q&A

Q: Does the employer need to check to see that an employee who has been advanced EIC has properly completed his individual tax return?

A: No, the employer is under no obligation to see that an employee who has received advance EIC files Schedule EIC with his tax return.

Payroll Accounting Procedures for Advance EIC

We will now discuss the specific steps taken to advance EIC to an eligible employee. The key document that an employer needs in order to advance the EIC on a prorated basis is the **Form W-5,** *Earned Income Advance Payment Certificate.* The certificate must be filled out by the eligible employee with one or more qualifying children. The employer who receives a signed W-5 form will calculate the credit, prorated by pay period, and advance it to the employee with each paycheck he receives.

The Form W-5 expires every December 31. An eligible employee must file a new form with the employer for each calendar year that the employee is eligible to receive the advance credit.

The employee is responsible for determining if he is eligible for the credit. The payroll professional is not required to verify the employee's eligibility in any way. The payroll professional, upon receiving a signed W-5 form, will use either the *EIC wage-bracket withholding method* or the *EIC percentage method* discussed below to calculate the prorated credit to be added to the employee's net pay each pay period.

Calculating the EIC

EIC, like federal income taxes that are withheld, can be figured using either wage-bracket withholding tables or the percentage method. The procedure for making the actual calculation is similar to the one discussed in Section B, Chapter 7, for calculating federal income taxes.

No matter which method is used to calculate EIC, the payroll professional will consult a table in order to figure the amount of EIC for the employee. Figures 5–3 and 5–4 show the wage-bracket and percentage tables to be used when calculating EIC for an employee paid weekly or biweekly. Tables are available for the following pay periods: daily or miscellaneous, weekly, biweekly, semimonthly, monthly, quarterly, semiannual, and annual.

Each pay period, employees with one qualifying child will receive only a portion of the total EIC to which they are entitled. The IRS wage-bracket and percentage EIC tables have been calculated based on this limit. Any additional EIC amount due the employee will be given to the employee after he files the 1040 or 1040A tax return.

EIC tables can be found in *Circular E*, known as the *Employer's Tax Guide,* or *Publication 15*. This guide is an essential reference and information source for the payroll accountant. This publication is available free of charge from any IRS office.

Using Form W-5 Information

Information to determine the amount of EIC to be advanced to an employee is found on the Form W-5. Look at Figure 5–2, and notice questions 1, 2, 3, and 4. Depending on how the employee answers these questions, the payroll professional will use one of two sections contained in each table to calculate the amount of the credit to be advanced.

FIGURE 5-3

EIC Wage Bracket Method Table

Tables for Wage Bracket Method of Advance EIC Payments (For Wages Paid in 200X)

WEEKLY Payroll Period

SINGLE or MARRIED Without Spouse Filing Certificate

Wages- At least	But less than	Payment to be made	Wages- At least	But less than	Payment to be made	Wages- At least	But less than	Payment to be made	Wages- At least	But less than	Payment to be made
$0	$5	$0	$75	$80	$15	$270	$280	$25	$420	$430	$11
5	10	1	80	85	16	280	290	24	430	440	10
10	15	2	85	90	17	290	300	23	440	450	9
15	20	3	90	95	18	300	310	22	450	460	8
20	25	4	95	100	19	310	320	21	460	470	7
25	30	5	100	105	20	320	330	21	470	480	6
30	35	6	105	110	21	330	340	20	480	490	5
35	40	7	110	115	22	340	350	19	490	500	4
40	45	8	115	120	23	350	360	18	500	510	3
45	50	9	120	125	24	360	370	17	510	520	2
50	55	10	125	130	26	370	380	16	520	530	1
55	60	11	130	135	27	380	390	15	530	- - -	0
60	65	12	135	250	28	390	400	14			
65	70	13	250	260	27	400	410	13			
70	75	14	260	270	26	410	420	12			

MARRIED With Both Spouses Filing Certificate

Wages- At least	But less than	Payment to be made	Wages- At least	But less than	Payment to be made	Wages- At least	But less than	Payment to be made	Wages- At least	But less than	Payment to be made
$0	$5	$0	$40	$45	$8	$135	$145	$12	$205	$215	$5
5	10	1	45	50	9	145	155	11	215	225	4
10	15	2	50	55	10	155	165	10	225	235	4
15	20	3	55	60	11	165	175	9	235	245	3
20	25	4	60	65	12	175	185	8	245	255	2
25	30	5	65	125	13	185	195	7	255	265	1
30	35	6	125	135	13	195	205	6	265	- - -	0
35	40	7									

BIWEEKLY Payroll Period

SINGLE or MARRIED Without Spouse Filing Certificate

Wages- At least	But less than	Payment to be made	Wages- At least	But less than	Payment to be made	Wages- At least	But less than	Payment to be made	Wages- At least	But less than	Payment to be made
$0	$5	$0	$145	$150	$30	$530	$540	$53	$820	$830	$25
5	10	1	150	155	31	540	550	52	830	840	24
10	15	2	155	160	32	550	560	51	840	850	23
15	20	3	160	165	33	560	570	50	850	860	22
20	25	4	165	170	34	570	580	49	860	870	21
25	30	5	170	175	35	580	590	48	870	880	20
30	35	6	175	180	36	590	600	47	880	890	19
35	40	7	180	185	37	600	610	46	890	900	18
40	45	8	185	190	38	610	620	45	900	910	17
45	50	9	190	195	39	620	630	44	910	920	16
50	55	10	195	200	40	630	640	43	920	930	15
55	60	11	200	205	41	640	650	42	930	940	14
60	65	12	205	210	42	650	660	41	940	950	13
65	70	13	210	215	43	660	670	40	950	960	12
70	75	14	215	220	44	670	680	39	960	970	11
75	80	15	220	225	45	680	690	38	970	980	10
80	85	16	225	230	46	690	700	37	980	990	9
85	90	17	230	235	47	700	710	36	990	1,000	8
90	95	18	235	240	48	710	720	35	1,000	1,010	7
95	100	19	240	245	49	720	730	34	1,010	1,020	7
100	105	20	245	250	50	730	740	33	1,020	1,030	6
105	110	21	250	255	51	740	750	32	1,030	1,040	5
110	115	22	255	260	52	750	760	31	1,040	1,050	4
115	120	23	260	265	53	760	770	30	1,050	1,060	3
120	125	24	265	270	54	770	780	30	1,060	1,070	2
125	130	26	270	500	55	780	790	29	1,070	1,080	1
130	135	27	500	510	55	790	800	28	1,080	- - -	0
135	140	28	510	520	54	800	810	27			
140	145	29	520	530	53	810	820	26			

F I G U R E   5–4

EIC Percentage Method Table

Tables for Percentage Method of Advance EIC Payments
(For Wages Paid in 200X)

Table 1. WEEKLY Payroll Period

(a) SINGLE or MARRIED Without Spouse Filing Certificate		(b) MARRIED With Both Spouses Filing Certificate	
If the amount of wages (before deducting withholding allowances) is:	The amount of payment to be made is:	If the amount of wages (before deducting withholding allowances) is:	The amount of payment to be made is:

Over-	But not over-		Over-	But not over-	
$0	$137 . . .	20.40% of wages	$0	$68 . . .	20.40% of wages
$137	$251 . . .	$28	$68	$125. . .	$14
$251	. . . . .	$28 less 9.588% of wages in excess of $251	$125	. . . .	$14 less 9.588% of wages in excess of $125

Table 2. BIWEEKLY Payroll Period

(a) SINGLE or MARRIED Without Spouse Filing Certificate		(b) MARRIED With Both Spouses Filing Certificate	
If the amount of wages (before deducting withholding allowances) is:	The amount of payment to be made is:	If the amount of wages (before deducting withholding allowances) is:	The amount of payment to be made is:

Over-	But not over-		Over-	But not over-	
$0	$274 . . .	20.40% of wages	$0	$137. . .	20.40% of wages
$274	$503 . . .	$56	$137	$251. . .	$28
$503	. . . . .	$56 less 9.588% of wages in excess of $503	$251	. . . .	$28 less 9.588% of wages in excess of $251

Table 3. SEMIMONTHLY Payroll Period

(a) SINGLE or MARRIED Without Spouse Filing Certificate		(b) MARRIED With Both Spouses Filing Certificate	
If the amount of wages (before deducting withholding allowances) is:	The amount of payment to be made is:	If the amount of wages (before deducting withholding allowances) is:	The amount of payment to be made is:

Over-	But not over-		Over-	But not over-	
$0	$297 . . .	20.40% of wages	$0	$148. . .	20.40% of wages
$297	$545 . . .	$61	$148	$272. . .	$30
$545	. . . . .	$61 less 9.588% of wages in excess of $545	$272	. . . .	$30 less 9.588% of wages in excess of $272

Table 4. MONTHLY Payroll Period

(a) SINGLE or MARRIED Without Spouse Filing Certificate		(b) MARRIED With Both Spouses Filing Certificate	
If the amount of wages (before deducting withholding allowances) is:	The amount of payment to be made is:	If the amount of wages (before deducting withholding allowances) is:	The amount of payment to be made is:

Over-	But not over-		Over-	But not over-	
$0	$595 . .	20.40% of wages	$0	$297 . . .	20.40% of wages
$595	$1,090 . .	$121	$297	$545. . .	$61
$1,090	. . . . .	$121 less 9.588% of wages in excess of $1,090	$545	. . . .	$61 less 9.588% of wages in excess of $545

Question 1

The IRS requires an answer to Question 1 to ensure that the employer has a signed statement from the employee that he is eligible for advanced EIC.

Question 2

EIC will only be advanced if the employee has one or more qualifying children. An employee who answers no to Question 2 will not be eligible for advance EIC payments on a pay period basis.

Questions 3 and 4

The answers to these questions will determine which sections of the EIC wage-bracket or percentage tables will be used. Look at Figures 5–3 and 5–4 to see that the tables are divided into sections based on one of the following two criteria:

- A single Form W-5 is being filed (for either single or married status).
- The taxpayers are married, they are filing a joint return, and both spouses file W-5s with their employers.

The key difference in using one of the two sections found in each table is the dollar amount of the EIC that will be advanced to the employee each pay period.

Steps in Calculating EIC

Whether the payroll professional is using the wage-bracket or percentage method, the following information is needed to figure the EIC to be advanced to the employee each pay period:

- The pay period involved.
- Gross earnings of the employee.
- Marital status selected on the Form W-5.

If you have trouble remembering these three items of information that are needed in order to calculate advanced EIC payments, try memorizing the phrase *PAYGEMS*. It is a mnemonic that stands for:

- *PAY* as in pay period.
- *GE* as in gross earnings.
- *MS* as in marital status.

So, advanced EIC payments for an employee are *paygems* each payday.

   The payroll accountant will not use the number of withholding allowances found on the employee's Form W-4 for the EIC calculation. If the employee has claimed an exempt status on Form W-4, EIC will still be advanced by the employer.

The Wage-Bracket Method

In order to use the **EIC wage-bracket withholding method**, the payroll professional will use EIC wage-bracket tables found in Circular E. **Circular E** is
an IRS publication also known as **The Employer's Tax Guide,** or **Publication 15.** This is a key Federal reference guide when working with a payroll.
The IRS prints withholding tables for Federal income taxes as well as EIC tables (two of which have been reproduced in Figures 5-3 and 5-4) in this guide.
We will discuss this valuable publication further in later chapters.

   Q&A

   Q: How can I obtain a copy of IRS Circular E?

   A: Local IRS offices will give you a copy of Publication 15. You can
       also call 1-800-TAX-FORM (1-800-829-3676) to receive a copy by
       mail or use the Internet to download an Adobe® pdf file copy at
       www.irs.gov. See Appendix 1 for more information about obtaining
       this publication and other IRS forms and instructions.

   Once the appropriate table has been found, based on the pay period,
marital status, and number of W-5 forms filed, the payroll professional
should find the correct line between the columns labeled "Wages at least
$ . . . but less than $." You will see in looking at Figure 5–3 that, for a weekly
pay period, no EIC is advanced if the employee earns more than $530 per
week. This is because if the employee is earning at least this much weekly,
the employee's gross earnings for the year will exceed the dollar maximum
for receiving EIC from the government.

E X A M P L E   1

Dan Jackson started as a shipping/receiving clerk for U.S. Route 66
Trucking, Inc., and filed a current Form W-5. He claimed a single status and
has one qualifying son. Dan is paid weekly.
   Jackson's starting rate of pay is $8.50 per hour, and he will normally work
a 40-hour week. How much EIC would be advanced to Dan Jackson under
the wage-bracket method?

Steps to Solve Example 1 Using Wage-Bracket EIC Tables

1. We must first obtain Dan's gross earnings on a weekly basis. Given a 40-hour week as an average, Dan Jackson's gross earnings will be $340 per week ($8.50/hour × 40 hours per week).

2. Using the wage-bracket EIC method, we first must choose the correct table for a weekly pay period with a single marital status. The correct table is found in Figure 5–3.

3. We must then determine if the gross earnings are over the maximum amount for advanced EIC purposes. By looking at the ranges found in the weekly table, we can see the earnings are not over $530 for a weekly pay period.

4. We now need to find the correct earnings range for Dan's weekly gross earnings. Dan's gross earnings falls on the line labeled "At least $340 but less than $350." The amount of EIC that Dan will receive weekly will be $19. The annual amount advanced to Dan will be $988.

The EIC Percentage Method

The **EIC percentage method**, also known as the *exact calculation method*, will rely on a set of tables *and* calculations to arrive at the amount of EIC to be advanced to an employee. The only difference between the percentage and wage-bracket methods is that the payroll professional must make calculations in order to arrive at the correct EIC for an employee as we see in Example 2.

E X A M P L E 2

Using the information found for Dan Jackson in Example 1, compute the amount of advanced EIC using the percentage method approach.

Steps to solve Example 2 using percentage EIC tables

1. Dan's weekly gross earnings are $340, using the same calculation found in the wage-bracket Example 1 above.

2. We now need to use the correct table. In looking at Figure 5–4, find that percentage method Table 1(a) applies to weekly pay periods and single employees.

3. We now need to find the correct line within Table 1(a) for our calcula-
    tion. We will use the line that states "Over—$251."

4. Per the instructions found for this line in Table 1(a), calculate Dan's
    advanced EIC by first finding the dollar amount of wages that are over
    $251 for the week:

$ 340.00	Dan's weekly earnings
− 251.00	subtract the base amount per the table
$ 89.00	earnings over $251 for the week

5. Now that the amount "over $251.00" has been found, multiply the
    amount by 9.588 percent, as follows:

$ 89.00	amount over $251 for the week
× .09588	percentage per the table
$ 8.53	9.588 percent of the amount over $251

6. Notice that the amount found in step 5 must now be subtracted from
    $28.00 per Table 1(a):

$ 28.00	Table amount
− 8.53	9.588 percent amount from Step 5
$ 19.47	dollar amount of EIC advanced weekly

Subtracting the 9.588 percent amount from $28.00, we find the EIC amount
that should be advanced to Dan weekly. If we use the percentage method
rather than the wage-bracket method, Dan will receive an additional
47 cents per week in advanced EIC, which amounts to an additional $24.44
for the calendar year ($.47 \times 52 = \$24.44$).

According to the Internal Revenue Code, EIC reaches a maximum
amount when an individual with one qualifying child earns $13,260 annu-
ally. The amount of EIC is then phased out for each additional dollar earned
during the year in excess of $13,260. The amount of EIC will reach zero if
more than $28,281 is earned during the year. This is why 9.588 percent of
the earnings over $251 must be subtracted from the $28 weekly maximum
EIC amount.

Comparing EIC Methods

Using the percentage EIC method will result in an exact amount of EIC to be
advanced. In looking at Dan Jackson's case, the percentage method calculation will result in advancing an additional $24.44 for the year.

Either EIC calculation method can be used by the payroll professional. The percentage method is the best method to use in a computerized
system, while the wage-bracket EIC method is easier to use when preparing
a manual payroll.

In this Chapter we have only summarized the general payroll administration aspects of the EIC and making advance payments to eligible employees. EIC is a topic addressed in many classes on individual income tax.
To gain a better understanding of the EIC, study IRS Publication
596—*Earned Income Credit.*

Calculating Withholding Taxes, Other Deductions, and Tips

CHAPTER 6
Social Security Taxes

In Section A of this book our payroll road map began with the activities connected with hiring employees and an overview of the major federal laws that affect payroll administration. Our next stop on our road map is an important one. We begin Section C by discussing how to calculate and withhold social security and Medicare taxes for employees.

We have been discussing the payroll accounting process and how to calculate the gross pay for employees in a typical business. In Chapter 6 we will now focus on calculating social security taxes for a business. This is the first of several payroll taxes we will consider in exploring the payroll accounting process.

1 SOCIAL SECURITY TAX BACKGROUND

What people commonly refer to as **social security tax** is also known as FICA tax. The term *FICA* stands for **Federal Insurance Contributions Act.** The terms *social security tax* and *FICA tax* are interchanged frequently by businesspeople and the general public.

The purpose behind collecting social security tax is to provide revenue that will be used for benefits for qualifying individuals. Benefits are paid when an individual retires or becomes disabled. Included in this benefit package is medical insurance. Survivor's benefits are paid to family members in the event of the individual's untimely death. These benefits are subject to certain rules and regulations.

The FICA tax collected for the U.S. government by the U.S. Treasury is used to fund programs that are administered by the government agency known as the *Social Security Administration* (abbreviated as SSA). The Social Security Administration uses the monies collected to fund four major program categories. These programs are officially referred to by the government as insurance:

- Old age or retirement insurance.
- Survivor's insurance.
- Disability insurance.
- Hospital insurance, also commonly called Medicare.

The first three programs—old age or retirement insurance, survivor's insurance, and disability insurance—are technically known by the acronym **OASDI.** The fourth program, hospital insurance or **Medicare**, technically is referred to as **HI.**

Each employee is currently required to pay social security tax as a percentage of his wages earned in a calendar year. The amount that is paid by an employee must be matched on a dollar-for-dollar basis by that person's employer as well.

Social security or FICA tax must be paid by both individuals and their employers according to federal law known as the **Social Security Act of 1935**. Employers are responsible for collecting the tax as outlined by the provisions of this law.

Employees must pay FICA on the earnings from each job for which they are employed. In a case where an individual works full-time for one employer and part-time for another, each employer must withhold FICA on the earnings each pay period, regardless of the other job.

Q&A

Q: Is it possible for an employee to have too much social security tax withheld if he works for two separate employers at the same time?

A: It is possible for this situation to occur. Neither employer is responsible to make any adjustment for social security withholding for the employee. The employee may claim a refund of overpaid social security taxes on his Form 1040, Individual Income Tax Return after the end of the calender year in which the overpayment occurs.

The Social Security Administration does not grant exemptions from paying social security tax to an individual who is a full-time student or an individual who supports a full-time student.

Self-employed individuals must also contribute to the social security fund by paying a tax on their net earnings from their self-employed activities. This tax is called **SE tax** (or *self-employed tax*).

Most types of compensation received by employees will be considered taxable for social security purposes. Commissions, wages, salaries, overtime pay, and bonuses are all types of income that are considered taxable.

2 THE BEGINNINGS OF THE FEDERAL INSURANCE CONTRIBUTIONS ACT (FICA)

As we mentioned above, employees and employers are required to pay social security or FICA tax based on a federal law known as the **Social Security Act of 1935.** This federal act was passed by Congress and was signed into law by President Franklin Delano Roosevelt as part of the government's attempt to provide some measure of insurance benefits for American workers. Up to that point in time, the majority of employees in the United States had no established program to help them financially in their retirement years or if they unexpectedly became disabled. Soon after the program started it was modified to include benefits for the surviving spouse and any dependents of a deceased worker. Certain conditions apply to these benefits. Figure 6–1 shows the major historical events before and after the signing into law of the Social Security Act.

Social security has provided millions of dollars in benefits to recipients. Although the act was signed into law in August 1935, 1940 was the first year that benefits were available to workers who were of retirement age and had paid into the fund a mere three years earlier. In that year, $325,000,000 was contributed to the fund, and $62,000,000 was paid out in benefits. (Please note that these amounts have not been adjusted to any inflation index.) Fifty years later, in 1990, the amount of contributions rose to $288,486,000,000, and the amount paid out in benefits was $252,209,000,000.

In the first year that contributions were required to be made by employees and employers (1937), the amount of the contribution was 1 percent of the first $3,000 the employee made during that year (or a maximum con-

F I G U R E   6–1

Major Historical Events Surrounding the Enactment
of the Social Security Act

1918	▪ World War I ends.
1929	▪ The Great Depression begins in the United States.
1932	▪ Franklin D. Roosevelt is elected President.
1935	▪ The Social Security Act is signed into law.
1937	▪ U.S. workers begin paying into the social security fund.
1939	▪ World War II begins in Europe.
1940	▪ Eligible recipients begin receiving benefits from the social security fund.

tribution of $30). Since 1937, the percentage rate for FICA contributions has risen over 11 times to its current level.

Social security has been a controversial political issue since its inception in 1935. The future of the system and its method of funding are debated frequently by Congress and business leaders. With the current discussion of balancing the federal budget and the budget surplus, there will probably be major changes made to parts of the social security system in the near future.

3 CALCULATING FICA:
THE SOCIAL SECURITY EARNINGS LIMIT

In order for us to learn how to calculate social security tax, we will need to look at how the tax is figured for an individual employee. Here we introduce the unique accounting concept of the *earnings limit.*

The Social Security Earnings Limit

FICA tax is one of three payroll taxes computed for an individual employee based on how much in earnings that person has made in a calendar year. An **earnings limit** is the maximum amount of an individual's earnings in a calendar year that will be subject to being taxed for social security purposes. From a payroll accounting standpoint, the earnings limit is the amount an employee (or self-employed person) earns from zero dollars on January 1 of the calendar year up to the point at which the employee (or self-employed individual) has reached the maximum amount.

Q&A

Q: What is a social security wage-base limit?

A: The term *wage-base limit* is synonymous with the term *earnings limit*. IRS publications will use this term in their literature. We use the term *earnings limit* as we believe it better describes how the limit works.

To better understand what an earnings limit is and its use in calculating FICA taxes, we need to point out that when we refer to FICA or social security taxes, we really are referring to two separate taxes, namely social security (or OASDI) and Medicare (or HI).

Even though social security and Medicare are actually two taxes, there is only one earnings limit for social security. Medicare has no earnings limit maximum for the current calendar year. The 2001 social security earnings limit for old age, survivors, and disability insurance programs has been set at $80,400 for both employees and employers as well as self-employed individuals. This is illustrated in Figure 6–2.

The earnings limit maximum for social security tax is set by the Board of Governors of the Social Security Administration in late fall of each year. Depending on the funding requirements for the upcoming fiscal year, the earnings limit and rate of FICA tax may be changed.

Tracking the Earnings Limit

As of January 1 each calendar year, our wages or pay will begin at zero dollars for the earnings limit calculation. As the year progresses, the payroll professional must keep a year-to-date total of wages earned by each employee, comparing this dollar amount with the current year earnings limit maximum in order to compute the correct amount of social security tax to be paid during any pay period.

Using Figure 6–2, let's visualize this accounting concept of the earnings limit for social security purposes. Keep the following key facts in mind when dealing with the earnings limits:

- The earnings limit for social security tax is figured on a calendar year basis, beginning with January 1.
- Each individual employee or self-employed person will be subject to the same earnings limit dollar maximum.

F I G U R E   6–2

Earnings Limit for OASDI FICA in 2001

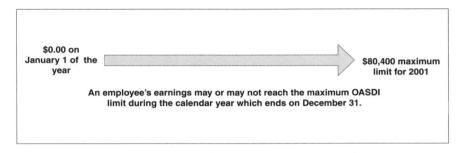

$0.00 on January 1 of the year

$80,400 maximum limit for 2001

An employee's earnings may or may not reach the maximum OASDI limit during the calendar year which ends on December 31.

- The earnings limit maximum for 2001 is $80,400 for social security contributions.
- There is no earnings limit for Medicare tax; the total amount earned by an individual employee each year will be subject to this tax.

Before 1991, there was one earnings limit for *both* social security and Medicare taxes. When calculating social security tax based on a single earnings limit, one was left with an impression that social security was a single tax. The reality is that FICA has been made up of two separate taxes since Medicare was signed into law in 1966.

From January 1, 1991, through December 31, 1993, there were two distinct earnings limits for social security taxes: one for social security and one for Medicare. During this period of time, the earnings limit for Medicare tax exceeded the earnings limit for social security tax. The result was that the payroll professional had to track and account for each tax separately.

Figure 6-3 is a chart showing the increase in the social security earnings limit from 1990 through 2001. In 1990 the limit was $51,300; in 2001 it is $80,400. On average, the limit has increased by $2,645 each year over the last 11 years. This trend is expected to continue into the twenty-first century.

We mentioned that the rate paid in social security tax varies depending on where an employee's cumulative year-to-date total earnings lies on the earnings limit line. We will now discuss FICA tax rates and how the rates relate to the social security earnings limit.

Social Security Earnings Limit Increases

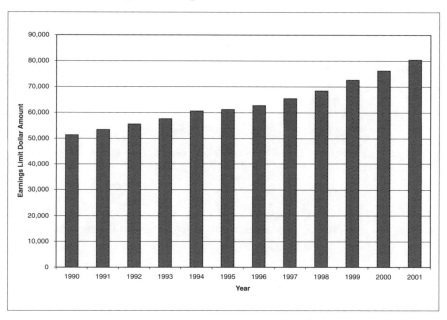

4   CALCULATING SOCIAL SECURITY FOR AN INDIVIDUAL EMPLOYEE

Calculating FICA for a single employee is a relatively simple task. We often see the current rate for social security tax stated as 7.65 percent. The percentage rate of 7.65 percent for FICA is actually the total of the two separate FICA tax rates. The FICA rate that employees pay for social security tax is 6.20 percent. The FICA rate paid for hospital insurance, or Medicare coverage, is 1.45 percent. Adding the percentages together then tells us that the combined rate for social security and Medicare is 7.65 percent (6.20 percent + 1.45 percent). This combined rate can be used in calculations when an individual's earnings in a calendar year do not exceed the current year's social security earnings limit (which is $80,400 for 2001).

If we look at the FICA earnings limits divided up into the social security and Medicare percentage rates, we see that an employee will pay social security tax on a cumulative year-to-date total of $80,400 in wages. If this

F I G U R E   6–4

Social Security, Medicare, and the Combined Earnings Limit

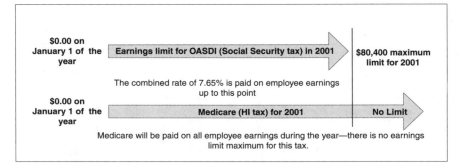

individual earns in excess of $80,400 in the calendar year, Medicare will still be paid at a rate of 1.45 percent for the total amount earned during the year, as is shown in Figure 6–4.

Q&A

Q: Why is there a social security earnings limit?

A: The limit is set based on the needs of the fund as analyzed and established by the Social Security Administration. Most likely such an earnings limit will continue to exist in the near future.

Let's compute the FICA tax to be withheld for one employee to illustrate what we have covered to this point.

E X A M P L E   1

Tom Sullivan works for U.S. Route 66 Trucking, Inc. During the current year he is paid a monthly salary of $2,500. For the pay period ending February 28 (note this is not a leap year), he earns $2,500 in wages and has no other earned income. Given these facts, compute the total social security and Medicare taxes that must be withheld for February.

Steps to Solve Examples 1 and 2

1. Find the year-to-date wages before the current pay period earnings.

2. Add the current pay period earnings to the year-to-date wages and obtain a new year-to-date total.

3. If the new year-to-date total is less than the current social security earnings limit, multiply the pay period wages by the combined rate of 7.65 percent.

Remember that the calculation in Step 3 will be based on the gross wages paid for the pay period. Based on the steps above, the following calculation is made for Example 1:

Solution to Example 1

1. The total year-to-date wages as of January 31 are $2,500. This amount is less than the social security earnings limit of $80,400, so the total amount will be subject to the combined rate of 7.65 percent.

2. The new year-to-date total as of February 28 is $5,000 (or $2,500 + $2,500). The new year-to-date total is less than the social security earnings limit of $80,400, so the total amount will be subject to the combined rate of 7.65 percent.

3. Calculate the social security and Medicare to be withheld for February.

$2,500.00	gross wages for February
× .0765	combined rate for social security and Medicare
$ 191.25	employee's portion of FICA tax

Use the same steps to find the answer for Example 2.

E X A M P L E 2

Tonya Smith also works for U.S. Route 66 Trucking, Inc. as an accountant. She earns $4,000 per month. She is paid her monthly salary on March 31. What amount should be withheld for social security and Medicare taxes on March 31?

Solution to Example 2

1. Find the year-to-date earnings:

$ 4,000	monthly salary
× 2	2-month time period (January and February)
$ 8,000	year-to-date earnings

2. Obtain the new year-to-date total:

$ 8,000	year-to-date earnings as of February
+ 4,000	March salary
$ 12,000	new year-to-date earnings total

3.   Calculate the FICA to be withheld for March:

$ 4,000.00	gross wages for March
× .0765	combined rate for social security and Medicare
$ 306.00	employee's portion of social security taxes

The above examples are straightforward and require little effort to arrive at the correct answer. In both cases, the employees' year-to-date earnings were under the social security earnings limit. However, in Example 3 the situation becomes more complicated when an employee's pay period earnings brings his year-to-date earnings over the social security earnings limit.

E X A M P L E 3

Todd Scott is vice president for operations at U.S. Route 66 Trucking Inc. He earns a monthly salary of $8,000. For the month of November, Todd's salary is $8,000. Find the year-to-date earnings for Todd as of October 31 and then calculate the amounts of social security and Medicare to be withheld from Todd's salary for November.

Steps to Solve Examples 3 and 4

1.   Find the year-to-date earnings *prior* to the current pay period.

2.   Add the current pay period earnings to the year-to-date wages and obtain a new year-to-date total.

3.   If the new year-to-date total is less than the current social security earnings limit, multiply the pay period wages by the combined rate of 7.65 percent and omit steps 4 through 7.

4.   If the current gross pay will bring the total year-to-date earnings over $80,400, find the dollar amount of earnings needed to bring the employee's year-to-date earnings up to the maximum social security limit.

5.   Calculate the social security tax by multiplying the dollar amount found in step 4 times 6.20 percent.

6.   Calculate the Medicare tax due by multiplying the *total* earnings for the pay period times 1.45 percent.

7. Add the two amounts found in Steps 5 and 6 together to arrive at the total social security and Medicare tax due for the pay period.

Solution to Example 3

1. | $ 8,000 | monthly salary. |
    | × 10 | number of months—January through October |
    | $80,000 | Todd's year-to-date earnings as of October 31 |

2. | $80,000 | year-to-date earnings as of October 31 |
    | + 8,000 | November salary |
    | $88,000 | Todd's new year-to-date earnings as of November 30 |

3. The new year-to-date earnings of $88,000 are above the $80,400 social security earnings limit. Go to Step 4 and calculate the portion of Todd's pay that brings his year-to-date earnings up to the $80,400 earnings limit

4. | $80,400.00 | social security FICA maximum for the year |
    | −80,000.00 | Todd's earnings as of October 31 |
    | $ 400.00 | amount of current period wage required to reach the social security maximum |

5. | $ 400.00 | social security FICA earnings for the pay period |
    | × .062 | social security percentage for 2001 |
    | $ 24.80 | social security FICA tax for the pay period. |

6. | $ 8,000.00 | Medicare earnings for pay period |
    | × .0145 | Medicare percentage for 2001 |
    | $ 116.00 | FICA Medicare tax for the pay period |

7. | $ 24.80 | social security FICA tax due |
    | +116.00 | Medicare tax due |
    | $ 140.80 | total FICA tax due for the pay period |

Please note that the situation in the example above occurs only when Todd's pay period earnings exceed the social security earnings limit for FICA, which happened in November. Todd's October total earnings were taxed at both the social security and Medicare rates because his year-to-date earnings were $80,000 as of October 31, under the social security earnings limit of $80,400. Todd's December wages will be taxed only on the Medicare rate as his year-to-date earnings as of November 30 now exceed the social security tax maximum of $80,400.

E X A M P L E 4

Judy Garcia is the controller for U.S. Route 66 Trucking, Inc. She is paid a semimonthly salary of $3,625. She will receive her regular paycheck on December 15. What is Ms. Garcia's year-to-date earnings as of November 30? What will be the dollar amount of social security and Medicare to be withheld from her paycheck on December 15?

Solution to Example 4

1. $ 3,625.00   semimonthly earnings
         × 22   total pay periods through November 30
     $79,750.00   year-to-date earnings through November 30

2. $79,750.00   Judy's earnings as of November 30
     +3,625.00   Judy's gross pay for December 15
     $83,375.00   Judy's new year-to-date earnings

3. Judy's December pay will cause her year-to-date earnings to exceed the social security earnings limit of $80,400. Go to step 4.

4. $80,400.00   social security FICA maximum for the year
     −79,750.00   Judy's earnings as of November 30
     $ 650.00   amount needed to reach the social security maximum

5. $ 650.00   social security earnings for pay period
         × .0620   social security percentage
     $ 40.30   social security tax for the pay period

6.
     $ 3,625.00   Medicare earnings for the pay period
         × .0145   Medicare percentage
     $ 52.56   Medicare tax for the pay period (rounded)

7. $ 40.30   social security tax due
         + 52.56   Medicare tax due
     $ 92.86   total social security taxes due for the pay period

Q&A

Q: How often does the social security earnings limit change?

A: If history repeats itself, it is likely that the earnings limit will change each year (go back and look at Figure 6–3 as an example). The trend is for it to increase each year. This means that the payroll person must pay close attention to the new earnings limit dollar amount when it is announced by the Social Security Administration. If you are working on a payroll for January, be certain to withhold at the current percentages for both social security and Medicare taxes and use the correct social security earnings limit!

5   CALCULATING SOCIAL SECURITY AND MEDICARE FOR A PAY PERIOD

The calculations discussed in Segment 4 are not complicated for one employee's pay period wages. However, the process can become quite tedious when calculating FICA taxes to be withheld for all the employees of a company for any given pay period.

The payroll accountant must complete the above steps for each employee of the company for every pay period because FICA is calculated on an individual employee basis. The payroll accountant must consult an accounting document called an **employee earnings record** for the year-to-date earnings information *before* calculating FICA to be withheld for that employee for the given pay period. This record is discussed in Section D of this book. The payroll accountant must also figure the company's FICA tax liability for the pay period involved. Recall that FICA tax is paid not only by an employee, but by the employer as well. The employer must match what the employee pays in FICA tax each pay period.

Q&A

Q: What is an employee earnings record?

A: This is one of several essential documents that the payroll professional must maintain for each employee. We discuss this document fully in Chapter 10, Section 3 of this book. Note here for our purposes in this chapter the amounts withheld for both social security and Medicare are recorded in each employee earnings record, and most importantly, the social security earnings limit for each employee *is tracked* using such documents.

The calculation for the employer's portion of FICA taxes will be made on *the sum of the gross pay for all employees paid each pay period*. The gross pay for each employee will be separated into amounts below and above the social security earnings limit based on each employee's year-to-date amounts. These employee dollar amounts for the social security earnings limit are added together to arrive at the total amount that will be multiplied by the appropriate rate for social security taxes. Medicare taxes will be calculated on the sum of all of the employees' gross pay for the pay period.

From the standpoint of the employer, this amount for FICA taxes represents one of several payroll taxes that the employer must pay. The payroll accountant will prepare a separate journal entry to debit the payroll tax expense account and credit FICA tax payable to reflect this expense at the same time the journal entry is prepared to record the payroll.

Rounding Differences

When the employer's FICA tax liability is calculated as outlined above, the total owed by the employer for a pay period will differ slightly from the total withheld from each employee's paycheck. This difference is merely due to the fact that the FICA calculation for each employee is based on that employee's gross pay, whereas the employer portion is calculated using the total earnings of all employees for the pay period. This slight difference between the two totals is referred to as the **FICA rounding difference.** This rounding difference will be noted on Form 941 which is a quarterly tax return that reports the amount of federal income and FICA tax withheld from employees and owed by the business. The Form 941 is discussed in Section F of the book.

The time involved and the accuracy required proves challenging to any payroll professional who must make such calculations manually without the aid of computerized payroll software. The majority of businesses today will use a computerized payroll program to assist in the preparation of a payroll because of the repetitive nature of the FICA calculations and the great need for accuracy and timeliness in completing the payroll each pay period.

A valuable feature that many computerized payroll programs offer is quarter-to-date and year-to-date earnings totals based on the earnings limit for all the employees on a company's payroll. The ability to obtain these figures easily is beneficial when preparing the payroll each period as well as when compiling the various tax reports.

A computerized payroll program may be part of a larger integrated software package that incorporates features used by a human resources department. Integrated packages are becoming popular because much of the information that is needed for payroll accounting is also required for human resource management purposes. This information can be easily shared in one software program.

CHAPTER 7

Calculating Income Taxes

In November of 1789, Benjamin Franklin commented in a letter to Jean-Baptiste Leroy that the new U.S. Constitution had an appearance that promised permanency. Franklin however was cautious in his observation about the new U. S. Constitution when he wrote his now famous words ". . . but in the world nothing can be said to be certain except death and taxes." Today's payroll accountants and administrators are involved with the latter: calculating and withholding income taxes for federal, state, and local governments. At this spot on our road map you will learn how to apply IRS tables to correctly calculate an employee's federal income tax withholding for payroll purposes.

1 THE W-4 AND FEDERAL INCOME TAX WITHHOLDING

The **Form W-4** provides an employer with essential information that is needed to calculate the amount of federal income tax to be withheld from an employee. This is the reason that employees are requested to fill out the form when they begin a new job or when the number of their withholding allowances changes. Figure 7–1 outlines the purpose for this important form. Be sure to review this table along with Figure 7–2 to better understand the function of the Form W-4 in payroll accounting.

F I G U R E   7–1

Frequently asked questions about the IRS Form W-4

Who prints and issues Form W-4?	The Form W-4 is an IRS form which is updated and issued each calendar year.
What is the purpose of the Form W-4?	The information captured on the form when completed by an employee is used to calculate federal income tax withholding. Many states also allow its use for state income tax withholding in lieu of a state form.
When is it filled out by an employee?	The Form W-4 is filled out when any employee begins a new job or has a change in withholding status (such as a change in marital status, birth of a child). A change in an employee's income could trigger a legitimate adjustment to withholding. Some employers ask employees to complete a new form each calendar year. (This request is optional on the part of the employer.)
Is the form sent to the IRS or other government agencies?	No. There is an exception, however if the employee claims greater than ten exemptions or if the employee claims an "exempt" status and earns more than $200 per week. See Section 2 of this chapter for more information.
Is the form retained by the employer?	Employers should retain the form for a minimum of two years per federal requirements. It may be kept indefinitely as part of an employee's personnel file if desired.
Does the employee get a copy of the completed form?	Usually not. This is not a requirement; however, an employer may give the employee a copy of his completed Form W-4.

There are two items of information on the Form W-4 that are needed to calculate an employee's income tax withholding:

- The marital status of the employee.
- The number of withholding allowances claimed by the employee.

The marital status of the employee is limited to one of three possible choices: married, single, or married but withhold at the single rate. The reason the form asks marital status is that the withholding calculation is made using different rates that are determined by the employee's marital status.

F I G U R E 7–2

200X W-4 Form for Stewart Gibson

The payroll professional needs to know the number of withholding allowances to properly calculate the amount of income tax to be withheld. In Segment 2 of this chapter, we will show how this information, when combined with the gross earnings for a given pay period, is used to calculate income tax.

Exemption from Withholding

The vast majority of employees must have federal income tax withheld from their paychecks. Certain employees may be exempt from income tax withholding. As indicated on the Form W-4, an employee who meets both of the following criteria *may* be exempt from federal income tax withholding for the year:

- The employee had no federal tax liability last year and received a full refund of all federal income taxes.
- The employee expects to have no federal tax liability for the current year, *an*d the employee expects a full refund of all federal taxes.

Employees who are full-time students *may* be exempt. The student must meet the criteria outlined above. It is important to note that a full-time student is not automatically exempt from federal income tax withholding. An employee who is also a full-time student must properly complete and sign a Form W-4 in order to claim an exempt status. Other employees who could be exempt from withholding would be employees who are retired and do not earn enough in a year to be taxed for federal purposes.

The criteria outlined above are printed on the Form W-4. It is the employee's decision and responsibility to claim an exempt status on the form. The payroll professional is not obligated to verify that the employee's circumstances qualify him for an exempt status. The responsibility of the payroll professional is limited to following the instructions found on the Form W-4 in determining how much income tax should be withheld.

Q&A

Q: What if an employee asks me advice regarding the number of withholding allowances to use in completing his Form W-4?

A: We strongly suggest that you not engage in giving tax advice to your employee. You may refer him to *IRS Publication 919*, "How Do I Adjust my Withholding?" which outlines the steps a taxpayer should use in arriving at the correct number of withholding allowances based on his earnings.

2 CALCULATING FEDERAL INCOME TAXES

As we stated previously, the vast majority of employees who work in the United States today must have federal income taxes withheld from their paychecks each pay period. Employers are required to withhold federal income taxes under the Internal Revenue Code of 1986.

In states where income taxes are collected for state purposes, state law generally requires that income tax be withheld and remitted to the state.

Q&A

Q: Is state income tax withholding a requirement in all states?

A: No. Currently there are nine states that do not require withholding on an employee's income. Please see Figure 7–6 in Section 4 of this chapter for a list of these states.

Information Needed to Figure Withholding

There are four items of information that are necessary in order to calculate federal income tax withholding. The payroll professional must obtain this information first before any calculation can be made. The four items of information are as follows:

- The pay period.
- The number of withholding allowances claimed by the employee.
- The gross earnings of the employee for the pay period.
- The marital status of the employee.

In Section 1 we found that marital status and the number of withholding allowances are found on an employee's Form W-4.

The payroll accountant *will know* the employee's pay period. The pay period, whether it is weekly, biweekly, semimonthly, monthly, or quarterly, will affect the amount of income tax to be withheld.

The amount of gross earnings for the pay period is essential when calculating the amount of taxes to be withheld. Income taxes are actually computed as a percentage of earnings, modified by adjustments the payroll accountant makes. We will discuss these calculations later in the chapter.

If you have trouble remembering these four pieces of information, here's a hint for you: Try remembering the phrase **PAY-WAGES.** It stands for

PAY as in *pay period.*

WA as in *withholding allowances.*

GE as in *gross earnings* of the employee.

S as in *marital status* of the employee.

Remember, we must calculate the federal income tax withholding before we can PAY-WAGES to employees.

Methods of Calculating Withholding

There are two ways or methods of manually calculating federal income tax withholding. The first method is known as the **wage-bracket method,** and the second method is called the *exact calculation* or **percentage method.** The payroll professional should familiarize himself with both methods, as occasionally one or the other could have to be used in order to properly figure withholding.

Both methods use IRS tables to arrive at the amount of federal withholding. The wage-bracket method only uses a table to arrive at the amount of withholding. In the percentage method, several calculations must be made in addition to using an IRS table to arrive at the income tax figure.

If the company uses computerized payroll software, the calculation for federal and any state or local income tax withholding will be made automatically. (The IRS provides formulas for calculating federal tax withholding that payroll software programs use.) An obvious question you might ask is, "If this is the case, why do I need to bother learning how to make the calculation by hand?" The answer is important: even if the payroll department is using computer software to process a company's payroll, the payroll professional must verify and check the integrity of the computer output. Income tax rates change frequently, and the new data will be input into the computer program to update it. The payroll professional will have to check the accuracy of the software's calculations using the new rates. It will be impossible for the payroll professional to audit or verify the computer's calculations without knowing how to manually calculate the amounts withheld.

The Wage-Bracket Method

The wage-bracket method relies on tables created by the IRS to determine the amount of federal income tax withholding. In order to use this method, the payroll professional needs the PAY-WAGES information. This method is easy and quick, and payroll professionals will use this method when they have to prepare or "cut" a paycheck manually.

The payroll professional will look up the amount of federal income tax to be withheld using one of several tables published by the IRS. These tables can be found in an IRS publication called the **Circular E Employer's Tax Guide,** or *Publication 15.* In this publication, the IRS has created tables that will list amounts of withholding based on marital status (single or married), and pay period (daily, weekly, biweekly, semimonthly, monthly).

The IRS also publishes a supplement to *Circular E* known as *Publication 15-A.* This publication features withholding tables that are used in software program calculations. This publication also contains combined withholding tables for federal income, social security, and Medicare taxes; and it discusses special rules and other less frequently encountered payroll topics.

A special situation exists for any payrolls made during the July–December, 2001 time period. Due to the passage of the George W. Bush administration's **Economic Growth and Tax Relief Reconciliation Act of 2001,** the IRS has issued new federal tax withholding tables for this six-month time period. These tables can be found in **Publication 15-T** (printed in June, 2001). Note that Figures 7-3 and 7-5 utilize two tax tables from Publication 15-T. It is expected that the IRS will issue a revised Publication 15 for calendar year 2002 to replace the *mid-year* Publication 15-T, which will reflect any new tax rates and amounts. It is important to note that

F I G U R E   7–3

MARRIED Persons—WEEKLY Payroll Period

If the wages are—		And the number of withholding allowances claimed is—										
At least	But less than	0	1	2	3	4	5	6	7	8	9	10
		The amount of income tax to be withheld is—										
$740	$750	93	85	76	68	60	51	43	35	26	18	9
750	760	95	86	78	70	61	53	44	36	28	19	11
760	770	96	88	79	71	63	54	46	38	29	21	12
770	780	98	89	81	73	64	56	47	39	31	22	14
780	790	99	91	82	74	66	57	49	41	32	24	15
790	800	101	92	84	76	67	59	50	42	34	25	17
800	810	102	94	85	77	69	60	52	44	35	27	18
810	820	104	95	87	79	70	62	53	45	37	28	20
820	830	105	97	88	80	72	63	55	47	38	30	21
830	840	107	98	90	82	73	65	56	48	40	31	23
840	850	108	100	91	83	75	66	58	50	41	33	24
850	860	110	101	93	85	76	68	59	51	43	34	26
860	870	111	103	94	86	78	69	61	53	44	36	27
870	880	113	104	96	88	79	71	62	54	46	37	29
880	890	114	106	97	89	81	72	64	56	47	39	30
890	900	116	107	99	91	82	74	65	57	49	40	32
900	910	117	109	100	92	84	75	67	59	50	42	33
910	920	119	110	102	94	85	77	68	60	52	43	35
920	930	120	112	103	95	87	78	70	62	53	45	36
930	940	122	113	105	97	88	80	71	63	55	46	38
940	950	123	115	106	98	90	81	73	65	56	48	39
950	960	125	116	108	100	91	83	74	66	58	49	41
960	970	127	118	109	101	93	84	76	68	59	51	42
970	980	129	119	111	103	94	86	77	69	61	52	44
980	990	132	121	112	104	96	87	79	71	62	54	45
990	1,000	135	122	114	106	97	89	80	72	64	55	47
1,000	1,010	138	124	115	107	99	90	82	74	65	57	48
1,010	1,020	140	125	117	109	100	92	83	75	67	58	50
1,020	1,030	143	128	118	110	102	93	85	77	68	60	51
1,030	1,040	146	131	120	112	103	95	86	78	70	61	53
1,040	1,050	148	133	121	113	105	96	88	80	71	63	54
1,050	1,060	151	136	123	115	106	98	89	81	73	64	56
1,060	1,070	154	139	124	116	108	99	91	83	74	66	57
1,070	1,080	156	141	126	118	109	101	92	84	76	67	59
1,080	1,090	159	144	129	119	111	102	94	86	77	69	60
1,090	1,100	162	147	132	121	112	104	95	87	79	70	62
1,100	1,110	165	150	134	122	114	105	97	89	80	72	63
1,110	1,120	167	152	137	124	115	107	98	90	82	73	65
1,120	1,130	170	155	140	125	117	108	100	92	83	75	66
1,130	1,140	173	158	143	128	118	110	101	93	85	76	68
1,140	1,150	175	160	145	130	120	111	103	95	86	78	69
1,150	1,160	178	163	148	(133)	121	113	104	96	88	79	71
1,160	1,170	181	166	151	136	123	114	106	98	89	81	72
1,170	1,180	183	168	153	138	124	116	107	99	91	82	74
1,180	1,190	186	171	156	141	126	117	109	101	92	84	75
1,190	1,200	189	174	159	144	129	119	110	102	94	85	77
1,200	1,210	192	177	161	146	131	120	112	104	95	87	78
1,210	1,220	194	179	164	149	134	122	113	105	97	88	80
1,220	1,230	197	182	167	152	137	123	115	107	98	90	81
1,230	1,240	200	185	170	155	139	125	116	108	100	91	83
1,240	1,250	202	187	172	157	142	127	118	110	101	93	84
1,250	1,260	205	190	175	160	145	130	119	111	103	94	86
1,260	1,270	208	193	178	163	148	133	121	113	104	96	87
1,270	1,280	210	195	180	165	150	135	122	114	106	97	89
1,280	1,290	213	198	183	168	153	138	124	116	107	99	90
1,290	1,300	216	201	186	171	156	141	126	117	109	100	92
1,300	1,310	219	204	188	173	158	143	128	119	110	102	93
1,310	1,320	221	206	191	176	161	146	131	120	112	103	95
1,320	1,330	224	209	194	179	164	149	134	122	113	105	96
1,330	1,340	227	212	197	182	166	151	136	123	115	106	98
1,340	1,350	229	214	199	184	169	154	139	125	116	108	99
1,350	1,360	232	217	202	187	172	157	142	127	118	109	101
1,360	1,370	235	220	205	190	175	160	144	129	119	111	102
1,370	1,380	237	222	207	192	177	162	147	132	121	112	104
1,380	1,390	240	225	210	195	180	165	150	135	122	114	105
1,390	1,400	243	228	213	198	183	168	153	137	124	115	107

$1,400 and over   Use Table 1(b) for a **MARRIED person** on page 3. Also see the instructions on page 2.

even though tax rates may change at least once a year, the steps required to arrive at the correct amount of withholding for an employee remain the same.

Once the correct table has been located, the payroll professional will locate the correct row based on the gross earnings of the employee, and then identify the correct column based on the number of withholding allowances for the employee. Figure 7–3 shows an example of the July 1, 2001 withholding table for married employees who earned $740 to $1,399 for a weekly pay period. The table rounds the amount of withholding to the nearest dollar.

Use the table in Figure 7–3 to work through the following example.

E X A M P L E 1

Stu Gibson filed his W-4 form as married, with three withholding allowances. He earns $1,150 per week as a shop foreman at U.S. Route 66 Trucking, Inc. How much should his federal income tax withholding be?

Steps to Solve Example 1

1. Obtain the PAY-WAGES information. Use the information as follows.

2. Choose either the single or married tax withholding table.

3. Find the correct table for the employee's pay period.

4. Using the "At least" and "But less than" columns at the left of the table, find the line (row) that the employee's gross earnings fall between.

5. Find the correct column based on the number of withholding allowances. Move down the column until you intersect with the gross earnings line (row). This is the amount of federal income tax to be withheld.

Solution to Example 1

1. PAY-WAGES = Weekly pay period, three (3) withholding allowances, $1,150 gross earnings, married.

2. We will find the married withholding tax tables in Circular E (IRS Publication 15 or IRS Publication 15-T for any payrolls made during July through December 2001).

3. We will use the WEEKLY payroll period tax table. (See Figure 7–3).

4. Stu's gross earnings are found between the "At least" $1,150 "But less than" $1,160 line of the table.

5. Moving down the "3" withholding allowance column, the column and line (row) intersect at $133. This is the amount of income tax to withhold from Stu's earnings.

Number of Withholding Allowances

The IRS tables have been designed to accommodate an employee who claims up to 10 withholding allowances. If an employee claims over 10 withholding exemptions, the payroll professional's best course of action is to use the percentage method to figure the income tax to be withheld.

When an employee claims in excess of 10 withholding allowances, the IRS requests that the Form W-4 be sent in with the next quarterly Form 941 report. The payroll professional is nonetheless obligated to withhold federal income taxes based on the W-4 information when more than 10 allowances are claimed by an employee.

From Example 1 you can see that the wage-bracket method is simple and quick to use. In looking at Figure 7–3, notice that if the gross earnings exceed $1,399, the table cannot be used to calculate the amount of income tax to be withheld. In this situation, we must use the percentage method to arrive at the correct amount of tax to be withheld.

The Percentage Method

The percentage method of calculating federal income tax is another manual calculation method used to arrive at employees' withholding. This method can be used as the primary method of figuring withholding, or the professional can use the wage-bracket method instead and use the percentage method only when necessary.

This method involves making several calculations and using an entirely different type of IRS table to arrive at the amount of income tax to be withheld.

The percentage method will start with the PAY-WAGES information for the withholding calculation, using this information as the basis for the calculations. As with the wage-bracket method, marital status and the pay period will determine which table will be used.

When we use the percentage method of withholding, we are actually *prorating on a pay period basis* the estimated annual amount of taxes an employee owes based on his earnings. The pay period determines how we prorate any annual amounts used in our calculations. In order to understand the steps involved in using the percentage method, we need to briefly discuss personal income taxation and the personal exemption.

The Personal Exemption

When individual taxpayers prepare their tax returns after the end of each calendar year, they are allowed to deduct a dollar amount from their income known as a **personal exemption**. The personal exemption is the basic amount of money that taxpayers can earn without being taxed. Congress originally allowed taxpayers this nontaxable amount for living essentials. The personal exemption for the 2001 calendar year is $2,900.

Q&A

Q: Why does the personal exemption change each year?

A: Congress has indexed the personal exemption to the cost of living and assumes that some adjustment will take place each year.

Personal exemption is the correct term used in income tax accounting. The synonymous term we use in payroll accounting is **withholding allowance**. In payroll accounting terms, a prorated personal exemption is really a prorated withholding allowance.

The taxpayer is allowed a personal exemption for each dependent claimed on his income tax return. Usually, the number of personal exemptions on the individual's tax return is the same as the withholding allowances claimed on the employee's W-4. (However, this does not always hold true as we discussed in Chapter 2.)

The 2001 personal exemption for income tax purposes is $2,900. This amount, shown in Figure 7–4, can be divided by the appropriate number of pay periods in a year to arrive at the prorated withholding allowance. This prorated amount is used in the percentage method tax calculations.

For payroll accounting purposes, we must take the number of withholding allowances and multiply by the prorated withholding allowance amount to arrive at the employee's nontaxable amount for the pay period. If an employee has claimed zero withholding allowances on his Form W-4, no calculation is necessary.

F I G U R E 7–4

Prorated Withholding Allowance Amounts for 2001

Pay period	Amount	Pay period	Amount
Daily or miscellaneous	$ 11.15	Monthly	$ 241.67
Weekly	$ 55.77	Quarterly	$ 725.00
Biweekly	$111.54	Semiannually	$1,450.00
Semimonthly	$120.83	Annually	$2,900.00

In Section G, the Information Resources Appendix features a table that lists the 2001 prorated withholding allowances. Amounts have been calculated for withholding allowances ranging from 1 to 10.

The Standard Deduction

Another amount that taxpayers are allowed to deduct from their income on their individual tax returns is known as the **standard deduction**. This is a dollar amount that is allowed as a deduction from income when an individual's itemized deductions are less than a standard amount allowed to taxpayers. The taxpayer is allowed to deduct the greater of the standard deductions or itemized deductions on his individual tax return.

In payroll accounting, a prorated standard deduction amount is used in the percentage withholding tables to adjust the pay period earnings for this nontaxable amount. We call this number found in the tables an **offset amount** because this dollar amount compensates for the employee's taxable income by a nontaxable amount. Without subtracting the offset amount from the employee's pay period earnings, too much income tax would be withheld from the employee every pay period.

Using the Percentage Method Tables

The percentage method also makes use of IRS tables. Keep in mind that tables used are different than the tables used for the wage-bracket method. These tables require that calculations are made in order to arrive at the amount of federal income tax to be withheld. Figure 7–5 shows four of the eight IRS percentage withholding tables that are effective July 1, 2001.

In looking at Figure 7–5, you will notice that each table is based on the pay period of the employee. Then each table is further divided by marital status, either single or married. Also notice that each table lists the offset amount for prorating the employee's standard deduction on a pay period basis.

Steps in the percentage method

To use the percentage method for an employee's earnings, follow these steps:

1. Obtain the PAY-WAGES information.
2. Using the prorated withholding allowance table in Figure 7–4, multiply the number of withholding allowances by the dollar amount of the pay period exemptions. (If no withholding allowances are claimed, skip this

step. The employee's gross pay period earnings will be the amount used in Step 3 below.)

3. Subtract the dollar amount of the pay period exemption from the employee's gross earnings. We can call this amount the *pay period taxable earnings (PTE)*.

4. Find the correct Percentage Method Table based on pay period and marital status. Use one of the eight tables available in *Circular E* (*IRS Publication 15*).

5. Once the correct table is found, locate the line that the PTE falls between, using the *"Over"* and *"But not over-"* columns.

6. Follow the instruction for the line regarding any offset amount to be subtracted from the PTE. The result of subtracting any offset amount will be called the *net taxable earnings (NTE)*.

7. Take the NTE and multiply it by the percentage found on the line. Add to this any dollar amount found in the column titled "The amount of income tax to withhold is." This is the amount of federal income tax to be withheld.

The best way to become familiar with this method is by working out the following examples. Use Figure 7–4 and one of the tables in Figure 7–5 to complete the following examples.

E X A M P L E 2

Let's take Stu Gibson's earnings and tax withholding information from Example 1 and calculate his withholding using the percentage method. Recall that Stu is married, has three withholding allowances, and is paid $1,150 weekly. What is the amount of Stu's federal income tax to be withheld?

Steps to Solve Example 2

1. Obtain Stu's PAY-WAGES information.

2. Calculate the prorated withholding allowance amount for Stu.

3. Subtract the prorated withholding allowance amount from Stu's gross earnings to arrive at pay period taxable earnings (PTE).

4. Find the Percentage Withholding table for married employees paid on a weekly basis.

5. Locate the line that the PTE falls between the "Over" and "But not over-" columns.

F I G U R E   7–5

Tables for Percentage Method of Withholding

TABLE 1—WEEKLY Payroll Period

(a) SINGLE person (including head of household)—

If the amount of wages (after subtracting withholding allowances) is:		The amount of income tax to withhold is:	
Not over $51 . . . . . $0			
Over—	**But not over—**		**of excess over—**
$51	—$552	15%	—51
$552	—$1,196	$75.15 plus 27%	—552
$1,196	—$2,662	$249.03 plus 30%	—1,196
$2,662	—$5,750	$688.83 plus 35%	—2,662
$5,750	. . . . .	$1,769.63 plus 38.6%	—5,750

(b) MARRIED person—

If the amount of wages (after subtracting withholding allowances) is:		The amount of income tax to withhold is:	
Not over $124 . . . . . $0			
Over—	**But not over—**		**of excess over—**
$124	—$960	15%	—$124
$960	—$2,023	$125.40 plus 27%	—$960
$2,023	—$3,292	$412.41 plus 30%	—$2,023
$3,292	—$5,809	$793.11 plus 35%	—$3,292
$5,809	. . . . .	$1,674.06 plus 38.6%	—$5,809

TABLE 2—BIWEEKLY Payroll Period

(a) SINGLE person (including head of household)—

If the amount of wages (after subtracting withholding allowances) is:		The amount of income tax to withhold is:	
Not over $102 . . . . . $0			
Over—	**But not over—**		**of excess over—**
$102	—$1,104	15%	—$102
$1,104	—$2,392	$150.30 plus 27%	—$1,104
$2,392	—$5,323	$498.06 plus 30%	—$2,392
$5,323	—$11,500	$1,377.36 plus 35%	—$5,323
$11,500	. . . . .	$3,539.31 plus 38.6%	—$11,500

(b) MARRIED person—

If the amount of wages (after subtracting withholding allowances) is:		The amount of income tax to withhold is:	
Not over $248 . . . . . $0			
Over—	**But not over—**		**of excess over—**
$248	—$1,919	15%	—$248
$1,919	—$4,046	$250.65 plus 27%	—$1,919
$4,046	—$6,585	$824.94 plus 30%	—$4,046
$6,585	—$11,617	$1,586.64 plus 35%	—$6,585
$11,617	. . . . .	$3,347.84 plus 38.6%	—$11,617

TABLE 3—SEMIMONTHLY Payroll Period

(a) SINGLE person (including head of household)—

If the amount of wages (after subtracting withholding allowances) is:		The amount of income tax to withhold is:	
Not over $110 . . . . . $0			
Over—	**But not over—**		**of excess over—**
$110	—$1,196	15%	—$110
$1,196	—$2,592	$162.90 plus 27%	—$1,196
$2,592	—$5,767	$539.82 plus 30%	—$2,592
$5,767	—$12,458	$1,492.32 plus 35%	—$5,767
$12,458	. . . . .	$3,834.17 plus 38.6%	—$12,458

(b) MARRIED person—

If the amount of wages (after subtracting withholding allowances) is:		The amount of income tax to withhold is:	
Not over $269 . . . . . $0			
Over—	**But not over—**		**of excess over—**
$269	—$2,079	15%	—$269
$2,079	—$4,383	$271.50 plus 27%	—$2,079
$4,383	—$7,133	$893.58 plus 30%	—$4,383
$7,133	—$12,585	$1,718.58 plus 35%	—$7,133
$12,585	. . . . .	$3,626.78 plus 38.6%	—$12,585

TABLE 4—MONTHLY Payroll Period

(a) SINGLE person (including head of household)—

If the amount of wages (after subtracting withholding allowances) is:		The amount of income tax to withhold is:	
Not over $221 . . . . . $0			
Over—	**But not over—**		**of excess over—**
$221	—$2,392	15%	—$221
$2,392	—$5,183	$325.65 plus 27%	—$2,392
$5,183	—$11,533	$1,079.22 plus 30%	—$5,183
$11,533	—$24,917	$2,984.22 plus 35%	—$11,533
$24,917	. . . . .	$7,668.62 plus 38.6%	—$24,917

(b) MARRIED person—

If the amount of wages (after subtracting withholding allowances) is:		The amount of income tax to withhold is:	
Not over $538 . . . . . $0			
Over—	**But not over—**		**of excess over—**
$538	—$4,158	15%	—$538
$4,158	—$8,767	$543.00 plus 27%	—$4,158
$8,767	—$14,267	$1,787.43 plus 30%	—$8,767
$14,267	—$25,171	$3,437.43 plus 35%	—$14,267
$25,171	. . . . .	$7,253.83 plus 38.6%	—$25,171

---

6. Subtract the offset amount found in the table from the PTE to arrive at the net taxable earnings (NTE).

7. Multiply the NTE by the percentage found on the line. Be sure to add to this figure any additional amount of tax for the line as instructed.

Solution to Example 2

1. Stu's gross earnings are $1,150.

2.
$$\begin{array}{ll} \$\ 55.77 & \text{weekly withholding allowance from Figure 7–4} \\ \underline{\times\ 3} & \text{Stu's withholding allowances} \\ \$167.31 & \text{prorated withholding allowances} \end{array}$$

3.
$$\begin{array}{ll} \$1{,}150.00 & \text{gross earnings for the week} \\ \underline{-167.31} & \text{prorated allowance amount} \\ \$\ 982.69 & \text{PTE} \end{array}$$

4. Use Table 1(b) from Figure 7–5.

5. Use the "Over" $960 "But not over" $2,023 line for calculations.

6.
$$\begin{array}{ll} \$982.69 & \text{PTE} \\ \underline{-960.00} & \text{offset amount for this line of the table} \\ \$\ 22.69 & \text{NTE to be multiplied by 27 percent rate} \end{array}$$

7.
$$\begin{array}{ll} \$\ 22.69 & \text{NTE} \\ \underline{\times\ .27} & \text{Tax rate for the line} \\ \$\ \ \ 6.13 & \text{Tax on the NTE} \end{array}$$

$$\begin{array}{ll} \$125.40 & \text{Base tax for this line of the table} \\ \underline{+\ 6.13} & \text{Tax on the NTE} \\ \$131.53 & \text{Total tax on Stu's earnings for the week} \end{array}$$

You will notice that the amount of Stu's tax as computed in Example 1 was an even $133, per the withholding table. Using the percentage method in Example 2, the amount is $131.53.

An advantage to using this method is that it is more accurate than the wage-bracket method. One drawback to the method is that with more calculations being made, there is a greater chance of error. Remember that no computations are made when using the wage-bracket method. For IRS purposes, using either method is acceptable for calculating withholding.

Q&A

Q: Where can I find current IRS federal income tax withholding tables?

A: IRS *Publication 15*, also known as *Circular E*, can be obtained from the IRS by calling 1-800-TAX-FORM (1-800-829-3676). Recall that you also can download *Publication 15* as an Adobe® pdf file from the IRS web site at www.irs.gov.

To reinforce your understanding of the percentage method, we will work through another example.

E X A M P L E 3

Jack Smith is another employee of U.S. Route 66 Trucking, Inc. Jack earns $800 weekly, is married, and claims three withholding allowances. What is the amount of income tax withholding using the percentage method?

Solution for Example 3

1. Jack's earnings are $800.

2.
$ 55.77	weekly withholding allowance from Figure 7–4
× 3	Jack's withholding allowances
$167.31	prorated withholding allowances

3.
$800.00	gross earnings for the week
−167.31	prorated allowance amount
$632.69	PTE

4. Use Table 1(b) from Figure 7–5.

5. Use the "Over" $124 "But not over" $960 line for calculations.

6.
$632.69	PTE
−124.00	offset amount for this line.
$508.69	NTE to be multiplied by the 15 percent rate

7.
$508.69	NTE
× .15	tax rate for the line
$ 76.30	income tax on Jack's earnings for the week

Notice that Step 7 in Example 3 has only one calculation, whereas Step 7 in Example 2 has two calculations to arrive at the total tax to be withheld. The reason for this is that as the NTE increases, the percentage of tax jumps from 15 percent to 27 percent, then from 27 percent to 30 percent, then from 30 percent to 35 percent, and stops at a maximum rate of 38.6 percent. This is in keeping with IRS rules for taxing income at several separate rates per the Economic Growth and Tax Relief Reconciliation Act of 2001; therefore, the more an employee makes, the more taxes that must be withheld.

The percentage method of withholding lends itself to being used when the payroll person desires a more exact withholding amount. Those employers who have computerized the payroll accounting function will use the software for normal payroll needs and resort to using the wage-bracket method when a paycheck must be figured and "cut" manually.

Q&A

Q: Can we always use the wage-bracket method to calculate an employee's federal income tax withholding for a pay period?

A: No, the wage-bracket tables have an upper limit of earnings. The percentage method must be applied for any employee who earns more than the upper limit listed on a wage-bracket table.

3 THE PURPOSE OF FEDERAL INCOME TAX WITHHOLDING

Federal income taxes are withheld from the majority of employees by employers per federal law. The federal law that originally mandated withholding was called the **Current Tax Payments Act of 1943**. This law is now part of the Internal Revenue Code of 1986 which is explained in Chapter 3.

Withholding income taxes from employee paychecks is known as the "pay-as-you-go" method, because as income is earned, federal income tax is withheld. As a historical note, before 1943, income tax withholding was voluntary and many employees accrued large income tax liabilities after the end of each year with no withholding to offset the debt. This is the reason the pay-as-you-go method was made law.

Remember that the amount of federal income tax withheld for the year is taken as a credit against the actual income tax liability and reduces any amount that could be due when the employee's 1040 return is filed. This method ensures that most employees have some dollar amount of credit ready to apply against their actual tax liability after the end of the year.

The Form 1040

The actual amount of federal income tax that employees will owe for a calendar year is determined by the filing of a *Form 1040*. Individuals may file simplified versions of the Form 1040 known as *Form 1040-A* and *Form 1040-EZ*. The individual's Form 1040 will list all the types of income received for the year as well as deductions that are allowed against income. Earnings from employment are only one of many types of income that the individual may receive in a year.

This chapter has to this point focused on the calculation and withholding of federal income taxes. We will now turn our attention to state income taxes and withholding methods.

F I G U R E   7–6

States That Do Not Require Withholding on Employee Earnings

▪ Alaska	▪ New Hampshire	▪ Texas
▪ Florida	▪ South Dakota	▪ Washington
▪ Nevada	▪ Tennessee	▪ Wyoming

4 STATE INCOME TAXES

Most of the 50 states require that state income taxes be withheld on employee earnings in the state in which they work. Most of these states have based their systems of withholding on the federal model with some modifications. We will look briefly at several states and discuss their withholding methods.

States That Do Not Require Withholding on Earnings

Not all states currently tax income on earnings. As of this writing, there are nine states that do not require withholding on employee earnings. These states are listed in Figure 7–6.

In these states other sources provide necessary tax revenues. For example, Alaska, Texas, and Wyoming levy severance taxes on natural resources such as natural gas, oil, and mineral deposits. Revenues for Florida, Nevada, and Washington come from sales taxes and other types of taxes such as taxes on interest and dividend income.

Nonresident Employees

In some locations in the United States, an employee may reside in one state but work in an adjacent state. An employee who works in one state but lives in another is commonly referred to as a **nonresident employee**. Geographic examples include employees who work in New York and live in New Jersey, those who live in Virginia but work in Maryland (and vice versa), and those who work in Kansas City, Missouri, but live in Kansas City, Kansas.

As a general rule, the payroll accountant will withhold state tax on the income of these employees as if they lived and worked in the same state.

The fact that the employee resides in another state does not change the withholding obligation of the employer. Likewise, the fact that the employee works in one state but lives in another does not relieve the employee from any tax obligation in the state of employment.

In most cases, the employee will have to file state tax returns in the state of residence *and* the state of employment. The employee could be entitled to a "credit for taxes paid in another state" on the residence state tax return, thus avoiding paying tax twice on income earned from employment in the other state. The matter of filing state tax returns is entirely the obligation of the employee, not the payroll professional or the employer.

State Reciprocity Agreements

There are exceptions to the general rule that requires withholding on nonresident employee earnings. Some states may set up a reciprocity agreement with other neighboring states where each state agrees not to tax the nonresident employees from the other neighboring state. The payroll professional should check for the existence of such agreements and comply with the specific requirements of any agreement.

5   COUNTY AND LOCAL WITHHOLDING TAXES

In addition to federal and state income tax withholding, a county or municipality may levy a tax on income or employment. An employer will be required to withhold these taxes from the employee's income in the same way federal and state income taxes are withheld.

City Tax

In some locations, the city where an employee works will require a city income tax to be withheld from earnings. Several hundred localities in the state of Ohio and several cities in Michigan impose income taxes on earnings. New York City also imposes such a tax. In the case of Ohio cities, the rate may range from 1 to 2.85 percent; over half of Ohio's rates are at 1 percent. Employees in such situations must file a city return along with state income tax returns after the end of the year. The city return may be part of the state return, or it may be a separate return. For example, the New York City return is part of the New York state income tax return that an employee will file.

Employment or Head Tax

In some municipalities and counties, an employee may pay a tax for the privilege of working in that particular city or county. Such taxes are levied to raise revenues for various reasons and may not necessarily be based on a percentage of employee earnings. Employers could also be required to pay or share in such a tax. Such taxes are sometimes called **head** or **employment taxes** because an employee is taxed (or charged a license fee) for working in a particular location, rather than being taxed on income.

Over 60 localities in the state of Kentucky levy income taxes which are called *occupational license fees.* Such taxes must be withheld from an employee's earnings. Many localities in the state of Pennsylvania currently levy income taxes. An example of localities in states that currently impose income or employment taxes are listed in Figure 7–7. Please note that this figure shows only a sample of localities nationwide.

One example of such an employment tax is the Denver, Colorado, *Occupational Privilege Tax (DOPT).* This tax is paid on a monthly basis by anyone who works within the boundaries of the city and county of Denver, Colorado. The tax is levied to help the city and county with road maintenance. Currently, any full-time employee who works within the city and county boundaries and earns a minimum amount each month is required to pay $5.75 per month in occupational privilege tax. The employer must pay its share of $4 per month for each employee who pays the tax.

F I G U R E   7–7

Localities That Tax Income or Have an Employment Tax

- **Alabama**—City of Birmingham, Jefferson County

- **Colorado**—Employee Occupational Privilege Tax

- **Delaware**—Wilmington Earned Income Tax

- **Indiana**—County Adjusted Gross Income Tax

- **Michigan**—Uniform City Income Tax Ordinance

- **Missouri**—Kansas City and St. Louis Earnings Tax

- **New York**—New York City income tax

- **Ohio**—Various locality income taxes

- **Pennsylvania**—Various locality income taxes

The payroll professional should check to see if any local or county taxes must be withheld from employee earnings and comply with any regulations that apply.

6 REPORTING REQUIREMENTS FOR INCOME TAXES WITHHELD

Employers who are required to withhold state income taxes will in most instances be involved with preparing and submitting the following state forms and tax returns:

- Individual state copies of employees' W-2 forms.
- State deposit forms for income taxes withheld.
- State withholding tax returns.

Generally speaking, any state that requires income tax withholding on employee earnings will also require that the employer prepare a state withholding tax return. These returns are also known as *information returns*. Although each state's return differs somewhat, the information usually requested on such a return will include the amount of income tax withheld, dollar amounts of state tax deposits made, and any balance due with the filing of the return.

The filing requirement for such withholding returns may be semimonthly, monthly, quarterly, or annually. Usually, the greater the amount of tax withheld, the more frequently tax deposits must be made and withholding returns filed.

The withholding return requirements for several states are listed in Figure 7–8. Please note the differences in the form numbers and titles. Most states require that employers who withhold state income taxes give their employees a *state copy* of federal Form W-2 that includes the amount of state withholding and any local withholding. These forms will cover the calendar-year period and should be given to employees no later than January 31 of the next calendar year.

A state may not accept a state copy of federal Form W-2 and may require that the employer prepare a special state version of the wage-and-tax statement form. The employer must still give these statements to their employees after the end of the year (no later than January 31). The employer can obtain the specific requirements for the form from these states, including its appearance and the information that must be stated on the form.

Examples of State Income Tax Withholding Returns

State	Withholding return form number	Return form name or title
▪ California	DE6	Quarterly Contribution Return
▪ Colorado	DR 1094	Income Withholding Tax Return
▪ Illinois	IL-941	Quarterly Illinois Withholding Tax Return
▪ Maryland	MW506	Return of Income Tax Withheld
▪ Massachusetts	M-941	Quarterly Return of Income Taxes Withheld
▪ New York	NYS-4-MN	Quarterly Combined Withholding and Wage Reporting Return
▪ Texas	None	No form required

State W-2 Forms

Most states also require that employers send copies of individual employee wage-and-tax statements (or state copies of the W-2 forms) to the state after the end of the calendar year. These forms may be accompanied by a state transmittal form, similar to the federal Form W-3.

Some states allow the employer an option: use magnetic tape or computer disk to file state wage-and-tax statements. Some states could require the employer to file using magnetic media if the employer is required to do so for federal purposes. Employers could have to file electronically if the number of state W-2 forms exceeds a certain total (250 being the usual threshold amount). The employer should check with the specific state as to its electronic filing options and requirements.

Electronic Funds Transfer Tax Deposits

Employers who withhold over a certain amount in state income tax per year may be required to make tax deposits electronically using the *electronic funds transfer* system (known as *EFT*) from the employer's bank account to the state treasury's bank account. For example, if an employer's New York State withholding is $400,000 or more annually, the employer must use the

EFT system, which is known as the *PrompTax* program, for tax deposits. In Colorado, any employer whose annual state tax withholding exceeds $11,000 must use the EFT system. Again, the payroll professional must check with each specific state regarding any EFT deposit requirements.

Because there are no rules that apply across the board to all 50 states, the payroll professional must check with each state where individuals are employed regarding withholding tax and report filing requirements. The competent professional will make every effort to keep current with changes in state laws that affect the payroll accounting function. Professionals who are members of an association can use their membership advantageously to keep up with federal and state or provincial withholding tax developments as they occur.

CHAPTER 8

401(k) Plan, Cafeteria, SEP, SIMPLE, and Other Deductions

This spot on the payroll accounting road map is a popular stop in our journey. It's essential for anyone involved in payroll to have an understanding of the mechanics of retirement and cafeteria plans, and before- and after-tax deductions. This chapter will explain how such deductions are calculated and tracked as part of the payroll accounting process. This chapter will also help you to better understand the area of employee benefits.

1 EMPLOYEE DEDUCTIONS

One of the many responsibilities of the payroll professional is calculating and withholding various deductions from employee earnings. The area of employee deductions has become complex, and today employees can have amounts taken from their pay for a variety of reasons.

Deductions can be separated into two groups: elective and required. Payroll professionals must know the difference between these two groups in calculating an employee's paycheck and accounting for the deductions. Figure 8–1 gives examples of elective (voluntary) and required (mandatory) deductions.

An **elective deduction** is one that an employee chooses to have withheld from his pay. Practically speaking, an employee could have an amount withheld by the employer for almost any reason as long as the employer is willing to make the deduction. Elective deductions are a convenient way for an employee to make loan payments to a credit union, buy U.S. savings bonds, or pay medical insurance premiums.

A **required deduction** is one that is imposed on an employee by a court order and enforced through law. Employees have no choice as to

FIGURE 8-1

Examples of Elective and Required Deductions

Elective Deductions:

- Medical insurance premiums
- Charitable contributions

- Labor union dues
- Credit union saving plans

- Credit union loan payments
- U.S. Savings Bond plans

Required Deductions:

- Child support payments
- Income tax levies
- Wage garnishments

whether these deductions are taken from their earnings. Payments for child support and delinquent income taxes as well as a court-ordered garnishment to pay an employee's creditor are examples of required deductions. The key point to remember in dealing with required deductions is the fact that these deductions are ordered by a court of law, and the employer must comply with the court order and withhold the amount requested. Several common types of required deductions are listed in Figure 8–1.

Legal Aspects of Required Deductions

Federal law has prioritized the order in which required deductions are made. Payments for child support are the top priority, tax levies are second in line, and wage garnishments then fall in line with any others.

The law also limits the amounts that can be withheld on a pay period basis for required deductions. Required deductions cannot exceed certain percentages of an employee's take-home pay each pay period. This rule allows an employee to take home enough money to live on while making the court-ordered payments.

EXAMPLE 1

James Johnson, the payroll accountant for U.S. Route 66 Trucking, Inc., has two court orders for the same employee. One court order is for child support, and a separate court order is for payment of an overdue doctor's bill. James must first comply with the court order for child support and make the appropriate deduction. Then, if the employee's take-home pay is sufficient after applying the percentage calculation for required deductions, James will make the appropriate deduction for payment of the doctor's bill.

Employer Deposits for Deductions

Amounts that have been withheld from employees' earnings will be paid under various timetables. For instance, the deductions for medical insurance premiums may have to be paid monthly on the last day of the month by the employer. Labor union dues may be paid on the fifteenth of each month. The payroll accountant should set up a regular timetable for paying employee deductions and comply with the payment deadlines.

Now that we have broken deductions into two general categories, we will shift our attention to the challenging concepts of before- and after-tax deductions, and their impact on employees' earnings and the payroll taxes of an employer.

2   BEFORE- AND AFTER-TAX DEDUCTIONS

Our discussion of employee deductions would be finished at this point except for the fact that certain payroll deductions can be made either *before* or *after taxes*. The payroll accounting for the tax effects of a before-tax deduction is considerably different than for an after-tax deduction. It is important in payroll accounting to understand and be able to calculate employee pay when these types of deductions are involved.

First, we must understand the concept of a **before-tax deduction.** By definition, such a deduction is taken from an employee's pay before income taxes are calculated on the pay. This means that a payroll professional will not compute taxes on the employee's gross pay, but on the employee's pay *after* subtracting the deduction which we refer to as the employee's **taxable pay**. The importance of a before-tax deduction lies in the fact that income taxes are computed on employee earnings *after* the deduction has been made. No federal or state income tax is computed on the amount of the deduction itself—so, the employee saves tax dollars by making the deduction "before tax."

Before-tax deductions are not taxable for federal or state income purposes. However, a before-tax deduction could be subject to social security and Medicare taxes. We will identify and discuss the types of before-tax deductions that are exempt from income taxes and those that are exempt from *both* income and social security taxes in Segments 3 and 4 of this chapter.

Please note that now we have three definitions for pay or earnings: *gross earnings,* the amount of regular and overtime earnings for a pay period *before* any taxes are withheld; *taxable earnings,* the amount upon which the payroll professional will calculate taxes (after subtracting before-tax deductions); and *net pay,* the amount the employee will receive after *all* taxes and deductions have been withheld.

E X A M P L E 2

An employee for U.S. Route 66 Trucking, Inc. earns $490 (gross pay) for the week. The employee has a $50 before-tax deduction withheld from his weekly pay. Jim Johnson in payroll will first subtract the $50 from the employee's gross pay of $490. The remaining amount, $440 (taxable income), will be the amount used to compute federal and state taxes. The $50 is then considered a *before-tax deduction.*

Let's look at the steps involved in calculating a before-tax deduction and an employee's net pay.

Steps to Compute Net Pay Using Before-Tax Deductions

1. Compute the employee's gross pay *before* any deductions or taxes.

2. Subtract the before-tax deduction from the gross pay amount found in Step 1. This is called *taxable pay.*

3. Using the taxable pay found in Step 2, calculate state and/or federal income taxes.

4. Subtract the taxes calculated in Step 3 from the taxable pay. Subtract any other deductions and payroll taxes. This then is the employee's *net* or *take-home pay.*

E X A M P L E 3

Jackie Williams earns $950 weekly as a terminal worker for U.S. Route 66 Trucking, Inc. in Adrain, Texas. Jackie has claimed "Married; two withholding allowances" on her current W-4 form. She has a before-tax deduction of $79.25 withheld weekly from her pay for an employee benefit plan in which she has decided to participate. The payroll accountant uses the wage-bracket method for income tax withholding. Jackie has no other deductions taken out of her pay. What will be the amount of Jackie's net pay?

Steps to Solve Example 3

1. Jackie's gross pay is $950.
2. Subtract the before-tax deduction from gross pay.
3. Use the taxable pay amount to compute federal income tax. (Texas has no income tax withholding.)
4. Subtract the tax withholding amount from taxable pay to arrive at net pay.

Solution to Example 3 (Before-Tax Deduction)

1. Jackie's gross earnings are $950.

2.
$950.00	gross pay
−79.25	before-tax deduction
$870.75	taxable pay

3.
$96	federal income tax from wage-bracket table (See Chapter 7, Figure 7–3.)

4.
$870.75	taxable pay
−96.00	federal income tax
$774.75	Jackie's net pay

After-tax deductions have no special direct tax benefit for an employee. An after-tax deduction is subtracted after income taxes are computed on an employee's earnings. Such a deduction will be subtracted from an employee's gross pay along with payroll taxes to arrive at net pay.

Garnishments, tax levies, and child support payments are required by court order and are always after-tax deductions. The before- or after-tax character of the deduction is determined by the purpose of the deduction—not the employee's desire to treat a deduction as before tax.

How much will Jackie pay in taxes if we change her $79.25 deduction to an after-tax deduction? We can answer the question by looking at the steps involved in calculating net pay when an after-tax deduction is withheld.

Steps to Compute Net Pay Using After-Tax Deductions

1. Compute the employee's gross pay *before* any deductions or taxes.
2. Using the gross pay found in Step 1, calculate the appropriate taxes.
3. Subtract the taxes calculated in Step 2 *and* the after-tax deductions from gross pay. This equals net pay.

Solution to Example 3 (After-Tax Deduction)

1. Jackie's gross earnings are $950.

2. $950.00   gross pay
          $108.00   federal income tax from wage-bracket table
                     (See Chapter 7, Figure 7–3.)

3. $950.00   gross pay
         −108.00   federal income tax
          −79.25   after-tax deduction
         $762.75   Jackie's net pay

In looking at the above computations, two things are obvious: Jackie pays more in taxes and takes home less in earnings when the $79.25 deduction is treated as an after-tax deduction—she pays a total of $108.00 in federal income taxes on her earnings. If Jackie's deduction is treated as before-tax, Jackie pays $96.00 in taxes. A before-tax deduction of $79.25 saves Jackie $12.00 in federal income tax ($108.00 − $96.00 = $12.00). Jackie "bought" a $79.25 deduction for $67.25 ($79.25 − $12.00 in tax savings = $67.25).

In the examples found in this chapter we ask you to calculate federal and state income taxes as a flat percentage of gross pay. The percentages given approximate the tax paid by many workers today. We ask you to make the tax calculations this way to save you time. Thus, you can devote your full attention to learning how to calculate before- and after-tax deductions. Keep in mind that in actual practice you would use either the wage-bracket or percentage withholding allowance method to calculate income taxes which we discussed in Chapter 7.

Figure 8–2 shows side-by-side calculations for a deduction that is taken before and after tax by another U.S. Route 66 Trucking, Inc. employee. We assume in this example that the employee will have federal income tax withheld at 15 percent and state income tax withheld at 5.95 percent.

There are no restrictions as to the kind of deductions that can be made on an after-tax basis. The amount deducted is taken from the employee's gross earnings along with income, social security, and Medicare taxes and other deductions. Because employees do not enjoy any tax savings from after-tax deductions, there are no special Internal Revenue Code rules that govern such deductions.

The majority of deductions are after-tax deductions. Generally, these deductions are a specific set dollar amount (rather than a percentage of pay) and are not based on the gross earnings of the employee. The employee normally approves a deduction by signing an authorization form. The deduc-

F I G U R E   8–2

Tax Impact on Net Pay of a Before- and an
After-Tax Deduction

	Deduction Made Before Taxes	Deduction Made After Taxes
Gross earnings for the week	$400.00	$400.00
Deduction taken before tax	−35.00	0.00
Taxable earnings	$365.00	$400.00
Federal income tax withheld at 15%	−54.75	−60.00
State income tax at 5.95%	−21.72	−23.80
Deduction taken after tax	0.00	−35.00
Employee's net (take-home) pay	**$288.53**	**$281.20**

tion can then be made at regular intervals, either on a pay period basis or on some other schedule.

3   SALARY REDUCTION PLANS AND DEDUCTIONS

Now that we understand the concepts of before- and after-tax deductions, we need to direct our attention to the question of what employee deductions can be made on a before-tax basis. This section and Segment 4 will answer this important question.

In order for workers to enjoy the benefit of before-tax deductions, an employer must set up a specific plan under the rules of the Internal Revenue Code and other federal laws in order to provide its employees the option of making before-tax deductions. Businesspeople refer to these plans by the Internal Revenue Code sections that establish and authorize such plans. Two very popular plans are called *Section 401(k)* and *Section 125 plans* by employers. Section 401(k) plans, which are the topic of this section, are called *salary reduction* or *deferral plans* by employees and the general public. Section 125 plans, referred to as *cafeteria* or *flexible benefit plans* by employees and the general public, are the topic of Segment 4. Both of these plans or arrangements will allow employees to make certain deductions before income taxes are calculated.

In law books and textbooks dealing with taxation, the symbol § is used as an abbreviation for the term *section*. We will use this symbol to refer to particular sections of the Internal Revenue Code when discussing these deduction plans.

A §401(k) or **salary reduction plan** allows employees to set aside retirement savings on a before-tax basis. The money that the employee contributes to the plan in the form of payroll deductions will not be subject to federal or state income taxes; it *will* be taxed for social security and Medicare taxes. Therefore, the §401(k) deduction is still subject to social security and Medicare taxes.

In order for an employee to participate in a salary reduction plan, he must first become eligible to enter the plan. Employees can enter, or become eligible, to participate in a plan after they work a required period, usually 12 months, and attain a certain age, usually 21. The payroll professional is often required to determine or verify such eligibility of employees. Once an employee is eligible, the employee then has the option of making §401(k) contributions to the plan.

Salary reduction or deferral plans are a convenient way for employees to set aside funds before taxes for their retirement years. Employers may also make their own contributions toward their employees' retirement. These contributions are known as **matching** or profit-sharing **contributions.**

E X A M P L E 4

Kara Jefferson works for U.S. Route 66 Trucking, Inc. She contributes 5 percent of her weekly pay into a §401(k) plan. U.S. Route 66 Trucking, Inc. will match her contribution with a 50 percent employer match. For the week ending June 3, Kara's gross pay is $400. Her §401(k) deduction is $20 ($400 × .05 = $20). U.S. Route 66 Trucking's matching contribution is $10 ($20 × .50 = $10).

The amount or percentage of matching contributions an employer makes on behalf of its employees is entirely optional. Most employers contribute a percentage of each dollar the employee has deducted and placed into the plan; however, the employer dollars contributed are usually limited to a set maximum dollar amount. The employer percentages can range anywhere from 1 percent up to 200 percent of employee §401(k) deductions (in the case of one highly successful company). Some employers do not make any matching contributions—such employers generally have lower participation rates in their plans.

Employer matching and/or profit-sharing contributions are a valuable employee benefit because employees can keep the money the employer contributes on their behalf if they work for the employer for a specific number of years. **Vesting** is the amount of employer money the employee owns. Vesting is based on the number of years the employee has been working for the employer. The length of time employees must work for an employer in order to keep employer contributions varies depending on the specific requirements of the plan.

Employee and employer money placed into a salary reduction plan is held in trust for employees and can only be withdrawn for a limited number of reasons; thus, employee §401(k) deductions are subject to strict rules determined by a plan document. A **plan document** is the written rules that govern how a salary reduction plan operates. All plans must have such a document.

When an employee terminates employment, the employee may take all §401(k) deductions that he contributed into the salary reduction plan. All employee §401(k) deduction amounts are "owned" by the employee. However, the employee may not be entitled to keep all matching contributions the employer made for the employee's benefit. The percentage of employee ownership of matching contributions is usually determined by using a *vesting schedule.*

E X A M P L E 5

In order for Kara to legally keep, or own, 100 percent of the matching contributions U.S. Route 66 Trucking, Inc. has made on her behalf, she must work for the company for at least five years. If she terminates her employment with U.S. Route 66 Trucking, Inc. before five years pass and she leaves the plan, she will only be able to keep a percentage of U.S. Route 66 Trucking's matching contributions. Figure 8–3 shows the vesting schedule that U.S. Route 66 Trucking, Inc. follows to determine an employee's ownership percentage of matching contributions.

Employees who are only partially vested at the time they withdraw their contributions from the plan will only be entitled to receive the percentage of matching contributions per a schedule similar to the one shown in Figure 8–3. The amount of matching contributions the employee leaves behind in

F I G U R E   8–3

U.S. Route 66 Trucking's Vesting Schedule for
Matching Contributions

Time Period in Years	Percent of Employee Ownership
▪ Less than 1 year	0%
▪ 1 year up to 2 years	20%
▪ 2 years up to 3 years	40%
▪ 3 years up to 4 years	60%
▪ 4 years up to 5 years	80%
▪ 5 years or more	100%

the plan is called a **forfeiture.** At an employer's option, forfeited amounts can be used to pay certain plan expenses or can be used to fund future employer contributions to the plan.

Deductions to §401(k) Plans Are Tax-Deferred

Deductions made into the plan are taxable for income tax purposes when the employee retires and begins to receive payments from the plan. The employee is *postponing* the payment of taxes on the amounts deducted and placed into a §401(k) plan. This arrangement is called a **tax-deferred deduction**.

Congress has placed two limits on employee deductions and employer contributions placed into plans each calendar year: one is a "dollar cap" and the other is a "percentage ceiling."

The IRS sets the maximum dollar cap on the total of each employee's before-tax deductions made in a calendar year. For 2001, the employee's deductions are limited to a maximum of $10,500.

The IRS also places a percentage ceiling on the *combined* total of employee deductions and employer contributions made into the plan each calendar year. This combined total for 2001 must be the lesser of $35,000 or 25 percent of an employee's total compensation.

The combined total of 25 percent of total compensation must include both employee deductions and employer matching and/or profit-sharing contributions. If an employee receives a 5 percent profit-sharing contribution based on the employee's gross earnings, the employee's deduction for the year cannot exceed 20 percent of his gross earnings. This combined total also affects the other before-tax deductions made by the employee. One such deduction is known as a *cafeteria plan deduction* which we will discuss in the next section. Other before-tax deductions will further reduce the maximum amount of an employee's §401(k) deductions for a year.

It is important for the payroll professional to be aware of the dollar cap and percentage ceiling maximums in working with employee deductions, because questions will be raised by employees and management regarding the maximum amounts that can be made into §401(k) plans.

E X A M P L E 6

John Downing earns $60,000 for the year as a fleet manager with U.S. Route 66 Trucking, Inc. He wants to contribute 20 percent into a §401(k) plan. U.S. Route 66 Trucking, Inc. will not make any profit-sharing or matching contributions on John's behalf, and John has no other before-tax deductions withheld from his pay. A 20 percent contribution would equal a deduction of $12,000 ($60,000 × .20 = $12,000). John cannot make a $12,000 deduction because his deduction is limited to a maximum of $10,500 for 2001 per IRS rules. On a percentage basis, John's maximum contribution is actually 17.5 percent ($10,500/$60,000 = .175)

In order to understand how a §401(k) deduction is applied in calculating an employee's net pay, let's look at two examples.

E X A M P L E 7

Donald Sullivan is a participant in a §401(k) retirement plan. He earns $3,000 monthly as a plant manager. He has a 5 percent deduction made for the §401(k) plan. Donald's employer will make a 50 percent matching contribution. Donald pays federal income taxes at a rate of 15 percent and state income taxes at a rate of 5.95 percent. Donald's year-to-date earnings (including the current monthly $3,000 salary) are under the current social security earnings limit. What will be Donald's salary reduction amount and Donald's net pay?

Let's analyze the steps involved in calculating Donald's §401(k) deduction and his net pay. Note the steps involved to figure federal and state income taxes and social security and Medicare taxes below.

Steps to compute net pay using a §401(k) deduction

1. Obtain the gross pay for the employee.
2. Determine the amount of the §401(k) deduction by multiplying its percentage times gross pay.
3. Subtract the §401(k) deduction from gross pay found in Step 1. This is the taxable pay for computing income taxes.
4. Calculate federal income taxes based on taxable pay. Recall that the employer may use the wage-bracket or percentage withholding methods. For this example, we will use the percentage given in Example 7.
5. Calculate state income tax (if any) based on taxable pay. Use the percentage rate given in the example.
6. Calculate social security and Medicare taxes on the employee's *gross pay* (not taxable pay).
7. Subtract the §401(k) deduction and the payroll taxes from the employee's gross pay. This includes all payroll taxes: federal income, state income, social security, and Medicare taxes. The result is the employee's net (or take-home) pay.

Steps to solve Example 7

1. Donald's gross pay is $3,000 for the month.

2.
$3,000.00	gross pay
× .05	§401(k) percentage
$ 150.00	amount of §401(k) deduction

3.
$3,000.00	gross pay
−150.00	§401(k) deduction
$2,850.00	Donald's taxable pay for income tax calculations

4.
$2,850.00	taxable pay
× .15	federal income tax percentage
$ 427.50	federal income tax

5.
$2,850.00	taxable pay
× .0595	state income tax percentage
$ 169.58	state income tax (rounded to the nearest cent)

6. $3,000.00   gross pay
            × .0765   combined rate for social security and Medicare taxes
            $ 229.50   total social security and Medicare taxes

7. $3,000.00   gross pay
            −150.00   §401(k) deduction
            −427.50   federal income tax
            −169.58   state income tax
            −229.50   social security and Medicare taxes
            $2,023.42   Donald's net pay

In Example 7, Donald's employer matches his §401(k) deduction at a 50 percent rate. Notice that the matching contribution is not used to compute Donald's taxable pay. Employer matching amounts do not reduce or increase the taxable earnings of employees.

In the above example, Donald will save the amount he would have paid in federal and state income taxes on the $150 deduction. The amount of income tax savings is actually 20.95 percent (15 percent federal and 5.95 percent state) on $150.00, or $31.43 ($150.00 × .2095 = $31.43).

E X A M P L E 8

Let's look at Sam Clark's §401(k) deduction for the week ending June 3. He contributes 5 percent of his weekly pay into a U.S. Route 66 Trucking, Inc. §401(k) plan. U.S. Route 66 Trucking, Inc. will match his contribution at a 50 percent rate. For the week ending June 3, Sam's gross pay is $495. If federal income taxes are withheld at a rate of 15 percent and state income taxes at 5.95 percent, what will be Sam's take-home pay for the week? The steps to solve Example 8 are identical to those used to solve Example 7.

Steps to Solve Example 8

1. Sam's gross pay is $495.00 for the week.

2. $495.00   gross pay
            × .05   §401(k) percentage
            $ 24.75   amount of §401(k) deduction

3. $495.00   gross pay
            −24.75   §401(k) deduction
            $470.25   Sam's taxable pay for income tax calculations

4.	$470.25	taxable pay
	× .15	federal income tax percentage
	$ 70.54	federal income tax (rounded to the nearest cent)
5.	$470.25	taxable pay
	× .0595	state income tax percentage
	$ 27.98	state income tax (rounded to the nearest cent)
6.	$495.00	gross pay
	× .0765	combined rate for social security and Medicare taxes
	$ 37.87	total social security and Medicare taxes (rounded to the nearest cent)
7.	$495.00	gross pay
	−24.75	§401(k) deduction
	−70.54	federal income tax
	−27.98	state income tax
	−37.87	social security and Medicare taxes
	$333.86	Sam's net pay

Salary reduction or deferral plans must comply with the applicable rules found in Internal Revenue Code section 401 as well as several other sections. These rules are enforced by the Internal Revenue Service. Employers who establish such plans must also comply with several federal laws that set rules for administering plans and protecting plan assets. The **Employee Retirement Income Security Act** of 1974 (ERISA) was the first major federal law that specifically provides guidelines that employers must follow in administering §401(k) plans. ERISA is enforced by the U.S. Department of Labor (DOL) and the IRS.

Employee Perspective

Once an employee joins a §401(k) plan, he as a plan participant must abide by the plan's rules regarding how his deductions can be invested. Special rules also exist regarding the conditions under which a participant may withdraw his funds. Some plans allow a participant to borrow a portion of his funds as a loan.

Generally, a participant may elect to take a cash distribution of the amount in a §401(k) plan when the participant terminates employment, retires, or becomes disabled. Such amounts could be subject to income tax and in some instances early-withdrawal penalties.

When an employee changes jobs, his new employer's §401(k) plan might allow the employee to take his money from the former employer's plan and roll over the funds into the new plan. Such rules are not global and vary with each §401(k) plan.

We will now discuss the other types of allowable before-tax deductions, known as *flexible benefit* or *cafeteria plan deductions*.

4   CAFETERIA PLANS AND DEDUCTIONS

An employer-sponsored plan that would allow employees to make before-tax deductions is commonly known as a *flexible benefit* or *cafeteria plan*. The terms *flexible benefit* or **cafeteria plan** are used because the employee has a degree of flexibility in the types of available benefits chosen. Such plans allow employees to pick and choose from among many options in the areas of medical insurance premiums, child day care expenses, or various kinds of insurance. From a technical viewpoint, these plans are called *employee welfare plans*.

Section 125 plans are also called *flexible spending arrangements (FSAs)*. In this situation employees are allowed to make a payroll deduction into a fund. The fund will later reimburse the employee for out-of-pocket medical and dental expenses such as prescriptions, eyeglasses, contact lenses, and other expenses that qualify under the guidelines of this plan. The employee must pay the initial cost of the acceptable expense and then submit a claim to be reimbursed (which may take up to 30 days to receive). Figure 8–4 gives examples of some of the types of expenses that can be reimbursed through a §125 plan.

Under the rules of Internal Revenue Code §125, a cafeteria or flexible benefit plan must be a formal written plan that does not favor highly paid employees. This means that executives and highly paid employees of the company cannot be treated any differently by the plan than other employees of the company.

§125 Deductions Are Tax Exempt

Employee deductions made to a §125 plan are *totally* **tax-exempt deductions** because the amounts deducted are before income *and* social security and Medicare taxes. The employer also does not pay any social security, Medicare, or state and/or federal unemployment taxes on deductions made

F I G U R E   8 – 4

Types of Employee Expenses That Are Paid by a §125 Cafeteria Plan

Insurance Premiums:	Reimbursable Out-of-Pocket Medical Expenses:	Other Reimbursable Normal Living Expenses:
▪ Medical insurance premiums	▪ Eyeglasses or contact lenses	▪ Child day care
▪ Cancer insurance premiums	▪ Vision and eye exams	
▪ Group term life insurance premiums	▪ Deductible portion of doctor and dentist visits not covered by insurance	
▪ Dental insurance premiums	▪ Prescriptions	

into this type of plan. Section 125 deductions could be subject to certain state and local taxes. Figure 8–5 summarizes the before- and after-tax treatment of various deductions for individual taxes.

The amounts reimbursed to employees for the expenses shown in Figure 8–4 are not taxable to the employee when received. The reimbursement amounts are *tax-exempt,* meaning they are not subject to tax. Contrast this to §401(k) contributions that are *tax-deferred,* meaning that an employee will pay tax on any amounts taken out of a §401(k) plan.

Calculating §125 deductions is simpler than calculating §401(k) amounts because cafeteria plan deductions are not subject to social security or Medicare taxes as we can see in the following example.

E X A M P L E   9

Deborah Scott signs up to participate in a §125 flexible spending arrangement plan. She works in Massachusetts. She earns $1,800 monthly. She contributes $250 per month into a cafeteria plan. Of this amount, $200 will be applied directly to her monthly medical insurance premiums; the remaining $50 will be put into her flexible spending account in the §125 plan. As the fund builds, she may make withdrawals to pay out-of-pocket medical or dental expenses during the current year.

F I G U R E   8–5

Before- and After-Tax Treatment of
Employee Deductions

Type of Tax	§125 Cafeteria Deductions	§125 Flexible Spending Arrangement	§401(k) Employee Deductions	Other Types of Elective Deductions	Required Deductions
Federal income	Before tax	Before tax	Before tax	After tax	After tax
State income	Before tax[1]	Before tax[1]	Before tax[1]	After tax	After tax
Social security	Before tax	Before tax	After tax	After tax	After tax
Medicare	Before tax	Before tax	After tax	After tax	After tax
Federal unemployment	Before tax	Before tax	After tax	After tax	After tax
State unemployment	Before tax[2]	Before tax[2]	After tax	After tax	After tax

1. Certain states and localities do not allow §125 and §401(k) deductions to be treated as before-tax deductions.
2. Calculation of state unemployment taxes will vary from state to state.

Deborah's year-to-date earnings are under the current social security earnings limit. Using a federal income tax rate of 15 percent and a state income tax rate of 5.95 percent, what will be Deborah's net pay for the month ending June 30?

Steps to Compute Net Pay Using a §125 Deduction

1. Obtain the gross pay for the employee.
2. Determine the amount of the §125 deduction.
3. Subtract the §125 deduction from gross pay found in Step 1. This is the taxable pay for computing federal and state income, social security, and Medicare taxes.
4. Calculate federal income taxes based on taxable pay.
5. Calculate state income tax (if any) based on taxable pay.
6. Calculate social security and Medicare taxes based on taxable pay.
7. Subtract the §125 deduction and the payroll taxes from the employee's gross pay. The result is the employee's net (or take-home) pay.

Steps to Solve Example 9

1.   Deborah's gross pay is $1,800 for the month.

2. $ 250   amount of the §125 deduction

3. $1,800.00   gross pay
       −250.00   §125 deduction
       $1,550.00   Deborah's taxable pay for tax calculations

4. $1,550.00   taxable pay
         × .15   federal income tax percentage
       $ 232.50   federal income tax

5. $1,550.00   taxable pay
        × .0595   state income tax percentage
       $ 92.23   state income tax (rounded to the nearest cent)

6. $1,550.00   taxable pay
        × .0765   combined rate for social security and Medicare taxes
       $ 118.58   total FICA taxes (rounded to the nearest cent)

7. $1,800.00   gross pay
       −250.00   §125 deduction
       −232.50   federal income tax
       −92.23   state income tax
       −118.58   social security and Medicare taxes
       $1,106.69   Deborah's net pay

The Key Benefit of §125 Plans

Employees save valuable tax dollars when making deductions into §125 plans because the expenses they pay from such plans are paid with before-tax dollars. These plans are popular with many people today because of their tax savings aspect, and a growing number of employers are choosing to participate in such plans to accommodate their employees.

Employee Perspective

Employees who participate in §125 plans must abide by certain rules established by the IRS. One rule states that if an employee does not request reimbursement for 100 percent of the amount he has paid into the plan during a calendar year, the amount not reimbursed is lost by the employee. (This is informally known as the "use it or lose it" rule.) The employer is entitled to keep such amounts. Also, medical expenses reimbursed through a §125 plan are not deductible on the employee's 1040 tax return.

It is obvious that additional calculations must be made in order to correctly figure an employee's take-home pay when the employee contributes to a before-tax plan. When payroll accounting software is used, the before- and after-tax deductions are automatically calculated to arrive at net pay. This is a distinct advantage that an automated payroll software program has over a manual payroll accounting system.

An employee can contribute to both a §401(k) and §125 plan each pay period. In such a situation the §401(k) and §125 deductions will be subtracted in arriving at taxable pay to be used in computing income taxes. The dollar amount used to compute social security and Medicare taxes will be different than taxable pay due to the fact that a §401(k) deduction is taxable for FICA, whereas a §125 deduction is not. In this situation we have two types of taxable pay: one for computing income taxes and the other for computing FICA taxes. In order to help us distinguish between these two taxable amounts, we will refer to the amount used to compute social security and Medicare tax as **FICA taxable pay**. Example 10 illustrates an employee who has both §401(k) and §125 deductions.

E X A M P L E   10

Joe Collins is an engineer for U.S. Route 66 Trucking, Inc. He earns $4,000 monthly. Joe's year-to-date earnings as of June 30 are $24,000. Joe pays 15 percent in federal and 5.95 percent in state income taxes. Joe's deduction into the U.S. Route 66 Trucking, Inc. §401(k) plan is 5 percent of his gross pay. Joe also has $400 deducted each month to be set aside in a §125 plan to pay for child day care expenses. What is Joe's net pay for the month of July?

Steps to Compute Net Pay Using §401(k) and §125 Deduction

1. Obtain the gross pay for the employee.
2. Determine the amount of the §401(k) deduction.
3. Determine the amount of the §125 deduction.
4. Subtract the §401(k) and §125 deductions from gross pay found in Step 1. This is the taxable pay for computing income taxes.

5. Calculate federal income taxes based on taxable pay. Use the percentage rate given in the example.

6. Calculate state income tax (if any) based on taxable pay. Use the percentage rate given in the example.

7. Calculate the FICA taxable pay for the employee. This is found by taking the gross pay and subtracting the §125 deduction only.

8. Calculate social security and Medicare taxes on the employee's FICA taxable pay.

9. Subtract the §401(k) and §125 deductions and the payroll taxes from the employee's gross pay. The result is the employee's net (or take-home) pay.

Steps to Solve Example 10

1. Joe's gross pay is $4,000.00 for the month.

2.
$4,000.00	gross pay
× .05	§401(k) percentage
$ 200.00	amount of §401(k) deduction

3.
$ 400.00	amount of §125 deduction (given in the example)

4.
$4,000.00	gross pay
−200.00	§401(k) deduction
−400.00	§125 deduction
$3,400.00	Joe's taxable pay for income tax calculations

5.
$3,400.00	taxable pay for federal income tax purposes
× .15	federal income tax percentage
$ 510.00	federal income tax

6.
$3,400.00	taxable pay for state income tax purposes
× .0595	state income tax percentage
$ 202.30	state income tax

7.
$4,000.00	gross pay
−400.00	amount of §125 deduction
$3,600.00	FICA taxable pay

8.
$3,600.00	FICA taxable pay
× .0765	combined rate for social security and Medicare taxes
$ 275.40	total social security and Medicare taxes

9.	$4,000.00	gross pay
	−200.00	§401(k) deduction
	−400.00	§125 deduction
	−510.00	federal income tax
	−202.30	state income tax
	−275.40	social security and Medicare taxes
	$2,412.30	Joe's net pay

5 TRUSTEES AND PLAN ADMINISTRATORS

Accounting for §401(k) and §125 before-tax deductions is a payroll function. The payroll professional must track the deductions and remit the amounts on a timely basis. The elements of accuracy and timeliness are important when dealing with employee deductions, and the payroll professional must act in a competent manner when accounting for these payroll deductions.

Section 401(k) deductions and matching contributions are invested in a trust. The trust can then invest in mutual funds, money market funds, or other types of investment options for long-term growth and asset appreciation. Many plans allow employees to choose from among several investment options for their deductions. Such a plan is referred to as a **self-directed plan**. Other §401(k) plans are more restrictive in that employees do not have a choice as to where their money is invested. Investment options and the self-direction feature of many §401(k) plans are decided when a plan is established.

Cafeteria and flexible benefit plans do not use a trust or place their funds into long-term investment options because it is expected that the funds will be used in the near future to pay for employee expenses. The majority of these plans operate with a separate checking account used only for this purpose.

ERISA requires that a salary reduction or deferral plan must appoint a trustee. A **trustee** is an individual who has legal title to plan assets and custody of the assets. Trustees are in a position of considerable responsibility because many §401(k) plans have hundreds of employees who participate in them. As a result, plans may grow to several millions of dollars of assets.

The trustee may appoint **agents** to calculate and account for the deductions and contributions placed into §401(k) plans. In many situations payroll professionals become agents of trustees because they are responsible for determining employee deductions and employer contributions each pay period.

Plan administrators are responsible for the day-to-day operation of §401(k) plans. A plan administrator can be an individual or the employer that sponsors a plan. Daily affairs of a plan administrator include record keeping, accounting, communicating with plan participants, and preparing reports for the IRS and DOL.

Because most plan administrators do not have the time or expertise to oversee the daily accounting and administration activities of the plans, they hire a **third-party** (or contract) **administrator** *(TPA)* to take care of the daily operation of the plan. TPAs are individuals or firms that specialize in administration of §401(k) and §125 plans. Some insurance companies and attorneys also offer their services as TPAs.

Payroll professionals should work closely with both trustees and TPAs in calculating §401(k) deductions, matching contributions, and §125 plan deductions. Working with trustees and TPAs makes the payroll accountant's job both challenging and rewarding and involves the type of knowledge and skills that today's payroll professional must possess.

6 SEP AND SIMPLE PLANS

Our stop at this point on the payroll road map would be incomplete without mention of two other types of retirement plans that many small businesses choose to implement. Unlike the §401(k) plans we have discussed, these plans are easier to create and operate and offer a viable alternative for a small business. These plans have less administrative burden than a §401(k) plan; however, the trade-off here is that neither plan offers as much flexibility as the §401(k) plan does. A SEP (known as a *Simplified Employee Pension*) can be implemented by a business for pension purposes. A SIMPLE (an acronym which stands for *Savings Incentive Match Plan for Employees*) is also a plan that a small business can adopt and use. We will now briefly touch on several of the major features of each of these plans.

The SEP plan can be an alternative to more costly and complicated §401(k) plans for a small business. The rules for such a plan differ in many respects from those of a §401(k) plan. For instance, all monies that flow into such a plan must be deposited into an Individual Retirement Account or Annuity (commonly known as IRAs) for each employee. Unlike a §401(k) plan, the employee is always 100 percent vested in any contribution made by the employer since the employee "owns" the IRA.

Under SEP rules, if the employer chooses to make a contribution on behalf of its employees, it must contribute into a worker's account if

- The worker has been employed by the business for three of the last five years.
- The worker is at least 21 year of age.
- The worker has earned a minimum of $450 for the 2000 calendar year.

Using a SEP, an employer can make a contribution into its employees' accounts up to 15 percent of each employee's earnings for all employees entitled to participate in the SEP. This amount is still subject to the overall contribution limit of the lesser of 25 percent of an employee's total compensation or $35,000 in 2001 (what is technically known as an Internal Revenue Code §415 limit). Another difference between a SEP and a §401(k) plan is that employers must make a "level contribution percentage" into a SEP (For example, 6 percent of the total compensation of *all* eligible employees). Please note here that the employer's contribution is discretionary; it can vary from year to year based on the performance of the company and management's expectations; and like a §401(k) plan, the employer's contribution into a SEP is deductible as a business expense and exempt from social security and Medicare taxes.

One type of SEP plan that was established before December 31, 1996, allowed employees to make their own contributions in addition to any employer contributions. Such a plan is called a SARSEP. Here the employee could contribute in a way similar to that of a §401(k) plan—a maximum of $10,500 for the 2001 year. However there are several restrictive rules that apply to a SARSEP including the fact that the employer must have fewer than 25 employees, one half of which must participate in the plan. Also, the employer is not allowed to make any matching contributions into the SARSEP in keeping with the "level contribution percentage" rule mentioned above. There are other regulations that apply to a SARSEP that we will not discuss in this chapter. Any SARSEP that was in existence and operational as of December 31, 1996, can still exist and operate today using the pre-1997 rules.

A new type of plan replaced the SARSEP beginning in 1997. This plan is known as a SIMPLE (or *Savings Incentive Match Plan for Employees*). It was another part of the federal Small Business Job Protection Act of 1996. The SIMPLE is designed *to be* simple to operate and maintain for a small business (i.e., a business having 100 or fewer employees who earned at least $5,000 during the calendar year). The SIMPLE differs from a SEP (or SARSEP) in several respects:

- Employees can make up to a $6,000 contribution of their earnings to a SIMPLE in a calendar year.
- An employer can make matching contributions on the first 3 percent of employee compensation for the calendar year or an employer can make an additional mandatory (non-elective) contribution up to 2 percent on behalf of its employees.

SIMPLEs are like SEPs from the standpoint that all plan participants must be 100 percent vested at all times, but they are different due to the fact any employee who earned $5,000 in the last two years of employment *and* who is expected to earn at least the same amount during the current year must be included in a SIMPLE. Also, the employer must not maintain any other type of pension plan (such as a §401(k) or a SEP plan).

SIMPLE contributions, like SEP contributions, are made into an employee's IRA account. Since the employee is 100 percent vested in all contributions, the employee may elect to withdraw some or all of the funds at any time. Likewise, an employee who does withdraw funds will be subject to similar federal and state tax penalties as an employee who withdraws his funds from a §401(k) plan.

Q&A

Q: Where can I obtain more information about starting a SEP or SIMPLE for my company?

A: IRS *Publication 560* "Retirement Plans for Small Business" deals with SEP and SIMPLE plans in more detail. You may also want to obtain IRS *Publication 590* "Individual Retirement Arrangements" that discusses IRAs. May we suggest that before you establish a SEP, SIMPLE, or §401(k) plan you contact a knowledgeable CPA, tax attorney, or pension plan administrator who can evaluate your specific business and recommend the best type of pension plan for both you and your employees.

7 EMPLOYEE BENEFITS

A current topic heard in the news media today is downsizing or rightsizing. Corporations are reducing their work forces through attrition and/or the elimination of jobs. Labor costs are a major expense for employers today, and employee benefits comprise a significant portion of labor costs.

An almost hidden element of the labor costs of a company are employee benefits. The cost of such benefits add to the total cost of employing a worker, yet many employees believe that their hourly wage or salary is the total cost of their employment.

Two decades ago employee benefit packages were commonplace, and companies competed for employees by offering comprehensive packages to prospective employees. The current trend is just the opposite, and benefit packages may be eliminated altogether to comply with a corporate downsizing move.

An employer may pay a part or all of the cost of an employee's medical or life insurance or some other expense. This is referred to as an **employee benefit.** Benefits differ from deductions in that typically the employer, not the employee, pays the cost of the expense. If the cost of a benefit is shared by employer and employee, the amount of the employee's expense can be considered a payroll deduction.

Consider the many types of benefits that an employee might receive. Technically, vacation days, paid holidays, and sick leave are employee benefits. Employees are usually paid for such time away from their jobs which can amount to a sizable payroll cost because the employee is not engaged in work activities while off the job. Any other costs that the employer pays for the employee (such as medical insurance premiums for the employee, spouse, and dependents) increase the total cost of keeping the employee on the job. Figure 8–6 gives examples of the many types of benefits employees might receive in the course of their employment.

Employers also incur their own payroll tax costs. As discussed in Chapter 3, social security taxes are matched and paid by employers. An employer must also pay federal and state unemployment taxes on the earnings of employees—a topic discussed in Chapters 12 and 14 of this book. These

F I G U R E   8–6

Examples of Employee Benefits

▪ Sick pay	▪ §401(k) or SIMPLE matching contributions	▪ Payment of professional license fees (RN, CPA)
▪ Vacation pay	▪ Tuition reimbursement programs	▪ §401(k) profit-sharing contributions
▪ Paid holidays	▪ Employer's portion of social security and Medicare tax	▪ Continuing professional education courses
▪ Medical insurance paid for employee	▪ Medical insurance paid for employee's spouse and dependents	▪ Paid life and disability insurance

mandatory expenses of hiring and employing workers can be considered a benefit.

Employee benefits may or may not be taxable to an employee. If a benefit is taxable, the cost of the benefit is considered income to the employee, and the employee will pay tax on the dollar value of the benefit. The dollar value of taxable benefits generally will be shown on the employee's **W-2 form**, known as the *Wage and Tax Statement*.

For some employers, the total cost of employing a worker could be as much as 40 percent greater than the wage the worker earns. Thus, the total cost to an employer to employ a worker is greater than just the employee's hourly wage or salary.

CHAPTER 9

Tips and Taxes

Our next stop on the payroll road-map is the I-40/Route 66 Truck Stop in Adrian, Texas, to get a cup of hot coffee, a slice of pecan pie, and to think about tip income and how it is dealt with in payroll accounting. The town of Adrian, Texas, is the half-way point on historic Route 66, and likewise this chapter is about half-way through our payroll journey as well.

This chapter is devoted to the area of how tips are treated from a payroll accounting standpoint. We cover the taxability of tips, reporting and tax withholding requirements for tipped workers.

1 TIP INCOME AND THE FAIR LABOR STANDARDS ACT

In Chapter 3 we discussed the minimum wage as set by the Fair Labor Standards Act (FLSA) and amended by various laws including the recent *Small Business, Health Insurance, and Welfare Reform Act of 1996.*

One special exception from payment of the current federal minimum wage exists for employees who receive tip income. Due to the fact that tip income is considered to be a part of the employee's hourly wage, employers are exempted from paying the full current minimum wage. This exemption is better known under FLSA as the *tip credit.*

Q&A

Q: What is defined as *tip income*?

A: A tip is a gratuity that is received by an employee from a customer for satisfactory performance of a service (such as service from a waiter, waitress, bartender, seating by a maitre d', etc.). In order for such a gift to qualify as a tip, it must be received in the form of cash, a check, or a credit card. Note that non-cash gifts by definition are excluded from tip income. Also note that a tip must be freely given by a customer to an employee; therefore, mandatory service charges imposed by a restaurant (such as a percentage assessed on a large group having a lunch or dinner) are not considered tip income. One other important characteristic of tip income is that it cannot be under the control of an employer at any time; any tip income that an employer requires to be handed-over by an employee is not considered true tip income and will not count toward the amount used to compute any tip credit.

The employer may use the tip credit in connection with employees who receive tips on a regular basis in an occupation in which it is customary to tip workers (e.g., food and beverage establishments where waitresses, waiters, buspeople, and bartenders work). The tip credit could not be applied to the employee who only occasionally receives a tip for his services (e.g., a cashier at a fast food restaurant or gas station or convenience store). The following specific rules must apply in order for the employer to legitimately use the FLSA tip credit:

- The employee must ordinarily receive tips of $30 or more each month.
- The employee must work in an occupation where it is customary to receive tips.
- The employee must be told he will not receive the full current minimum wage due to the tip credit.

E X A M P L E 1

For several of our examples in this chapter we go to the imaginary town of Oakdale, Illinois, and find a small restaurant known as Tom's Cafeteria. Tom's is open for breakfast and lunch and employs 12 people. Vinnie Vitello works for Tom's Cafeteria as a waiter. When Vinnie was hired, he was told that he would receive an hourly wage of $2.13 (which is less than the current minimum wage) due to the fact that he would receive tips. Tom Smith, the owner of Tom's Cafeteria, is correct to apply the tip credit when paying Vinnie Vitello weekly.

E X A M P L E 2

Gayle Edwards works as a cashier at the I-40/Route 66 Truck Stop & Power Wash in Adrain, Texas. She does not receive tips on a regular, recurring basis, nor is it customary for her to receive tips as a cashier. The I-40/Route 66 Truck Stop cannot offset the current minimum wage with the FLSA tip credit when paying Gayle.

Q&A

Q: Do employers have to keep track of tips in order to claim the tip credit?

A: Employers do not have to maintain records of employees who receive tips merely to comply with FLSA when applying the tip credit; *however*, employers must keep track of the amount of tips earned by each employee during each calendar year in order to properly compute and pay the appropriate payroll taxes.

The Amount of the Tip Credit

The actual tip credit depends on the average hourly amount the employee receives in tips. Employers are allowed to count the tips employees receive towards the hourly minimum wage amount paid to tipped employees. The employer's base minimum wage for tipped employees is $2.125 per hour (rounded to $2.13). The $2.13 minimum was 50% of the previous federal minimum wage of $4.25 (prior to 1993). Under the provisions of the Small Business Job Protection Act of 1996, this amount for tipped employees currently remains at $2.13 per hour. This means that the current maximum federal tip credit is $3.02 per hour ($5.15 – $2.13 = $3.02 per hour).

In order for the employer to properly comply with FLSA, the tip credit should be applied using the employee's workweek as a measuring tool. In other words, the tipped employee should receive at least $3.02 per hour in tips during a 40-hour workweek in order for the employer to claim a tip credit of $3.02 per hour for that workweek ($3.02 + $2.13 = $5.15).

An employer may not be able to claim the maximum tip credit of $3.02 per hour if on average the tips a tipped employee receives is less than $3.02 per hour in any given workweek. In such cases, the employer should claim a tip credit that is less than this maximum. If the amount of tips received by the tipped employee is less than $3.02 per hour for the workweek, the employer is obliged to pay the employee the difference in order for the employee to receive at least $5.15 minimum wage per hour (so the tip credit would be less than the $3.02 per hour maximum in such a situation).

E X A M P L E 3

Big Bob's Belly Buster Burgers is across the street from Tom's Cafeteria. Big Bob's accountant, Johnny Debit, has figured that on average waitpeople only receive $1.50 per hour in tips. This means that Big Bob's can only claim a tip credit of $1.50 per hour and must pay its waitpeople at least $3.65 per hour for all hours worked ($5.15 – $1.50 = $3.65).

Overtime and Tip Income

The overtime provision of FLSA still applies to tipped employees, given that they are classified as nonexempt employees. (See Chapters 3 and 4 for a complete discussion of nonexempt employees.) Any hours worked in excess of 40 during the workweek must be compensated at 1.5 times the regular hourly rate of pay, regardless of the amount of tip income earned during the time period.

E X A M P L E 4

Vinnie Vitello had to work two shifts at Tom's Cafeteria due to a snowstorm over a weekend. Vinnie worked 52.30 hours during the workweek and made a substantial amount in tip income during this same period. Tom Smith must pay Vinnie 1.5 times the minimum wage for the final 12.30 hours worked, less the maximum tip credit of $3.02. Therefore, Vinnie will receive $4.71 per hour for the 12.30 overtime hours worked ($5.15 ×1.50 = $7.73 – $3.02 (tip credit) = $4.71 overtime rate).

2 TAXABILITY OF TIPS

Employees who regularly receive tips as a part of their income for services provided must report the amount of the tips to their employer at least once per month. Tips may be reported more frequently than monthly if the employer requests such an accounting and provides a way for the employee to report tips (such as an entry on a time card or a nightly tip tally sheet).

E X A M P L E 5

The owner of the Joe's Diner, Joe Johnson, requires all tipped employees to report their tips each week. Joe pays his employees weekly. Joe gives each employee Form 4070, shown in Figure 9–1, to use in reporting tip income. These forms are available in a coupon-book format known as *IRS Publication 1244.*

Tips are taxable to the employee as well as other types of remuneration. Any employee receiving $20 or more in tip income must report the actual amount received as income to the employer. Employees who report $20 or more in tip income per month must pay federal income tax as well as social security and Medicare taxes on tip income. Generally tips are taxable on a state level as well except for the nine states that currently do not tax income.

Q&A

Q: Why is there a $30 per month minimum for the employer tip credit and a $20 per month minimum for an employee when reporting tips to his employer?

A: Under FLSA a $30 per month minimum was established in order for an employer to claim a tip credit for an employee when paying minimum wage. However, for a tipped employee's reporting purposes, a

F I G U R E 9–1

Form 4070

Form **4070** (Rev. June 1999) Department of the Treasury Internal Revenue Service	**Employee's Report of Tips to Employer** ▶ For Paperwork Reduction Act Notice, see back of form.	OMB No. 1545-0065
Employee's name and address *Tina Dutton* *1233 Broadway #112, Oakdale, IL 66999*	Social security number *923 45 6781*	
Employer's name and address (include establishment name, if different) *Joe's Diner* *554 Grand Avenue* *Oakdale, IL 66999*	1 Cash tips received *112.16*	
	2 Credit card tips received *65.94*	
	3 Tips paid out *0*	
Month or shorter period in which tips were received from *September 15* , to *September 22, 200X*	4 Net tips (lines 1 + 2 - 3) *178.10*	
Signature *Tina Dutton*	Date *9-23-200X*	

lower $20 per month amount is used. Note also that the lower $20 per month tip income minimum is used for calculating employee earnings for federal unemployment tax purposes.

The employer must also pay his share of social security, Medicare, federal, and state unemployment taxes on reported tip income of $20 or more per month. For employer payroll tax purposes, tips are treated no differently than any other type of income earned by employees.

Q&A

Q: Do employees who receive credit card tips have to report such tips immediately as income, or can they wait until the credit card payment has been received by the employer?

A: It makes no difference whether the tip is received in cash or via a credit card. The employee must report the tip as if it has been received in cash at the time of the credit card purchase. Employees cannot defer reporting of their credit card tips. Employers should pay employees credit card tips no later than one pay period after the credit card purchase.

Federal Income Taxes

If the tips reported by an employee are added to the amount paid to the employee by the employer each pay period, federal income tax can be computed on the tip and hourly income as one dollar amount. Either the wage-bracket, percentage, or formula method can then be used to compute the amount of federal taxes to be withheld on the employee's gross pay.

If tip income is not added regularly to the employee's pay period earnings, the tip income can be treated as supplemental wages. If the employer chooses to treat tip income in this way, the amount of tip income will be subject to a flat 27.5 percent withholding for federal income tax.

E X A M P L E 6

If Joe Johnson chooses, he can calculate the amount of tip income received by each employee on a monthly basis even though he pays employees weekly for the hours they work. The federal income tax rate Joe must use for calculating federal income taxes on the tip income is a flat 27.5 percent regardless of withholding allowances or marital status.

Social Security and Medicare Taxes

As we have mentioned, tip income is also subject to social security and Medicare taxes. As we discussed in Chapter 6, the employee must pay his portion of these taxes just like the employer. The tax calculation will be subject to the current social security earnings limit for the year in which the tip income is earned. Again, the FICA and Medicare tax calculations for tip income are the same as for any other type of employee earnings.

Employee Payment of Taxes

The employee is responsible for his payment of federal and state income, social security, and Medicare taxes on all tip income received if it is over the $20 per month threshold. Ordinarily, the amount of these employee taxes will be deducted from the hourly pay of the employee, given that most tip income received by tipped workers is received in cash at the time their services are performed.

A question arises when the amount of hourly earnings of a tipped employee for a pay period is less than the taxes due for federal and/or state income, social security, and Medicare taxes. If this occurs, the employer has several options available. First, the employer can ask the employee to pay the amount of tax due in cash from tip income. If the employee cannot pay the amount in cash, the employer must remit the payment of these taxes in the following order:

1. Calculate and pay the social security or Medicare withholding due on the hourly (non-tip) earnings of the employee. There is no priority as to whether social security or Medicare is paid first in this instance.
2. Calculate and pay any federal income tax withholding due on the hourly (non-tip) earnings of the employee.
3. Calculate and pay the social security or Medicare withholding due on the tip income of the employee. Again, there is no priority as to whether social security or Medicare is paid first at this stage in the ordering of payment of these taxes.
4. Calculate and pay any federal income tax withholding due on the tip income of the employee.
5. If after following Steps 1 through 4 above, any amount in federal income, social security, and/or Medicare taxes still

remains unpaid, the liability should be made up with the employee's next pay period earnings.

3   SOCIAL SECURITY AND MEDICARE TAXES FOR FOOD AND BEVERAGE ESTABLISHMENTS

Special rules apply to restaurants and lounges (termed *food and beverage establishments* in IRS publications) when calculating FICA on the earnings of employees who receive tips. Waiters, waitresses, bus people, and bartenders are some of the employees who usually receive tip income.

When tips are reported to an employer by an employee using Form 4070 or another tracking method (e.g., time card entry or tip talley sheet), it is the employer's responsibility to withhold social security and Medicare taxes from the employee using the social security earnings limit rules discussed in Chapter 6. The FICA to be withheld must come out of any money the employer pays the employee for wages earned. Remember that the employer must also match the FICA withholding of the employee dollar for dollar, subject to the same earnings limit as the employee.

Allocated Tips and the 8 Percent Rule

Any restaurant or lounge that employs 11 or more people is classified by the IRS as a *large* food or beverage establishment. To determine whether this definition applies to a particular enterprise, the total number of employees on a regular business day during the preceding year must be counted. The count of employees must include *all* employees working on the day chosen whether they receive tips in the course of their work or not.

A large food or beverage establishment is required to calculate 8 percent of its annual sales (or gross receipts) as the assumed amount of tips its employees received for the year.

The employer (in this case, the restaurant or lounge) must take the 8 percent computed amount for the year and compare it to the actual dollar total of tips that have been reported by employees. If the total tips reported are less than 8 percent of the sales for the year, it is the employer's responsibility to allocate the difference between these two amounts to the employees. This allocated amount, called **allocated tips,** must be prorated to each employee.

The amount for allocated tips can be calculated and applied using one of three approved IRS methods. These methods are known as the following:

- A "good faith agreement"
- The "hours worked" method
- The "gross receipts" method.

A good faith agreement is a written document made by the employer and at least two thirds of the employees who receive tips (such as waiters, waitresses, maitre d's) at the time the agreement is approved and adopted. Generally speaking, the agreement will state that the difference between the tips reported and 8 percent of the gross receipts for the same time period will be considered to be allocated tips. The agreement will have an effective date as of the beginning of the next pay period after adoption. All parties must also concur that such an agreement can be revoked at a later date by a two-thirds vote of the employees affected by such an agreement.

If a food and beverage establishment does not have a good faith agreement in place with its tipped employees, the establishment is required to make allocated tip calculations using either the "hours worked" or "gross receipts" methods. Both methods are more complicated to apply than a good faith agreement calculation for allocated tips.

An establishment having fewer than 25 full-time (or the equivalent of full-time, 40-hours per week workers) employees on its payroll (this number includes both tipped and non-tipped employees) has the option of using either the "hours worked" or "gross receipts" method for allocated tips. An establishment with 25 or more full-time employees should use the "gross receipts" method in lieu of a valid written good faith allocated tip agreement.

In discussing allocated tips, the IRS distinguishes between *directly* and *indirectly tipped employees.* A directly tipped employee will receive tips in direct connection with the services he performs (such as a waiter, waitress, or maitre d'). Indirectly tipped employees contribute to the overall operation of the establishment but are not tipped directly (cooks, bus-people, dish washers, etc.). This distinction is important when working through Example 7 below.

In Example 7 we will illustrate the "hours worked" method for Joe's Diner, an establishment that employs 12 full-time workers. Note that the steps to finding the amount of allocated tips for a pay period is a series of individual calculations applied to the directly tipped employees of Joe's.

E X A M P L E   7

Joe's Diner is a restaurant that serves only breakfasts and lunches. Joe's employs 12 people full-time: 8 waitresses and waiters (*tipped employees*), 2 cooks, and 2 bus-people (*indirectly tipped employees*). These employees report their tip income on a weekly basis to Joe Johnson, the owner, using IRS Form 4070 (see Figure 9-1). Joe's does not have a good faith agreement in place with its tipped employees, and he chooses to use the "hours worked" method to report allocated tips each pay period.

For one weekly pay period ending on September 22, 200X, the employees of Joe's reported $921.50 in tips. Indirectly tipped employees received a total of $201.50 in tips for the pay period. The gross receipts for meals and beverages served by each of his tipped employees for the week is $19,297.25. Joe's payroll accountant calculated 495 hours worked by all employees for the weekly pay period, of which 330 were worked by directly tipped employees. One employee, Tina Dutton, worked 41.25 hours for the week, and in the same week she reported $178.10 in tips to Joe using a Form 4070. Will Tina have any allocated tip amount for this weekly pay period?

Steps to Solve Example 7

Joe's payroll person will need to make the following calculations in order to determine if an amount will be allocated for tips for Tina Dutton for the weekly pay period. The calculations are as follows:

1. Figure 8 percent of the meal and beverage sales of the restaurant for the weekly pay period.

2. Subtract from the 8 percent amount (calculated in Step 1) the amount of tips reported by *indirectly tipped employees* (the cooks and bus-people in Joe's Diner). The net amount is the amount of tips to be allocated among the *tipped employees* (the waitresses and waiters at Joe's Diner).

3. For each weekly pay period the payroll accountant must compute what is known as the **hours worked ratio.** This ratio is the total of all hours worked by each tipped employee for the week divided by the total hours worked by all tipped employees for the same week.

4. The hours-worked ratio for each tipped employee (found in Step 3) will be multiplied by the allocated tip amount (found in Step 2) to arrive at

each **directly tipped employee's allocated tip amount.** This step must be repeated for each tipped employee for the weekly pay period.

5. When the allocated tip amount for each tipped employee has been found, it must be compared to the actual tip amount reported by each waitress and waiter (Joe's tipped employees) for the same pay period. If the allocated tip amount is greater, the difference between the allocated tip amount and the actual reported tip amount will be computed. This amount is known as the individual **directly tipped employee shortfall allocation amount.**

6. The total **tip shortfall allocation amount** will be prorated and allocated to each tipped employee who had an individual shortfall for the pay period. Please note here that some employees could have reported more than the tipped employee shortfall amount found in Step 5. When this happens, the individual tipped employee will not receive any allocated tip amount for the pay period (see the calculation for "Sloppy" Joe Williams in Steps 5 and 6).

Now in order to better understand how all of these calculations work, let's find out if Tina Dutton will receive an allocated tip amount for the weekly pay period described in Example 7 at Joe's Diner.

Solution to Example 7

1. 8 percent of sales for the pay period is calculated:

$19,297.25	sales for the pay period
× .08	8 percent threshold amount per the IRS
$ 1,543.78	8 percent of sales for the pay period

    The 8 percent amount of $1,543.78 is greater than the reported amount of $921.50.

2. We must deduct any tip amount attributed to the indirectly tipped employees from the 8 percent figure found in Step 1 above to obtain the directly tipped employees net amount. In Example 7 the total amount of tips for the indirectly tipped employees is $201.50; so the directly tipped employees amount will be $1,342.28 ($1,543.78 – $201.50). The $1,342.28 figure will be used in Steps 3, 4, and 5 below.

Note also that of the 495 total hours worked for the pay period, indirectly tipped employees worked 165 hours; therefore, the directly tipped employees worked 330 hours for the pay period (495 hours – 165 hours). The 330 hour figure appears in Step 3 below.

3. In this step we must compute the **Hours Worked Ratio** for each directly tipped employee for the pay period. Note that we use the total hours for all directly tipped employees (330 hours; see Step 2) as the denominator for each employee's percentage calculation:

Directly Tipped Employee	Individual employee hours worked for the pay period **divided by:**	**From Step 2:** The total hours worked by directly tipped employees for the pay period	**Equals** the Directly Tipped Employee **Hours Worked Ratio** for the pay period
Stuart W.	40.00	330.00	0.1212
Jeff S.	45.00	330.00	0.1364
Wanda B.	40.00	330.00	0.1212
Debra A.	39.50	330.00	0.1197
Carol Ann C.	40.00	330.00	0.1212
Erin K.	44.25	330.00	0.1341
"Sloppy" Joe W.	40.00	330.00	0.1212
Tina Dutton	41.25	330.00	0.1250
Column Totals:	330.00 Hours	330.00 Hours	1.00

4. In this step we must find the directly tipped employees' **Allocated Tip Amount** for the pay period. Note that we will use the directly tipped employees 8% net amount from Step 2 and the percentages found in the Step 3 calculation to determine each employee's allocated tip amount:

Directly Tipped Employee	**From Step 3:** Directly tipped employee hours worked ratio for the pay period **multiplied by:**	**From Step 2:** Directly tipped employees net amount	**Equals** the **Allocated Tip Amount** for each directly tipped employee
Stuart W.	0.1212	$1,342.28	$ 162.68
Jeff S.	0.1364	1,342.28	183.10
Wanda B.	0.1212	1,342.28	162.68
Debra A.	0.1197	1,342.28	160.67
Carol Ann C.	0.1212	1,342.28	162.68
Erin K.	0.1341	1,342.28	180.00
"Sloppy" Joe W.	0.1212	1,342.28	162.68
Tina Dutton	0.1250	1,342.28	167.79
Column Totals:	1.000		$1,342.28

5. In this step we must find the Tipped Employee Shortfall Allocation amount for each employee for the pay period. Note that we use the amounts found in Step 4 (the 8 percent net amount for each directly tipped employee) and deduct the actual tips reported by each employee to determine any shortfall. Please pay particular attention to "Sloppy" Joe William's situation and the footnote at the bottom of this table for an explanation as to why he will not receive any shortfall allocation amount.

Directly Tipped Employee	From Step 4: Allocated Tip Amount for each Tipped Employee **minus**	Actual Tips Reported by each Tipped Employee for the Pay Period	**Equals** the **Directly Tipped Employee Shortfall Allocation** amount
Stuart W.	$162.68	$85.90	$76.78
Jeff S.	183.10	101.50	81.60
Wanda B.	162.68	60.73	101.95
Debra A.	160.67	85.75	74.92
Carol Ann C.	162.68	149.78	12.90
Erin K.	180.00	111.14	68.86
"Sloppy" Joe W.	162.68	171.50	**0.00
Tina Dutton	167.79	155.20	12.59
Column Totals:	$1,342.28	$921.50	$429.60

**Note that because "Sloppy" Joe reported more than the 8 percent net allocated tip amount ($8.82), he will not receive any portion of the Employee Shortfall Allocation. His difference is actually reallocated among the remaining directly tipped employees who reported less than their allocated amount ($1,342.28 – $921.50 = $420.78 + $8.82 ["Sloppy" Joe's reallocation] = $429.60).

6. In this final step, we prorate the **Tip Shortfall Allocation** amounts to individual "shortfall" employees (those workers who reported less than their individual 8 percent net allocation figure) for the pay period. Again see that "Sloppy" Joe Williams does not receive any allocation as he reported more than his individual 8 percent figure (refer back to Step 5). Notice as well that the amount of the shortfall is $622.28 which is obtained by subtracting the actual tips reported from the gross 8 percent tip allocation figure found in Step 1.

Directly tipped employees with shortfall amounts	Amount to be Allocated to "Shortfall" Tipped Employees ($1,543.78 − $921.50) multiplied by	From Step 5: The individual employee shortfall ratios	Equals the Amount of Tip Shortfall Allocation to directly tipped "shortfall" employees
Stuart W.	$622.28	$76.78 / $429.60	$111.22
Jeff S.	622.28	81.60 / 429.60	118.20
Wanda B.	622.28	101.95 / 429.60	147.67
Debra A.	622.28	74.92 / 429.60	108.52
Carol Ann C.	622.28	12.90 / 429.60	18.69
Erin K.	622.28	68.86 / 429.60	99.74
Tina Dutton	622.28	12.59 / 429.60	18.24
Totals:		$429.60 / $429.60	$622.28

In answer to our original question, Tina Dutton will have an allocated tip amount of $18.24 (look at the table in Step 6) for the weekly pay period ending on September 22, 200X at Joe's Diner.

If Joe's Diner employed more than 25 full-time (or full-time equivalent) employees *and* it did not have a good faith agreement in place with its tipped employees, the payroll accountant would have to use the "gross receipts" method of allocating tips. The steps to computing allocated tips using this method are the same as for the "hours worked" method, except that instead of using hours worked as the numerator and denominator in our series of calculations, we substitute the gross receipts for each tipped employee for the pay period as the numerator and the total gross receipts of the establishment for the pay period as the denominator, beginning in Step 3.

Please remember that the payroll accountant will make these computations for all directly tipped shortfall employees on a pay period basis for each pay period during the calendar year. However, for reporting purposes the total of all individual pay period allocated tip amounts will be shown in Box 8 of the employee's Form W-2 after the end of the calendar year.

Notice also that tipped employees must report the total of *all* of their tips, even if such an amount exceeds an 8 percent computed amount. The fact that the IRS uses the 8 percent figure does not relieve any tipped employee from reporting any actual amount of tips over and above this amount during any pay period.

The food or beverage establishment will report the totals for reported tips, gross sales, service charges, and allocated tips each calendar year to the IRS using **Form 8027** (see Figure 9-2). This form is an information return

F I G U R E   9–2

Form 8027

Form **8027** Department of the Treasury Internal Revenue Service	**Employer's Annual Information Return of Tip Income and Allocated Tips** ▶ See separate instructions.	OMB No. 1545-0714 **200X**

Use IRS label.
Make any
necessary
changes.
Otherwise,
please type or
print.
	Name of establishment
	Joe's Diner 12-3456789
	Number and street (See instructions.) Employer identification number
	554 Grand Blvd.
	City or town, state, and ZIP code
	Oakdale, IL 66999
		Type of establishment (check
		only one box)
		☐ 1 Evening meals only
		☐ 2 Evening and other
		   meals
		☒ 3 Meals other than
		   evening meals
		☐ 4 Alcoholic beverages

Employer's name		Establishment number (See instructions.)
Number and street (P.O. box, if applicable.)	Apt. or suite no.	
City, state, and ZIP code (If a foreign address, see instructions.)		

Check the box if applicable: Final Return ☐   Amended Return ☐

1	Total charged tips for calendar year 200X	**1**	
2	Total charged receipts (other than nonallocable receipts) showing charged tips	**2**	
3	Total amount of service charges of less than 10% paid as wages to employees	**3**	
4a	Total tips reported by indirectly tipped employees	**4a**	
b	Total tips reported by directly tipped employees	**4b**	49,782
	Note: *Complete the Employer's Optional Worksheet for Tipped Employees on page 4 of the instructions to determine potential unreported tips of your employees.*		
c	Total tips reported (Add lines 4a and 4b.)	**4c**	49,782
5	Gross receipts from food or beverage operations (other than nonallocable receipts). . .	**5**	829,700
6	Multiply line 5 by 8% (.08) or the lower rate shown here ▶ _____ granted by the district director. Attach a copy of the district director's determination letter to this return .	**6**	66,376
	Note: *If you have allocated tips using other than the calendar year (semimonthly, biweekly, quarterly, etc.), put an "X" on line 6 and enter the amount of allocated tips from your records on line 7.*		
7	Allocation of tips. If line 6 is more than line 4c, enter the excess here	**7**	16,594
	This amount must be allocated as tips to tipped employees working in this establishment. Check the box below that shows the method used for the allocation. (Show the portion, if any, attributable to each employee in box 8 of the employee's Form W-2.)		
a	Allocation based on hours-worked method (See instructions for restriction.) . . . ☐		
	Note: *If you checked line 7a, enter the average number of employee hours worked per business day during the payroll period. (See instructions.)* _____		
b	Allocation based on gross receipts method . . . . ☒		
c	Allocation based on good-faith agreement (Attach copy of agreement.) . . . . . ☐		

8   Enter the total number of directly tipped employees at this establishment during 200X ▶

Under penalties of perjury, I declare that I have examined this return, including accompanying schedules and statements, and to the best of my knowledge and belief, it is true, correct, and complete.

Signature ▶ *Joe Johnson*   Title ▶ Owner & operator   Date ▶ 1/25/200X

For Privacy Act and Paperwork Reduction Act Notice, see page 4 of the separate instructions.   Cat. No. 49989U   Form **8027** for the food and beverage establishment; no tax is due or is paid with the filing of this return. This return should be sent to the IRS no later than the last day of February each year for the prior calendar year's reporting period.

FICA Is Not Paid on Allocated Tips

Note that even though an employee finds a dollar amount for allocated tips on his W-2 form, the employee will not pay FICA on allocated tips. The employee pays FICA only on the actual amount of tips reported to the employer for the year. This is considered to be an information item on the W-2 form, and as such no FICA tax is paid on this amount by an employee.

For more information on the filing requirements for employees who receive tip income, request *Publication 1244, Employee's Daily Record of Tips and Employee's Report of Tips to Employer from the IRS.*

Q&A

Q: Do I file Form 8027 with the closest regional IRS Service Center to my business?

A: No, all IRS Forms 8027 should be submitted and filed with the IRS Service Center, Andover, MA 05501.

Reporting Tips Directly to the IRS

Under certain circumstances an employee might not have reported tips to his employer. When this situation occurs, the employee must report the tips earned during the year when filing Form 1040. A special form known as *Form 4137, Social Security Tax on Unreported Tip Income* will be prepared to calculate the FICA tax due on the tip income. The employee must pay the FICA due on the tip income when the Form 1040 is filed with the IRS.

4 REPORTING REQUIREMENTS FOR TIPS ON FORM W-2

Tips may be reported on the Form W-2, *Wage and Tax Statement,* in several different boxes depending on the employee's situation. Figure 9–3 summarizes the required reporting of tip income, tax liability, and allocated tip amounts.

F I G U R E   9–3

Summary of Tip Amounts Reportable on 2001 Form W-2

Tip Amount to Be Reported	Report in Form W-2 in Box
Tip income reported by employee and taxed on a recurring pay period basis with no exceptions occurring.	Show all reported tip income amounts in Boxes 1, 5, and 7. Note that any wage amount is also reported along with reported tips in Box 1.
Total wages paid subject to social security tax.	Report any wage amount in Box 3. **Do not** report social security tips or allocated tips in box 3.
Tips reported by employee subject to Medicare tax.	Show any reported tip amount in Box 5.
Tips reported by employee to employer.	Show any reported tip amount in Box 7. Note that the sum of the amounts reported in Boxes 3 and 7 should not exceed $80,400 for 2001 (the social security earnings limit).
Any allocated tips for the an individual employee (as computed and reported in total on Form 8027).	Show any allocated tip amount in Box 8. Note that the amount reported in this box should **not** be part of any amounts reported in Boxes 1, 3, 5, or 7.
An uncollected social security and/or Medicare tax liability exists for the employee due to reported tips at the end of the calendar year.	In Box 12a, 12b, 12c, or 12d: (1) Use a code "A" for any uncollected social security tax amount. Report the uncollected total in the amount section of the box. (2) Use a code "B" for any uncollected Medicare tax amount. Report the uncollected total in the amount section of the box.

Paychecks and Record-Keeping Activities

Summarizing Payroll Information

At this spot on the payroll road map, we pause to study two essential accounting documents used in payroll accounting/administration: the payroll register and the employee earnings record. These two documents will be used to record payroll activities in an accounting system. We also discuss the process of issuing paychecks to employees.

1   RECORDING PAYROLL ACTIVITIES

You might recall from Chapter 1 in Section A that payroll accounting is *a process where activities occur in cycles*. These cycles are coordinated with the many deadlines that must be met in payroll accounting and administration. The payroll professional's job is centered around this process and the activities that take place within this process.

One important cycle within the payroll accounting process is the *cycle of paying employees*. Figure 10–1 is shown here to help us in reviewing the cycle.

In Figure 10–1, Step 4 involves paying employees and issuing their paychecks. Step 5 is the part of the cycle that involves recording payroll activities. Step 5 will be discussed in Segment 3 of this chapter. We begin this section by defining payroll registers and employee earnings records.

F I G U R E   10–1

Summary of the Steps Taken in the Cycle of
Paying Employees

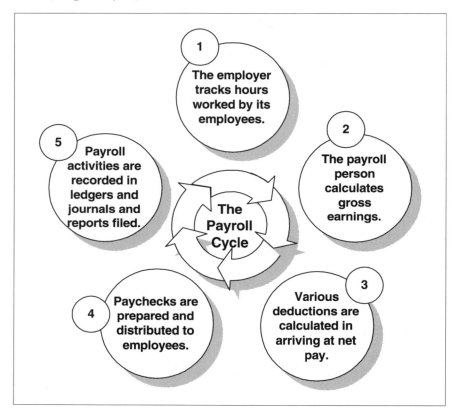

In other chapters of this book we have referred to the payroll register and discussed its purpose in payroll accounting. The **payroll register** is the multicolumn accounting document that provides a summary of the payroll information for a pay period. The payroll register will list all employees who were paid during the pay period along with each employee's gross earnings, taxes withheld, and various deductions. A payroll register will be prepared each pay period.

The document we call the **employee earnings record** provides a comprehensive history of the amounts earned by each individual employee during a calendar year. An employee's earnings record will be maintained for every employee who is issued a paycheck during the year. Employee earnings records, along with payroll registers, are important tools used in the recording of payroll activities.

We review these definitions at this point in the chapter to help you understand the payroll accounting process and the cycle of paying employees. Segment 3 will discuss both of these accounting documents.

Recording payroll activities is a requirement of various federal employment laws. It is also part of properly accounting for the payroll activities of any business that employs workers. The specifics of how a company goes about this task are determined partly by traditional accounting methods and partly by the decisions of the financial managers of a company. Federal law requires that a company maintain specific payroll accounting information, but it does not detail *how* it must be maintained.

Traditionally, creating and maintaining accounting records has been a "hands-on" activity. During the Renaissance, quill pen and paper were used by Italian merchants to determine their profits or losses in trading. There are still many businesses that use manual accounting systems today. However, this trend is changing due to the availability and low cost of personal computer technology.

Manual Systems

We begin this section by studying a manual system because it provides us with a good insight into the steps in the cycle of paying employees. Whether a company uses a manual or computerized system, the same general steps are necessary in order to properly process payroll information and record payroll activities. Note that computer accounting software is designed and written for the same steps that we take in recording a payroll by hand.

Figure 10–2 illustrates one approach to the flow of payroll information through a manual accounting system. We have referenced the various steps found in Figure 10–1 into this diagram to give you an idea of how this flow of information ties into the cycle of paying employees. This figure shows one way that payroll information flows through a manual system—it is not the only way a payroll system could work. A system could be designed in another way that would produce similar results.

Looking at Figure 10–2, you can see that in Step 1 the employee's hours worked must be tracked using time cards or some other method. At the end of the pay period, the hours must be totaled and segregated into "regular" and "overtime" or "premium" hours. In Step 2 the payroll profes-

F I G U R E   10–2

The Flow of Payroll Information in a
Manual Accounting System

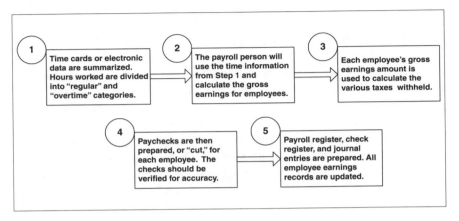

sional will make the calculations to arrive at the gross earnings for each employee. The various taxes and other deductions will be calculated to arrive at the net earnings or take-home pay of each employee (Step 3). Once these calculations have been made, the payroll professional can then prepare each employee's paycheck (Step 4) and complete the payroll register and the individual employee earnings records for the pay period (Step 5). Additional step 5 activities may include recording the paychecks issued in a check register and preparing journal entries that will be posted into the appropriate general ledger accounts.

There are several types of payroll accounting systems that can be placed within the general category of *manual systems*. These systems are listed in this category because each one requires a hands-on approach on the part of a payroll accountant to some degree. The manual systems we focus on here are as follows:

- Pencil-and-paper systems.
- Pegboard systems.

Pencil-and-paper systems consist of paper documents and are maintained by recording transactions by hand. A payroll accountant can buy printed payroll registers, employee earnings records, general journal columnar paper, general ledger sheets, and hardcover binders. The payroll accountant has then all the accounting tools necessary to set up a functional system. Many small businesses use this approach in recording payroll activities. Anyone who has a working knowledge of accounting—and exercises due care when making entries—will obtain excellent results from it.

One drawback of this system is the time that must be spent in maintaining payroll accounting records by hand. A company that has a large number of employees will probably choose another system over pencil and paper because of the time factor involved in recording payroll activities.

A **pegboard system** is also known as a One-write system® because it has been designed to allow the payroll accountant to write out an employee's paycheck *once* while simultaneously recording the information in the employee's earnings record *and* in a payroll register for the pay period.

The pegboard system consists of a writing board with pegs on the left side of the board. Specially printed checks, payroll registers, and employee earnings records are perforated on the left, and can be aligned and positioned to fit into the pegs on the board. These forms are carbon-backed so that when they are written on, a copy is made underneath the form.

Placing the payroll register on the pegboard first, then placing an individual employee earnings record on top of the payroll register, and finally placing the employee's paycheck on top of the employee earnings record will allow the payroll accountant to write out the check and check stub *and* simultaneously complete both the individual employee earnings record and a line on the payroll register.

When used properly, the pegboard system works well and provides the necessary documentation for payroll accounting purposes. The user of a pegboard system will save time because the system is designed to eliminate making repetitive entries by hand. There are several brands of pegboard systems on the market today.

Computerized Payroll Accounting Systems

In the last decade the personal computer revolution has made it possible for a sole proprietor businessperson to have the computing capability that 20 years ago was only possible on a large mainframe computer costing several hundred thousand dollars. Because of this high tech revolution, accounting software is now better than ever before and priced well within the budget of the small-business proprietor.

Computerizing payroll accounting tasks will save the payroll professional considerable time and take much of the drudgery out of recording payroll activities. For many employers, not to computerize payroll accounting activities would be a major mistake.

A computerized payroll accounting system can often be obtained as an add-on program (or module) that will complement an existing general ledger software program, or it can be purchased and used as a stand-alone system. In either case, it will be necessary for payroll accounting information to be entered into the program before it can be processed. The output can then be channeled into any number of various reports or formats. Figure 10–3 illustrates how payroll information will flow through a typical PC-based computerized system.

Q&A

Q: What is a computerized module?

A: It is a software program that, when added to another existing program, will make the entire program more useful. Modular software programs are popular because the user can pick and choose features and options within a software package.

In Step 1 of Figure 10–3, the essential input for the computer is the hours the employees work. Hours can be tracked using time cards or time sheets, or by some electronic means. Once the data are input, the program will merge the data with other information about each employee (the rate of pay for each employee, various deductions for each employee, etc.). This employee information usually has already been entered into the program. Once the program has merged the time data with the employee information, the system can generate various reports and forms.

Printing paychecks in Step 4 of Figure 10–3 is a simple task for computerized payroll accounting software—a major benefit of using such a software program. As the diagram points out, any number of reports can be printed out at various times during the year. Printing quarterly reports like 941 forms and annual reports like W-2 forms is also a simple matter with many payroll accounting software programs.

Payroll accounting programs that can be used as part of (or a module of) a larger general ledger software package will create and post the appropriate journal entries as well. Convenience, speed, and accuracy are tangible benefits of using a computerized program to process a company's payroll.

Companies that use a pegboard or pencil-and-paper payroll accounting system may choose to enter the payroll information in a computer program at a later date to generate the various quarterly and annual reports.

F I G U R E   10–3

The Flow of Information in a Computerized Payroll
Accounting System

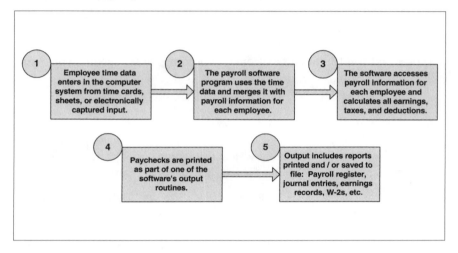

"After-the-fact" payroll software programs are designed to allow the payroll professional to use the employee information from paychecks to generate payroll registers, employee earnings records, quarterly reports such as the 941, and annual forms like the W-2.

2 PAYING EMPLOYEES

There are three ways for employers to pay their employees:

- In cash.
- By check.
- Using the electronic funds transfer system.

During most of American history, employees were generally paid in cash. In the earlier part of last century, many people did not have checking accounts. Payment of earnings in cash was the custom of the time and the expectation of employees.

Some employers today still pay employees in cash. Some retail stores and food and beverage establishments may still have a cash payroll because of the amount of cash they receive daily from their sales.

If an employer pays its employees in cash, certain steps should be followed for **internal control** purposes. The employer should require all employees to sign a receipt verifying that they have received their net pay. This procedure will confirm any question about the payment of wages at a later date. Employee earnings should be recorded in both the payroll register and the employee earnings records, as outlined in this chapter, for accounting purposes and also for the calculation, withholding, and subsequent payment of income and social security taxes.

Q&A

Q: What is *accounting internal control?*

A: The term refers to building and maintaining a series of checks and balances into an accounting system that will make the system more efficient and less subject to fraudulent activity and waste.

Today the vast majority of employers pay their employees by paycheck. There are two distinct advantages in paying employees by check rather than in cash. First, paying by check is safer for both employer and employees. Second, when employees cash paychecks, the canceled checks provide evidence that the employees have been paid, and the dollar amounts are verifiable.

When employees are paid by check, the employer will usually write (or "cut") the checks using a checking account separate from the company's general checking account. An account used only for one type of transaction or specific purpose is known in accounting as an **imprest account.** For payroll accounting purposes, this separate account will be used exclusively to clear paychecks.

Employers set up a separate checking account for internal control purposes. It is easier for the payroll accountant to keep track of checks not cashed. Also, once the employer transfers the net amount of the payroll to the payroll checking account, the payroll is "covered" for the pay period, and the funds will not be used to pay other operating expenses of the company.

When a special payroll checking account is used, only the net amount of each payroll is transferred into the account—payroll tax deposits will be paid from the company's general checking account.

Unclaimed Earnings

What happens when for some reason an employee does not cash a paycheck? This situation does occur in payroll accounting. An employee might not cash a paycheck because it is lost or the employee believes he has already cashed the check. In some instances some employees who terminate with a company will never pick up their last paycheck. What becomes of the employee's money? The answer depends on state escheat laws.

The area of unclaimed employee earnings is covered by **escheat law**. This area of law provides guidance on how unclaimed property should be disposed of or distributed. Each state sets its own regulations in this area. Under many state escheat statutes, an employee's unclaimed earnings will eventually be distributed to the state.

Q&A

Q: I have an unclaimed paycheck from an employee who recently terminated and left me no forwarding address.   What is my next step in this situation?

A: The answer will be specific to the state in which your business is domiciled.   You will need to contact your state treasurer's office to find out the specific time limits, rules, and procedures you need to follow in your state.   Since there are substantial penalties for failure to comply with state escheat law, it is to your advantage to become familiar with your state's laws in this area as soon as possible and follow them.

The Electronic Funds Transfer System

An employee may wish to be paid by having his paycheck deposited directly into his checking account. This method is commonly called direct deposit and is technically known as the **Electronic Funds Transfer (EFT)** system.

The EFT system has advantages for both the employee and employer. It is efficient, uses less paper, and allows the employee to immediately draw against funds deposited into his account.

When an employee requests to have paychecks deposited using EFT, the employer will make arrangements with the local bank. Figure 10–4 shows how a direct deposit of a paycheck works. The employer's bank uses an entity known as an **automated clearing house (ACH)** to have the employee's funds electronically sent to her bank.

There are several advantages to using the direct deposit method for employee paychecks: employees no longer have to make a trip to the bank to deposit their checks and stand in line; the employees' local bank may credit their deposit immediately, making the funds available to the employees without any delay; employees' checks are automatically deposited to their accounts while they are on a vacation or out of state; and, in some ar-

F I G U R E   10–4

How the Direct Deposit of a Paycheck Works . . .

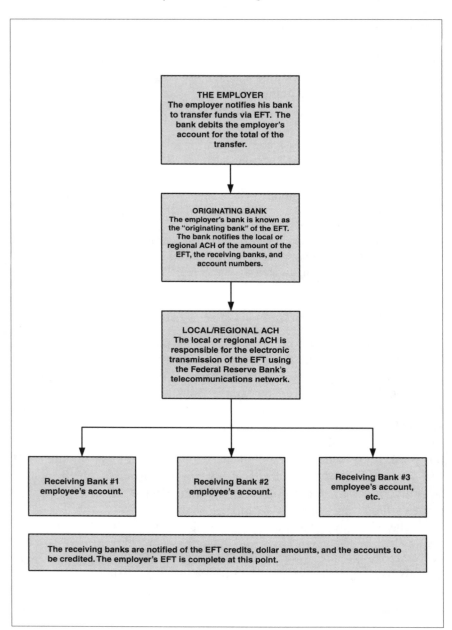

eas, banks may reduce or eliminate any service charges when paychecks are directly deposited into employees' checking accounts.

There are multiple ACHs nationwide that work together to electronically clear funds from one bank account to another. Look at Figure 10–4 to see that when the employer's local bank, called the "originating financial institution," notifies the local or regional ACH of the funds transfer, the ACH is responsible for handling the transfer. The ACH will use the Federal Reserve telecommunications system to transmit or "wire" the transfer to the employees' banks. The employees' banks are known as the receiving financial institutions. Each receiving bank will credit the employees' accounts for their amount of net pay.

In certain states, if an employer chooses to use the EFT system, *all* employees must be paid using EFT. In the other states, an employee can choose whether to have his paycheck directly deposited using EFT.

EFT is a growing trend and will probably be the standard in the near future because it offers convenience and flexibility to employees and employers alike. State payroll tax deposits can also be made using EFT, which we discuss in Chapter 13 of Section E. The IRS has also started a federal payroll tax deposit program using the EFT system. (Chapter 13 discusses who has to currently use the federal EFT system.)

3 PAYROLL REGISTERS AND EMPLOYEE EARNINGS RECORDS

Whether a manual or computerized payroll system is used, keeping track of payroll activities will require the use of several "special-purpose" accounting records or documents. Three such records are the payroll register, the employee earnings record, and various special-purpose ledgers.

The Payroll Register

At the beginning of this chapter, we stated that a payroll register is the multicolumn accounting document used to record the payroll activity for a company for a pay period. Figure 10–5 shows a payroll register that is maintained for a manual payroll of six employees. The payroll register like the one in Figure 10–5 will be prepared after the employees' gross earnings and deductions have been calculated (Step 3 of Figure 10–1). Note that Figure 10–5 has been separated into two parts for printing purposes—the actual payroll register would extend horizontally well past the pages of this book.

F I G U R E   10-5

Payroll Register

WEEKLY PAYROLL REGISTER - *for pay period 1/7/0X – 1/13/0X*

EMPLOYEE TIME CARD AND EARNINGS DATA / DEDUCTIONS

Employee Name	I.D. No.	W-4 Status/Allow.	Regular Hours	Regular Rate of Pay	Regular Earnings	Overtime Hours	Overtime Rate of Pay	Overtime Earnings	Total Earnings	OASDI FICA	HI FICA
Adams, D.	4199	S/0	40.0	14.84	593.60	2.4	22.26	53.42	647.02	40.12	9.38
Davis, P.	4135	M/2	40.0	18.39	735.60	0.0	27.59	00.00	735.60	45.61	10.67
Nelson, B.	0716	M/0	40.0	10.48	419.20	0.0	15.72	00.00	419.20	25.99	6.08
Garcia, M.	4105	S/1	40.0	12.54	501.60	3.8	18.81	71.48	573.08	35.53	8.31
Nguyen, J.	2346	M/2	40.0	8.40	336.00	2.1	12.60	26.46	362.46	22.47	5.26
Jones, W.	0725	M/4	40.0	5.48	219.20	3.9	8.22	32.06	251.26	15.58	3.64
Totals					2,805.20			183.42	2,988.62	185.30	43.34

DEDUCTIONS / CHECK DATA

FIT	SIT	Total Other Deductions	Net Pay	Check No.
115.61	25.52	25.00	431.39	15381
79.31	13.13	50.00	536.88	15382
44.12	5.73	50.00	287.28	15385
82.09	21.42	25.00	400.73	15383
37.23	1.66	50.00	245.84	15386
0.00	0.00	50.00	182.04	15384
358.36	67.46	250.00	2,084.16	

LABOR DISTRIBUTION / EMPLOYER TAXABLE EARNINGS

Acct. #645 Plant Wages	Acct. #650 Office Salaries	Acct. #654 Admin. Salaries	FUTA Taxable Earnings	SUTA Taxable Earnings	OASDI FICA Taxable Earnings	HI FICA Taxable Earnings
647.02			647.02	647.02	647.02	647.02
735.60			735.60	735.60	735.60	735.60
	419.20		419.20	419.20	419.20	419.20
573.08			573.08	573.08	573.08	573.08
		362.46	362.46	362.46	362.46	362.08
	251.26		251.26	251.26	251.26	251.26
1,955.70	670.46	362.46	2,988.62	2,988.62	2,988.62	2,988.62

Looking at Figure 10–5, you can see that information about each employee is entered in the payroll register, line by line. Each employee's name, ID number (or social security number), and W-4 status information are entered on a line, along with the regular and overtime earnings. The deductions from the employee's paycheck are listed along with net or take-home pay. The paycheck number for each employee's check can be listed to tie each line in the payroll register to the issuing of each employee's paycheck. The "Labor Distribution" and "Employer's Taxable Earnings" will be used by the payroll accountant in preparing journal entries for the pay period.

After the last employee has been listed in the payroll register for the pay period, the amount columns should be footed, and the "totals" line should be cross-footed to verify the arithmetic. The "totals" row of amounts from the payroll will be used to prepare the payroll journal entries for the pay period. Preparing journal entries for payroll purposes will be discussed in Section D, Chapter 11.

Q&A

Q: What is footing?

A: In accounting terminology, to *foot* a column means to add or subtract the amounts found in the column (vertically). To *cross-foot* a row means to add or subtract the amounts horizontally.

The payroll register is useful for accounting purposes because it is the only special journal in an accounting system that documents the payroll activity on a pay period basis. The payroll register fulfills part of the record-keeping requirements of the Fair Labor Standards Act and other employment laws. The information contained in a typical payroll register, along with the employee earnings record and other documents, is sufficient to meet these legal record-keeping requirements. Payroll registers will also be used by a company's management to help with budgeting and cost containment measures.

Q&A

Q: What is a special journal?

A: A special journal is an accounting term that is used to describe a book of original entry, or the spot where source document information is first entered into an accounting system. A payroll register can be considered a special journal because it is the first place payroll information will be entered into a company's accounting system.

The payroll register shown in Figure 10–5 is only one example. Payroll registers can be customized to meet the specific needs of a company. Additional information, such as department or job-cost identification numbers or year-to-date earnings limits, can be added for managerial accounting purposes. Social security numbers or codes used to identify employees or their job duties could be easily added to a payroll register.

In Figure 10–5 note that the gross earnings of employees are distributed (and debited) to three separate expense accounts, based on department. Each employee's gross earnings could also be distributed to various expense accounts depending on his/her occupation. Each expense account would have its own column in the register. This is known as a **labor distribution**, which is beneficial when recording the payroll register information in journal entry format.

There are no specific requirements regarding the media used to maintain payroll registers—registers can be stored as text or graphics files on computer disk or tape. Payroll registers for prior periods could be photographed and placed on microfilm or microfiche for storage purposes.

The payroll register is a simple document to maintain. Once prepared, it can be used as the basis for preparing another special-purpose accounting record known as the *employee earnings record.*

The Employee Earnings Record

The accounting record that provides an employer with specific payroll information for each employee during a calendar year is the *employee earnings record.* Each employee who receives a paycheck should have an earnings record. A new record will be started each January 1 for each worker currently employed. The employee earnings record provides a historical summary of what each employee earns, pay period by pay period. Figure 10–6 illustrates an employee earnings record.

The employee earnings record in Figure 10–6 shows identification information for the employee at the top of the form. The employee's name and social security number are needed at a minimum. Other information (such as home address, phone numbers, and emergency contact) can be added depending on the requirements of the employer. Below this section of the record will be columns for the payday and week of the year, the total of regular and overtime hours worked, and the gross earnings of the employee for the pay period. Several columns can be used to record the various taxes and deductions made to arrive at the employee's net pay.

One feature of an employee earnings record is the *year-to-date earnings* column. These year-to-date totals are important in the calculation of the amount of social security taxes that will be withheld due to the earnings limit maximum for social security taxes. (This concept can be reviewed in Chapter 6 of Section C.)

Year-to-Date Amounts Are Cumulative

Please note that the **year-to-date** amounts are cumulative totals, like the balance in a general ledger account. For example, assume that an employee had $50 deducted as a one-time deposit for uniforms in January. Once this amount has been deducted from the employee's paycheck, it will appear as a $50 deduction for the rest of the year—it is a $50 *year-to-date deduction*.

Like the payroll register, employee earnings records can be customized to meet the specific needs of an employer. The earnings information contained in the record in Figure 10–6 will be required for record-keeping purposes; however, a company can add additional information to the record as needed. The column totals can all be calculated to reflect year-to-date totals at the payroll professional's option.

As is the case with the payroll register, a company should maintain employee earnings records for all workers on payroll as part of federal and state employment law requirements. This information is required as part of the *Fair Labor Standards Act (FLSA)* and other laws. Employee earnings records should not be destroyed after the end of each year but should be retained for at least four years *after* the year of the record itself. Today many legal and accounting professionals advise that employers retain these records indefinitely.

In a manual payroll accounting system, the employee earnings records can be prepared directly from paycheck stubs or from the payroll register. A payroll professional could also prepare the employee earnings records first and then, using this information, prepare employee paychecks and the payroll register. The important point to remember is that preparing employee earnings records is required, and all payroll records must agree in terms of dates and dollar amounts with employee paychecks for each pay period.

Special-Purpose Ledgers

In addition to payroll registers and the employee earnings records, the payroll professional might wish to set up a special *tax deposit ledger* to track

F I G U R E 10-6

Employee Earnings Record

Employee Name Adams, David		Hire Date 06/21/89			Date Terminated -----					Emp. I.D. No. 4199	

Dept. No. 0645 Rate of Pay $14.84/Hour SSN 975-00-9991

Married/Single S   W-4 Allow. 0

	TIME CARD AND EARNINGS DATA						DEDUCTIONS				
Week No. & Date Ended	Total Regular Hours/Rate of Pay	Regular Earnings	Total Overtime Hours/Rate of Pay	Overtime Earnings	Gross Earnings	Year-to-Date Earnings	OASDI FICA	HI FICA	FIT	SIT	Medical Insurance	Net Pay
---	---	---	---	---	---	---	---	---	---	---	---	---
#1-1/7	40/14.84	593.60	00/22.26	00.00	593.60	593.60	36.80	8.61	101.29	24.17	25.00	397.73
#2-1/14	40/14.84	593.60	2.4/22.26	53.42	647.02	1,240.62	40.12	9.38	115.61	25.52	25.00	431.39

payroll tax deposits. This type of **special-purpose ledger** can be created using standard columnar paper. A tax deposit ledger, although not required in a payroll accounting system, can be useful to the payroll professional for the following reasons:

- To track payroll tax deposits and the dates of the deposits.
- To reconcile the balances in the federal tax payable accounts to the payroll tax reports each quarter.
- To aid in reconciling tax payable accounts and cash balances to the general ledger.

The payroll professional may design and use special-purpose tax deposit ledgers as required in a payroll accounting system. A special-purpose ledger can be used any time that organizing information in a unique way will save time or increase the effectiveness of a payroll accounting system.

Recording Payroll Information

At this spot on our road map we pause to review some basic accounting theory and preparation of the journal entries associated with recording a payroll for a pay period. You may want to stop here and go over this chapter to refresh your memory of double-entry accounting and basic accounting principles.

1 ACCOUNTING THEORY AND CONCEPTS

Payroll accounting, like any other specialized area of accounting, follows the general rules and principles of the profession. These rules, which many people refer to as *accounting theory*, provide the basis for the way transactions are recorded in journals and ledgers. This segment will review basic accounting theory and several concepts that provide us with the foundation to account for payroll activities.

Accounting Theory

The accounting rules (or theory) on which accountants rely and follow when recording transactions and preparing financial statements are called *GAAP*, or **Generally Accepted Accounting Principles**. Figure 11–1 lists various assumptions, principles, and concepts that make up a part of GAAP. The list in Figure 11–1 only focuses on some of the better-known rules and concepts; accounting theory is a vast technical area of academic study. We

F I G U R E   11-1

Examples of Generally Accepted Accounting
Principles (GAAP)

Assumptions	Principles	Bases of Accounting	Other Concepts
■ Business entity	■ Matching	■ Accrual	■ Internal control
■ Going concern	■ Revenue recognition	■ Cash	
■ Currency	■ Cost		
■ Time period			

will briefly describe the rules and concepts found in this list in the paragraphs below.

An accountant must be able to *identify and separate* the business activities of a given enterprise from those of its owners, shareholders, or other businesses. This concept is known as the **business entity assumption.** When the business activities of an enterprise can be separated, the accountant can record the accounting transactions that relate to the business as *distinct and separate* from other enterprises.

Payroll transactions must relate to a specific employer or business for legal and accounting purposes; the business entity assumption allows the accountant to link the payroll transactions of a specific employer to that employer as a business entity.

When recording transactions, the company's accountants assume the business entity, or employer, is a *thriving, ongoing enterprise* that will be here tomorrow and continue into the future. Accountants refer to this idea as the **going concern assumption.** The company's accountants generally believe that the business will have a long life. In payroll accounting, this assumption allows the accountant to record the obligations incurred for payroll expenses with the understanding that the company will be in business to pay these liabilities in the future.

The **currency assumption** recognizes currency as the common denominator that should be used to record accounting transactions. Payroll accountants must *use dollars or some other currency* as the basis for recording payroll transactions. Whether accountants in Russia and England use rubles or British pounds to account for transactions, they are following GAAP.

This assumption allows accountants to divide the business transactions of an enterprise into time periods for measurement purposes. Separating accounting activities in this way is called the **time period assumption.** The longest time period for accounting purposes is a fiscal or calendar year or operating cycle, and the shortest time period is usually one month.

The time period assumption is important to payroll accounting because payroll transactions must be measured and accounted for in terms of a calendar year. A calendar year will be used for payroll purposes even if the employer adopts and uses a fiscal year or some other operating cycle for financial statement purposes.

These two accounting rules that are closely related and work together with the time period assumption for GAAP purposes are known as the *matching* and *revenue recognition principles.*

The **matching principle** states that the accountant must match expenses, or the costs of doing business, with the revenues that the business earned during the same period of time.

The **revenue recognition principle** states that the accountant must recognize revenue as the earnings process is completed—that is, the company has earned the revenue, and payment either has been received or will be received in the near future. The account "Accounts Receivable" is used based on this principle.

Recognizing revenues and matching that revenue with the appropriate expenses should be done within the same time period. Accountants "link together" the revenue recognition and matching principle with the time period assumption to comply with GAAP.

In payroll accounting, a company that incurs payroll costs such as wages and payroll tax expense must match these costs to the revenues that the employee efforts help to produce during the same period of time.

The **cost principle** states that, in general, accountants must value the cost of assets, liabilities, revenues, and expenses at their *historical cost,* rather than use another valuation method, such as an appraised value. Accounting theory allows for several exceptions from the cost principle in certain situations; however, the great majority of accounting transactions use historical cost as a base for recording purposes. From a payroll accounting viewpoint, this means that the dollars actually paid to employees will always be the amounts recorded on the employer's books.

Accrual and Cash Accounting

Two methods, or bases, that accountants commonly use are the accrual and the cash methods of accounting. A company's accounting will generally use one of these two methods to record accounting transactions. The payroll professional should be familiar with both of these **bases of accounting**.

The **accrual basis** of accounting requires that a revenue should be recognized when it is earned, as opposed to received, and an expense should be recognized when it is incurred, as opposed to paid. Receivable and payable accounts usually indicate that the accrual (or modified accrual) basis of accounting is being used. Typically, payroll transactions are made using the accrual basis of accounting. Accrual accounting is an appropriate method for GAAP purposes.

The **cash basis** of accounting relies on the flow of cash to record business transactions. Using the cash method, a revenue is not recorded until a business actually receives the cash from the transaction, and likewise an expense will not be recorded until it is actually paid. The cash basis is a popular method used by many small businesses. The cash method is not considered an appropriate method for GAAP purposes because it does not accurately match all revenues earned with expenses incurred during the same time period.

For payroll purposes, the accountant will use payable accounts to record the liabilities incurred each pay period. The **modified cash basis** of accounting permits the use of receivable and payable accounts for recording payroll activities while using the cash basis for recording other business transactions.

Q&A

Q: How does accounting for a transaction using the accrual basis differ from using the cash basis method?

A: The key difference between the two methods is the *timing* of when the transaction is entered in the general journal and general ledger. Remember that accrual accounting recognizes a transaction before the movement of cash, whereas the cash basis *only* recognizes a transaction when a movement of cash has occurred. You might have studied the concept of internal control in an accounting principles course. The area of internal control might be difficult to understand, yet our lives are both directly and indirectly affected by internal control in business and at school. It is a vital necessity in operating a business efficiently and effectively. Understanding internal control will help you understand why payroll accounting operates the way it does.

Internal control is defined theoretically as a means to ensure the efficient operation of a business. This definition is not limited to the area of accounting but includes all areas of a business: administrative, executive, production, and finance. All areas of a business should operate with a system of internal control in place.

Because internal control is somewhat abstract, the concept is probably best understood by analyzing examples of internal control in payroll accounting. The following procedures illustrate good internal control in a payroll accounting system:

- Employees, if paid in cash, must sign a receipt for the cash payment when they receive it.
- Employees must sign time cards or time sheets.
- Paychecks will be written and cleared using a separate checking account.
- Paychecks should be distributed to employees in person on payday.
- Payroll activities are recorded using journal entries and double-entry accounting.

These examples seem simple and are commonsense measures, yet following these procedures establishes and maintains good internal control. Consider, for example, the requirement that employees who are paid in cash should sign a receipt stating that they received their earnings. Cash payments are more easily tracked and potential problems eliminated when a receipt system is in place and used by management.

The same holds true for having employees verify the hours they work by signing time cards or time sheets. This establishes a line of accountability from the employee to the employer and generally results in more accurate reporting of the actual hours worked by each employee.

Using an imprest checking account (like a payroll checking account) provides good internal control because funds are immediately segregated, and the process of reconciling the account and identifying outstanding paychecks is simplified.

Paychecks should be physically handed out to employees on payday to verify that the employee actually does exist and works for the company. If paychecks are mailed to employees on a regular basis, the chance of "phantom employees" (i.e., individuals who have not been hired by the company) appearing on a company's payroll can increase. Good internal control requires that faces and paychecks be matched on any given payday.

Finally, recording payroll activities using journal entries is an excellent example of internal control. Journal entries, as part of the double-entry method of accounting, provide a system of controls over the entries made into the general ledger accounts. This is one primary reason that the double-entry system of accounting has not changed much in over five centuries of use.

Internal control can also be defined in another way as a system of checks and balances designed to keep the business operating efficiently. These checks and balances will also help prevent fraud from occurring, and well-designed systems will help prevent waste and mismanagement.

2   JOURNALIZING PAYROLL ACTIVITIES

Paying employees is a typical, routine activity of most businesses. Recording business transactions, whether the transactions deal with payroll or some other aspect of operating a company, will require the preparation of journal entries.

Whether an employer is using a manual or a computerized system for accounting purposes, both rely on the journal entry to initially record accounting transactions. In a manual hands-on system the accountant will prepare journal entries and then post the entries into the general ledger. In a computerized environment much of this activity may be automated, as is typically the case with payroll accounting software programs. In either case, journal entries represent the transactions of a business stated in monetary terms.

We discuss preparing journal entries in this chapter based on the assumption that the payroll professional is using a manual accounting system. This will afford you with the best opportunity to understand the process of journalizing payroll activities.

Chart of Accounts

Please recall that any accounting system uses a **chart of accounts** to organize and identify the accounts that can be used to record business transactions. An example of the typical accounts that are used to record payroll activities is shown in Figure 11–2. This illustration shows a partial chart of accounts because we will only focus on the accounts that are used for payroll accounting.

F I G U R E   11–2

Partial Chart of Accounts Listing the Accounts Used in
Recording Payroll Activities

ASSET ACCOUNTS	
#110	Cash—Checking
#125	Cash—Payroll

LIABILITY ACCOUNTS	
#220	Salaries and Wages Payable
#225	Employee Social Security Tax Payable
#230	Employee Medicare Tax Payable
#235	Employee Federal Income Tax Payable
#240	Employee State Income Tax Payable
#247	Medical Insurance Premiums Payable
#255	Employer Social Security Tax Payable
#260	Employer Medicare Tax Payable
#265	Federal Unemployment Tax Payable
#267	State Unemployment Tax Payable

EXPENSE ACCOUNTS	
#610	Payroll Tax Expense
#645	Plant Wages Expense
#650	Office Salaries Expense
#654	Administrative Salaries Expense

3 JOURNALIZING A PAYROLL

Please recall from earlier chapters that we referred to payroll accounting as
a *process within which there are activities that occur in cycles.* Journalizing
payroll activities is one of the final steps taken in the cycle of paying employees.

Journal entries are prepared based on the steps we take in paying employees. We have identified the journal entries tied to these activities in Figure 11–3. Note that in this figure we reference each journal entry by number.
We will refer to these journal entries by number throughout this chapter.

F I G U R E　11–3

Journal Entries Follow the Steps Taken in Paying Employees and Remitting Taxes

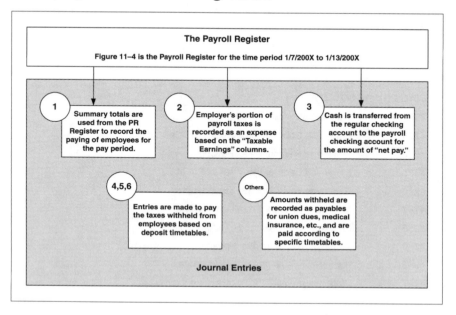

To begin journalizing a payroll, we rely on the **payroll register**. Looking at Figure 11–3, notice that journal entries 1, 2, and 3 are generated from a completed payroll register. Recall that the payroll register is completed by listing each employee who is paid for a given pay period. The amounts deducted for taxes and other items will also be listed for each employee. The payroll register's columns are footed, and the summary totals are cross-footed to verify the accuracy of the amounts. The summary totals at the bottom of the payroll register form the basis of the first journal entry. In Figure 11–4, we illustrate the payroll register we will use in preparing journal entries 1, 2, and 3.

Journal Entry 1

The purpose of Journal Entry 1 is to record the payroll for a pay period. An entry like this must be made each pay period. In our example the company pays its employees weekly, and this entry is made for the pay period ending on January 13, 200X.

FIGURE 11-4

WEEKLY PAYROLL REGISTER - *for pay period 1/7/200X - 1/13/200X*
EMPLOYEE TIME CARD AND EARNINGS DATA

Employee Name	I.D. No.	W-4 Status/Allow.	Regular Hours	Regular Rate of Pay	Regular Earnings	Overtime Hours	Overtime Rate of Pay	Overtime Earnings	Total Earnings	DEDUCTIONS OASDI FICA	DEDUCTIONS HI FICA
Adams, D.	4199	S/0	40.0	14.84	593.60	2.4	22.26	53.42	647.02	40.12	9.38
Davis, P.	4135	M/2	40.0	18.39	735.60	0.0	27.59	00.00	735.60	45.61	10.67
Nelson, B.	0716	M/0	40.0	10.48	419.20	0.0	15.72	00.00	419.20	25.99	6.08
Garcia, M.	4105	S/1	40.0	12.54	501.60	3.8	18.81	71.48	573.08	35.53	8.31
Nguyen, J.	2346	M/2	40.0	8.40	336.00	2.1	12.60	26.46	362.46	22.47	5.26
Jones, W.	0725	M/4	40.0	5.48	219.20	3.9	8.22	32.06	251.26	15.58	3.64
Totals			240.0		2,805.20	12.20		183.42	2,988.62	185.30	43.34

JOURNAL ENTRY 1

DEDUCTIONS FIT	SIT	Total Other Deductions	CHECK DATA Net Pay	Check No.
115.61	25.52	25.00	431.39	15381
79.31	13.13	50.00	536.88	15382
44.12	5.73	50.00	287.28	15385
82.09	21.42	25.00	400.73	15383
37.23	1.66	50.00	245.84	15386
0.00	0.00	50.00	182.04	15384
358.36	67.46	250.00	2,084.16	

JOURNAL ENTRY 1
Credit amounts to payable accounts

JOURNAL ENTRY 3

LABOR DISTRIBUTION Acct. #645 Plant Wages	Acct. #650 Office Salaries	Acct. #654 Admin. Salaries	EMPLOYER TAXABLE EARNINGS FUTA Taxable Earnings	SUTA Taxable Earnings	OASDI FICA Taxable Earnings	HI FICA Taxable Earnings
647.02			647.02	647.02	647.02	647.02
735.60			735.60	735.60	735.60	735.60
	419.20		419.20	419.20	419.20	419.20
573.08			573.08	573.08	573.08	573.08
		362.46	362.46	362.46	362.46	362.08
	251.26		251.26	251.26	251.26	251.26
1,955.70	670.46	362.46	2,988.62	2,988.62	2,988.62	2,988.62
			×.008	×.029	×.062	×.0145
			23.91	86.67	185.29	43.33

JOURNAL ENTRY 1
Debit amounts to expense accounts

JOURNAL ENTRY 2
Credit amounts to payable accounts

225

This journal entry is prepared based on the summary totals at the bottom of the payroll register. In Figure 11–4, notice that the amounts in the section labeled **"Labor Distribution"** become the debits to the expense accounts for employee earnings. In preparing the payroll register, the payroll professional will distribute the gross earnings of each employee into the appropriate expense accounts. This simplifies the preparation of the debit side of the journal entry.

JOURNAL ENTRY 1			
Date	**Description**	**Debit**	**Credit**
1/13/200X	Plant Wages (#645)	1,955.70	
	Office Salaries (#650)	670.46	
	Administrative Salaries (#654)	362.46	
	Employee Social Security Tax Payable (#225)		185.30
	Employee Medicare Tax Payable (230)		43.34
	Employee FIT Payable (#235)		358.36
	Employee SIT Payable (#240)		67.46
	Med. Ins. Premiums Payable (#247)		250.00
	Cash—Payroll (#125)		2,084.16
	—To record payroll for week ending 1/13/200X		

The amounts withheld for taxes are credits to payable accounts. The "Total Other Deductions" column is used for medical insurance premiums withheld from employees. The *Medical Insurance Premiums Payable* account (#247) is credited for this amount. The final credit is to the *Cash—Payroll* account (#125) for the amount of the net pay.

Q&A

Q: Who thought of the idea of journal entries and double-entry accounting?

A: Although no one is certain who created this system, the first person to document and explain how double-entry accounting works and its importance to business was a mathematician and theologian of the fifteenth century named Fra Luca Paciolo (or Pacioli).

Journal Entry 2

The purpose of this entry is to record the employer's portion of payroll taxes as liabilities. Again, the payroll register provides the amount of employee earnings that will be taxable for the various payroll taxes.

In Figure 11–4 the summary totals from the "Employer Taxable Earnings" section of the payroll register will be multiplied by the various tax rates to determine the actual tax liability of the employer for this pay period. Looking at the lower right side of Figure 11–4, you can see that we have multiplied the appropriate rates by the amount of taxable earnings in each column to arrive at the employer's payroll tax expense. These dollar amounts are credited to the *Employer Tax Payable* accounts. The sum of the credits then becomes the debit to *Payroll Tax Expense* (#610) in Journal Entry 2.

JOURNAL ENTRY 2			
Date	Description	Debit	Credit
1/13/200X	Payroll Tax Expense (#610)	339.20	
	FUTA Tax Payable (#265)		23.91
	SUTA Tax Payable (#267)		86.67
	Employer Social Security Tax Payable (#255)		185.29
	Employer Medicare Tax Payable (#260)		43.33
	—To record payroll tax expense for the weekly pay period ending 1/13/200X		

Journal Entry 2 will be prepared each pay period in which the employer incurs a payroll tax liability based on the employees' earnings for the pay period. Note that the taxable earnings found in the payroll register are determined on an individual employee basis. If an employee's year-to-date earnings exceed the earnings limit for federal or state unemployment taxes or social security tax, no amounts will be listed for that employee in the payroll register. The employer will only pay tax on the employee earnings that are taxable, based on each individual employee's year-to-date earnings limit.

Journal Entry 3

The purpose of this journal entry is to transfer the net amount of the payroll for the pay period from the regular checking account to the payroll checking account. Recall that the sole purpose of the payroll checking account is to pay employees. (See Segment 2 in Chapter 10.) As each pay period occurs, the payroll professional will transfer funds to the payroll checking account to cover the net payroll. In this example, the transfer of cash into the payroll checking account will bring the account into a zero balance.

JOURNAL ENTRY 3			
Date	**Description**	**Debit**	**Credit**
1/13/200X	*Cash —Payroll (#125)*	*2,084.16*	
	Cash—Checking (#110)		*2,084.16*
	—To transfer cash for the pay period ending 1/13/200X		

The payroll checking account is known as an **imprest checking account**. Such a checking account is used for only *one specific purpose,* such as paying employees' earnings or sales commissions.

In Journal Entry 1 we credited the payroll checking account for the amount of the net pay, and in Journal Entry 3 we debit the account for the same dollar amount. Effectively, the general ledger shows a zero balance in *Cash—Payroll* (#125), unless a minimum balance is maintained in the account. Keep in mind that these entries are made concurrently by the payroll professional.

Journal Entry 4

Figure 11–3 shows that additional journal entries will be made as the various payroll taxes are paid. As we pointed out in Chapter 9, payroll tax deposits must be made according to established timetables. When the liability is paid for Form 941 taxes (employee and employer social security, Medicare, and federal income taxes), the payroll accountant will make the following entry:

JOURNAL ENTRY 4			
Date	**Description**	**Debit**	**Credit**
1/19/200X	Employee Social Security Tax Payable (#225)	185.30	
	Employee Medicare Tax Payable (#230)	43.34	
	Employee FIT Payable (#235)	358.36	
	Employer Social Security Tax Payable (#255)	185.29	
	Employer Medicare Tax Payable (#260)	43.33	
	Cash—Checking (#110)		815.62
	—To pay Form 941 taxes for pay period ending 1/13/200X		

Entries to Pay Liabilities

The amounts found in the *Employee/Employer FICA Tax Payable* accounts (#225, 230, 255, and 260) will be debited along with the *Employee Federal Income Tax Payable* account (#235). The *Cash—Checking* (#110) account will be credited for the total amount of the payroll tax deposit. Note that the regular checking account is used to pay tax deposits as they become due—the payroll checking account is used solely to "clear" employee paychecks.

The same procedure will be followed for paying federal and state unemployment taxes to the government. Debiting the various payable accounts eliminates the liabilities which are paid by crediting the regular cash account.

This procedure will customarily be followed for each pay period in a year. There will be occasions when the payroll accountant must make accrual entries to record the payroll tax expense incurred at the end of an accounting period before the employees are actually paid. We refer to these entries as *end-of-period* entries.

Accruing Payroll Tax Expense

When the end of an accounting period occurs prior to the end of a pay period in the same week, an **end-of-period accrual** entry must be made. This entry will record the payroll tax expense incurred but not yet paid at the end of the accounting period. The accounts listed in the *labor distribution section* of the payroll register will be debited for the expense. The credit side of this entry will be to *Salaries and Wages Payable* (#220).

EXAMPLE 1

> U.S. Route 66 Trucking, Inc. pays its hourly workers weekly. The work-week and pay period both end Saturday at midnight. Employees are paid each Monday for the previous week's pay period. Looking at Figure 11–5, you can see that March 31 is a Wednesday, which is the end of the accounting period. The payroll accountant must accrue three days' earnings (Monday, Tuesday, and Wednesday—no employees worked on Sunday, March 28, in our example) as of Wednesday, March 31, for the salaries and wages earned but not yet paid.

The payroll accountant will make the accrual entry based on 24 hours worked (three 8-hour days) for each employee listed on the payroll register in Figure 11–4. The payroll accountant will multiply each employee's regular hourly rate of pay by 24 hours to arrive at the amount of each employee's earnings to be accrued.

FIGURE 11–5

End-of-the-Month Accrual for Salaries

SUNDAY	MONDAY	TUESDAY	WEDNESDAY	THURSDAY	FRIDAY	SATURDAY
			End of month			
March 28	March 29	March 30	March 31 →	April 1	April 2	April 3
Salaries and wages are accrued for Sunday, Monday, Tuesday, and Wednesday.						The payperiod ends at midnight Saturday.
April 4	April 5	April 6	April 7	April 8	April 9	April 10

Note that this entry does not account for any overtime hours worked during this period of time because time card data will not be available until the pay period ends. In this situation it is appropriate for the accountant to make an entry that *estimates* the amount of salaries and wages payable based on regular hours worked as of March 31.

Journal Entry 5

Based on the total of the employee earnings for this time period, the payroll accountant will make the following entry:

JOURNAL ENTRY 5			
Date	**Description**	**Debit**	**Credit**
3/31/200X	Plant Wages Expense (#645)	1,098.48	
	Office Salaries Expense (#650)	383.04	
	Administrative Salaries Expense (#654)	201.60	
	Salaries and Wages Payable (#220)		1,683.12
	—To accrue earnings for week #14 at 3/31/200X		

On April 1, the payroll accountant will make a reversing entry to eliminate the accrual. The usual entry (Journal Entry 1) will then be made on April 3 to record the payroll for the weekly pay period.

Q&A

Q: How does an accrual entry for salaries or wages affect employees' Form W-2s and payroll tax reporting?

A: Such an entry does not affect either an employee's Form W-2 or the various payroll tax reports prepared because all amounts found on these documents are reported under the *cash basis* of accounting. Such an entry is made using the accrual basis to comply with GAAP.

4 JOURNAL ENTRIES FOR OTHER
EMPLOYEE DEDUCTIONS

Journal Entry 6

In Figure 11–4, the "Total Other Deductions" column in the payroll register represents an elective deduction for medical insurance premiums. Journal Entry 1 recorded this summary total as a credit to *Medical Insurance Premiums Payable* (#247). When the medical insurance premiums are remitted to the insurance company, the payroll accountant will make the following entry:

JOURNAL ENTRY 6			
Date	**Description**	**Debit**	**Credit**
2/1/200X	Medical Insurance Premiums Payable (#247)	250.00	
	Cash—Checking (#110)		250.00
	—To pay med. ins. for week ending 1/13/200X		

There are numerous other deductions that employees can elect to have withheld from their paychecks. The payroll accountant will make the appropriate deduction for these amounts and track them by crediting the appropriate payable accounts. When these deductions are paid, the payroll accountant will debit the payable account and credit *Cash—Checking* (#110).

Charitable contributions and payments to credit unions are among the many deductions that employees will have withheld from their paychecks on a regular basis. These types of deductions are often referred to as **elective deductions.** Elective deductions generally require the employee to complete and sign a form that authorizes the deduction, the amount of the deduction, and the length of time the amount will be withheld from the employee's paychecks. Payable accounts will be set up to accommodate the amounts withheld for each type of elective deduction.

Likewise, certain other deductions may be taken from the employees' pay without employee authorization. Mandatory payments to a labor union, court-ordered garnishments, child support payments, and federal or state tax levies are typical **required deductions.** In such cases the payroll accountant is required to make the deduction based on a labor union contract or by the order of the court or the IRS. There are specific rules that govern how much can be withheld from an employee for required deductions. This protects an employee from having the majority of his earnings taken which would cause a considerable hardship.

Q&A

Q: What is a garnishment?

A: A garnishment is a court-ordered action on behalf of a creditor to collect an outstanding debt from an employee through the use of pay period deductions.

Again, in such cases the payroll accountant will establish the appropriate payable account to record and track the amounts withheld. The amounts will be paid based on timetables specified in the document(s) that orders the deduction.

Employer Payroll Taxes and Tax Deposits

CHAPTER 12

Unemployment Taxes

This stop on our payroll journey focuses on the topic of unemployment taxes. Few employers are exempt from unemployment tax on federal and state levels. This chapter is devoted to this important subject.

1 BACKGROUND OF UNEMPLOYMENT TAXES

The idea of establishing a tax to provide funds for unemployed workers came out of the economic chaos of the depression years of the 1930s. The federal government, under the leadership of President Franklin Delano Roosevelt, proposed such a tax as part of the **Social Security Act**, which was signed into law in 1935. Federal unemployment tax is commonly referred to as **FUTA,** because it is authorized by the *Federal Unemployment Tax Act.*

The funds that the federal government collects from federal unemployment taxes are used for running the federal unemployment tax program. The main purpose of this administrative program is to see that states are complying with unemployment tax laws. Because the main purpose of the federal program is the administration of unemployment tax law, the amount of FUTA taxes paid by employers is small when compared with the amount that is paid into state unemployment programs.

Businesses that employ eligible workers will pay FUTA taxes on the earnings of those workers, up to certain dollar limits. Under current federal unemployment law, unemployment taxes will be paid on the earnings of workers only if the work performed by the workers is covered under law. An employee's earnings are subject to FUTA taxes if:

- The worker is classified as an *employee* using the **common law test**; and
- The company employs at least one worker for one day (or part of a day) for 20 or more weeks in the current or previous year; or
- The company has paid employees $1,500 or more in any calendar quarter during the current or previous year.

The rules listed above are broad enough to cover the majority of employment situations. The law applies to small companies that employ only a few workers as well as gigantic companies such as General Motors and IBM.

Employers will pay FUTA taxes on the earnings of the workers that qualify under this law. Federal unemployment law refers to such earnings as *wages*. Any compensation that is classified as wages under unemployment law will be subject to unemployment tax. Figure 12–1 gives several examples of the types of earnings or wages paid to workers subject to federal unemployment taxes. This is only a partial listing of the various types of earnings classified as wages under FUTA.

Employers who must pay FUTA on the earnings of their employees generally will pay state unemployment taxes on those earnings as well. The term **SUTA** is the acronym for *state unemployment tax acts*, which are laws that cover the area of unemployment on a state level. Employer contributions to SUTA programs provide funds for unemployment insurance coverage and worker's compensation insurance, which we will discuss in Segment 3. Currently, all 50 states, Puerto Rico, the Virgin Islands, and Guam have state unemployment laws in effect.

The employer is responsible for paying unemployment taxes on workers' earnings to both the federal government and one or more state governments under unemployment tax laws. Employees currently do not have to contribute to the federal fund. Likewise, the majority of states do not require employees to pay state unemployment taxes on their own behalf. (As of this writing only Alaska requires employee state unemployment tax withholding.)

Q&A

Q: Not all states tax income. Do all states have unemployment tax laws in effect?

A: All states plus other U.S. jurisdictions must comply with FUTA and have some program in place.

F I G U R E   12-1

Examples of the Types of Earnings Subject to
FUTA taxes

▪ Advances	▪ Guaranteed wages or salaries
▪ Back pay of wages	▪ Jury duty pay
▪ Bonuses	▪ Idle-time or stand-by pay
▪ Commissions	▪ Wages or hourly pay
▪ Dismissal pay	▪ Salaries

2   CALCULATING FEDERAL UNEMPLOYMENT TAXES

In order to calculate FUTA for an employer, we need to look at the amount
of the tax that is due on each individual employee's earnings. To make such
a calculation properly, we need to understand the unique accounting concept of the *earnings limit*.

The amount of FUTA tax an employer will pay is based on the amount
of earnings for each individual worker paid in a calendar year. An **earnings
limit** for FUTA purposes is the amount of the individual's earnings in a calendar year that will be subject to being taxed for federal unemployment purposes.

The maximum amount of an employee's earnings subject to federal
unemployment taxes in a calendar year is currently $7,000. This means that
an employer must pay FUTA on the first $7,000 of wages or salaries that
each employee earns in a calendar year. Any amounts earned over the
$7,000 limit maximum are not subject to FUTA tax.

E X A M P L E   1

Gary Scott is an employee of U.S. Route 66 Trucking, Inc. He was employed
full-time last year, and as of April 30 of the current year his year-to-date gross
earnings are $6,543.23. U.S. Route 66 has paid federal unemployment tax on
the entire $6,543.23 as it is under the $7,000 FUTA earnings limit. For the
pay period ending on May 6, Gary's gross pay is $592.19. How much of
Gary's May 6 gross pay is subject to FUTA tax?

Steps to Solve Example 1

1. Find the year-to-date wages before the current pay period earnings.

2. Add the current pay period earnings to the year-to-date wages and obtain a new year-to-date total.

3. If the new year-to-date total is less than the current federal unemployment earnings limit, the entire pay period gross pay will be subject to FUTA.

4. If the new year-to-date total is more than the current federal unemployment earnings limit, the portion of the pay period gross pay that brings the year-to-date earnings up to the $7,000 limit will be subject to FUTA.

Based on the steps above, the following calculation is made for Example 1.

Solution to Example 1

1. The total year-to-date earnings as of April 30 are $6,543.23. This amount is less than the federal unemployment earnings limit of $7,000.

2. Gary's new year-to-date total as of May 6 is $7,135.42 ($6,543.23 + $592.19). The new year-to-date total is more than the federal unemployment earnings limit of $7,000, so only a portion of Gary's May 6 pay will be subject to FUTA tax.

3. This step does not apply based on the result found in step 2. Go to step 4.

4. If we subtract the April 30 year-to-date total of $6,543.23 from the $7,000 FUTA earnings limit, we obtain the amount of Gary's May 6 gross pay that will be taxed for federal unemployment purposes:

$7,000.00	Current FUTA earnings limit
−6,543.23	Gary's April 30 year-to-date earnings
$ 456.77	May 6 earnings subject to FUTA

We can use the same steps to find the answer for Example 2 below.

E X A M P L E 2

Kara Proctor started her job at U.S. Route 66 on February 13. Kara's year-to-date earnings as of May 27 are $6,121.88. Kara's gross wages for the pay period ending on June 3 are $482.70. How much of Kara's June 3 pay will be taxable for FUTA?

Solution to Example 2.

1. Obtain the year-to-date wages before the current pay period earnings.

    $6,121.88   Kara's May 27 year-to-date earnings

2. Obtain the new year-to-date total:

$6,121.88	year-to-date earnings as of May 27
+482.70	June 3 earnings
$6,604.58	June 3 new year-to-date earnings total

3. All of Kara's June 3 gross pay will be subject to FUTA tax, because her new year-to-date total is less than $7,000.

Figure 12–2 shows the amounts for six other employees of U.S. Route 66 Trucking whose earnings will be subject to FUTA taxes. The amounts subject to FUTA are determined according to the $7,000 FUTA earnings limit maximum. U.S. Route 66 Trucking will only calculate federal unemployment tax based on the FUTA earnings of each employee, not the total amount that the employee earns during the year.

The payroll professional must keep track of each employee's earnings on a pay period basis in order to determine the amount of FUTA taxes due to the government at any point in time. In a manual payroll system, the **employee earnings record** provides the necessary year-to-date earnings information for each employee, which the payroll accountant will use to determine the amount of taxable FUTA earnings. When the payroll function is computerized, a payroll software program will automatically track the amount of each employee's earnings that will be subject to the FUTA earnings limit maximum.

F I G U R E   12–2

Employee	Employed since	Year-to-date earnings as of October 31	FUTA taxable earnings
Ernie Ball	1/1/98	$21,563.23	$7,000.00
Jeff Johnson	10/5/00	3,542.90	3,542.90
Sarah Cannon	1/1/01	25,106.50	7,000.00
Freda Jones	7/1/99	5,281.90	5,281.90
Tina Martinez	12/1/99	893.12	893.12
Jennifer Yang	5/1/95	8,891.60	7,000.00

The rate of tax that the employer will pay on each employee's earnings depends on the employer's unemployment tax payments to a state (or states') fund(s). The actual rate for federal unemployment tax is 6.2 percent on each employee's earnings (or FUTA wages), up to the earnings limit maximum of $7,000 per employee. However, this amount is offset by a **state unemployment tax credit** of 5.4 percent. This credit is referred to as the *normal FUTA credit.* An employer will receive this state unemployment tax credit if it meets both of the following conditions:

- The employer must make payments into at least one state unemployment fund on the FUTA taxable earnings of its employees.
- The employer must be current in its tax payments to the state fund.

When both of the conditions are met by the employer, it automatically will receive the state unemployment tax credit of 5.4 percent against the current year's FUTA rate of 6.2 percent. This results in a net FUTA tax rate of .8 percent:

6.2 percent	Current FUTA tax rate
− 5.4 percent	state unemployment tax credit
.8 percent	net FUTA tax rate for the employer

Keep in mind that the net FUTA rate is eight-tenths of 1 percent. Remember that this is less than 1 percent so it must be entered into a calculator as .008, not .8 or .08.

If the employer does not pay into one or more state funds or is behind in its payments to a state fund, it is not entitled to receive the state unemployment tax credit and must pay 6.2 percent in FUTA taxes. The IRS will verify that the employer has met the two conditions listed above when it examines the Form 940-EZ (or 940), *Federal Unemployment Tax Return,* that the employer prepares and files after the end of each calendar year to report the amount of federal unemployment taxes paid.

E X A M P L E 3

Carol Burns works for U.S. Route 66 Trucking, Inc. U.S. Route 66 Trucking's rate for FUTA tax is .008. Carol has earned $6,721.95 as of June 3. For the weekly pay period ending on June 10, Carol earned $459.11. How much will U.S. Route 66 pay in FUTA tax on Carol's June 10 gross pay?

Steps to Solve Example 3

1. Find the year-to-date wages before the current pay period earnings.
2. Add the current pay period earnings to the year-to-date wages and obtain a new year-to-date total.
3. If the new year-to-date total is less than the current federal unemployment earnings limit, the entire pay period gross pay will be subject to FUTA.
4. If the new year-to-date total is more than the current federal unemployment earnings limit, the portion of the pay period gross pay that brings the year-to-date earnings up to the $7,000 limit will be subject to FUTA.
5. Multiply the amount found in either step 3 or 4 by the current FUTA rate. The result is the amount of FUTA tax for the employee's pay period earnings.

Based on the steps above, the following calculation is made for Example 3.

Solution to Example 3

1. Carol's total year-to-date earnings as of June 3 are $6,721.95.
2. Carol's new year-to-date total as of May 6 is $7,181.06 ($6,721.95 + $459.11). The new year-to-date total is more than the federal unemployment earnings limit of $7,000, so only a portion of her June 10 pay will be subject to FUTA tax.
3. This step does not apply based on the result found in step 2. Go to step 4.
4. If we subtract the June 3 year-to-date total of $6,721.95 from the $7,000 FUTA earnings limit, we obtain the amount of Carol's June 10 gross pay that will be taxed for federal unemployment purposes:

$ 7,000.00	Current FUTA earnings limit
– 6,721.95	Carol's June 3 year-to-date earnings
$ 278.05	June 3 earnings subject to FUTA

5. Calculate the FUTA tax on the amount found in step 4.

$278.05	Carol's FUTA earnings for June 10
× .008	U.S. Route 66 Trucking's FUTA rate
$ 2.22	FUTA tax on Carol's June 10 FUTA taxable earnings

Employers receive the state unemployment tax credit against their federal unemployment tax liability because the majority of the unemployment taxes paid by employers goes to state funds. The intent of the federal unemployment law is to make state unemployment funds responsible for providing benefits to unemployed workers. The state unemployment tax credit is given to employers due to this fact.

Under federal law, the employer will be given the 5.4 percent credit against FUTA tax regardless of the rate paid to a state unemployment tax fund on employee earnings. Example 4 shows this point.

E X A M P L E 4

U.S. Route 66 Trucking, Inc., pays into the Texas state unemployment tax fund. U.S. Route 66 has paid into the fund timely and is not delinquent in any payments to the SUTA fund. The state has assigned a rate of 3.5 percent on employee earnings subject to SUTA tax. Under FUTA law, U.S. Route 66 will still receive the 5.4 percent credit against its FUTA tax rate of 6.2 percent, even though it did not pay 5.4 percent into a SUTA fund. In the case of U.S. Route 66, its total federal and state unemployment tax rate is 4.3 percent (3.5 percent for SUTA plus .008 for FUTA).

The calculation for FUTA should be made each pay period so that the employer knows what the liability for this payroll tax is at any point in time. This way an accurate accounting for the liability is made and journalized. Chapter 11 discusses the journal entries that must be made to record the employer FUTA tax liability.

If an employee works at two different jobs, each employer will calculate and pay federal and state unemployment taxes on the employee's earnings independently of the other. The fact that the federal and state unemployment funds are receiving additional amounts for the same employee has no bearing on the amount of unemployment tax each employer pays. In this situation, an employer cannot claim any credit or refund from the federal or state unemployment funds.

Federal unemployment tax payments can be made quarterly using the deposit rules established under FUTA. If the employer's liability for FUTA tax is more than $100 by the end of a calendar quarter, the employer must make a deposit for the amount of tax due no later than one month after the end of that calendar quarter. If the liability is $100 or less at the end of any calendar quarter, the employer can carry the liability for FUTA into the next quarter, until it reaches more than the $100 threshold amount. Please see Section E, Chapter 13, Segment 3, which discusses the FUTA deposit rules in detail.

3   STATE UNEMPLOYMENT TAXES

As we discussed in Segment 2 of this chapter, the state in which the unemployed worker was employed is responsible for distributing benefits to that worker. As a result, the amount of contributions paid to various state funds is greater than the amount paid by employers into the federal fund.

Each state must comply with the basic rules established under the Federal Unemployment Tax Act. Federal and state laws work together in partnership to oversee that employers are complying with unemployment tax law and that benefits are properly distributed to eligible workers who become involuntarily unemployed.

This does not mean that each state has identical unemployment laws. State unemployment laws vary as to the percentage rate of employer contributions, the employee earnings limit maximums, and the amounts of benefits that are paid to unemployed workers. Each state has the right to set its own specific rates and limits, as long as it is in compliance with the basic rules of FUTA.

State Unemployment Earnings Limit Maximums

Each state may set its own earnings limit maximum for state unemployment purposes. The maximum will be based in part on the current monetary condition of the state unemployment fund and its anticipated future needs in providing benefits to unemployed workers. Currently, the 2001 state unemployment earnings limit maximums range from a low of $7,000 per employee to a high of $28,400. Figure 12–3 shows the 2001 unemployment earnings limit maximums for several states.

The payroll professional should always check with the specific state department of labor and employment for the current unemployment earnings limit maximums for that state.

As with the federal unemployment earnings limit maximum, the payroll professional must track the amount of employee earnings subject to any state's unemployment earnings limit maximum. A manual system will rely on the computations found on each employee earnings record, and an auto-

F I G U R E   12–3

2001 State Unemployment Earnings Limit Maximums

Alaska	$25,500	Massachusetts	$10,800
California	7,000	Maryland	8,500
Colorado	10,000	New York	8,500
Hawaii	28,400	Vermont	8,000

mated system will rely on the tracking features of payroll accounting software to provide accurate earnings limit information for SUTA purposes.

Unemployment Benefits

An employee may be eligible for unemployment benefits depending on several factors. Major factors that determine whether a worker will be eligible to receive unemployment benefits include:

- The length of time the employee was employed and the dollar amount earned during this length of time.
- The reason for the employee's unemployment.
- The time period the worker has been unemployed.
- The availability of the worker to accept new employment.

Most state rules are similar regarding a worker's eligibility for unemployment benefits. The state department of labor and employment is responsible for determining if a former employee is entitled to receive any benefits under state unemployment law. A worker's former employer may be contacted to verify the reason for unemployment; however, it is the state unemployment agency that determines payment of unemployment benefits to a former worker.

To claim unemployment benefits, most state laws require that an employee must have been employed for at least four out of the last five calendar quarters before the date that an unemployment claim is filed. During this time period, the employee must also have a certain minimum amount of earnings in order to be considered for unemployment benefits. The specific amount of earnings will vary with each state.

Reasons for a Worker's Unemployment

In most states, the only reason an employee is eligible for unemployment benefits is if the employee is **involuntarily unemployed** through no fault of the employee. Typically, involuntary unemployment occurs when an employee is laid off due to the downsizing of the employer or the employer goes out of business. Usually, a worker will not be eligible for unemployment benefits if the worker is terminated with cause or voluntarily leaves his job. Each state has its own definition and criteria for deciding whether a worker has been involuntarily terminated or not.

Most states have a **waiting period** requirement before any worker can receive benefits. The waiting period is at the beginning of the time the worker has been unemployed. The waiting period is usually one week in the majority of states; some states have no waiting period requirement.

Another factor that determines if a worker will receive unemployment benefits is the availability of the worker to accept new employment. The unemployed worker must be actively seeking employment in his or her career field or be willing to accept employment in another area that utilizes the existing skills the worker possesses. In most states, the worker must register with the department of labor and employment, actively submit applications and résumés, and make contacts with prospective employers in order to receive unemployment benefits. Again, each state has specific rules regarding a worker's availability for future employment.

4   CALCULATING STATE UNEMPLOYMENT TAX

Unlike the federal unemployment tax rate, the rate of state unemployment tax that an employer pays varies from state to state and from employer to employer. States may have different rates for unemployment tax depending on their specific funding requirements. Within each state, the rate paid by an employer will vary by employer due to the employer's *experience* or *merit rating.*

The Experience or Merit Rating

The rate of state unemployment tax that an employer pays depends on its **experience or merit rating.** This rating that an employer receives is calculated by the state based on several factors, such as the dollar amount of benefits paid to former employees under the employer's account.

An employer's experience or merit rating will change with time and the dollar amount of benefits paid to former employees. The rate may be adjusted annually by a state.

A new employer may be given a specific rate until the state can establish an experience or merit rating for the employer. Some states may establish a rate for an employer based on the industry in which the employer is engaged. The amount of state funds available for payment of benefits will also affect the rate an employer pays in state unemployment tax.

E X A M P L E 5

U.S. Route 66 Trucking, Inc., has opened a terminal in Colorado Springs, Colorado. Because U.S. Route 66 Trucking is a new company doing business within Colorado, the state's Department of Labor and Employment has assigned a new employer rate of 3.5 percent to the company. The earnings limit maximum for Colorado unemployment purposes is the first $10,000 each employee earns in the state. As time passes, U.S. Route 66 Trucking's rate for Colorado unemployment tax may vary as the state's Department of Labor and Employment establishes an experience or merit rating for the company.

There are several methods that states will use to calculate an experience or merit rating for an employer. The most popular method is commonly known as the **reserve ratio method.** This method takes into account both the amounts paid into a state unemployment fund as well as benefits paid to former employees under the employer's account. The amounts may be cumulative from the time the employer began paying unemployment tax, or the calculation may be based on either annual amounts or amounts over a three-year period of time. The basic calculation is expressed as:

$$\frac{\text{Employer tax payments} - \text{Benefits paid to former employees}}{\text{Average payroll}}$$

Keep in mind that the state is responsible for calculating and assigning an experience rating to an employer—the employer does not have to make any calculations on its own.

Other Types of Insurance Coverage

In some states employers may be required to participate in other types of insurance coverage for their employees. The other types of insurance coverage are disability insurance and worker's compensation insurance.

Disability insurance will provide benefits to workers who are unable to work due to a *non–job-related* injury, illness, or accident. In some states this coverage is mandatory; in other states this coverage is voluntary. Employees as well as employers may be required to pay toward the disability coverage.

Worker's Compensation Insurance

If a worker is unable to work due to an *on-the-job* injury, accident, or illness, in the majority of states the worker will be covered by some type of worker's compensation insurance. Employers are required to pay for such coverage, either through a state-sponsored fund or through a private insurance company. The laws regarding eligibility for benefits under a worker's compensation insurance plan differ in many states.

Currently, most states require that an employer prepare and file a return for unemployment taxes one month after the end of each calendar quarter. The return is submitted along with a listing of the employees on the company's payroll for the quarter and each employee's quarterly earnings. Chapter 14 in Section F discusses these quarterly reports in more detail.

Generally, any state unemployment tax liability should be paid with the filing of a state unemployment tax return. Depending on the dollar amount of the liability, some states may require that payment be made more often than every quarter. The payroll professional should check with the state in question to determine the current unemployment tax deposit requirements.

CHAPTER 13

Payroll Tax Deposits

This is a required stop in our payroll journey. It is essential that anyone involved with payroll accounting or administration understand the topic of payroll tax deposits. Move on to the next stop on our road map after having reviewed this important chapter.

1 EMPLOYER RESPONSIBILITIES FOR PAYROLL TAXES

Since the enactment of federal and state laws requiring the withholding of income taxes on earnings, employers have been placed in the position of collecting and remitting these taxes to the federal, state, and local governments on a timely basis. The area of payroll tax deposits is important to both the employer and the government.

One step in our payroll accounting process is making payroll tax deposits. Income taxes collected from employee earnings technically are payments that will be made to the federal, state, and local governments.

The employer is placed in a fiduciary position as both the collector of these taxes and payer of these taxes to the governments on behalf of its employees. Payroll taxes are known as **trust fund taxes** because of the position of trust that the employer assumes.

The responsibility for remitting trust fund taxes to various governments lies with the employer. Two key components of this responsibility are *accuracy* in the dollar amounts of the deposits and *timeliness* in making these deposits. The employer should always attempt to meet these two components or goals. The accuracy of the deposits results from the correct calculations for income, social security, and Medicare taxes. The element of timeliness in making the actual deposits is the topic of this chapter.

2   DEPOSIT RULES FOR FORM 941 TAXES

The term **Form 941 taxes** refers to the taxes that the employer reports on Form 941, the *Employer's Quarterly Federal Tax Return.* As discussed in Chapters 6 and 7 in Section C, these taxes are known as *social security, Medicare,* and *federal income taxes.*

Form 941 Deposits

A Form 941 payroll tax deposit is comprised of three parts:

- The *employees'* social security and Medicare taxes withheld for a given time period.
- The *employer's share* of social security and Medicare taxes for the same time period.
- The *employees'* federal income tax withheld for the same time period.

The employer must match employee social security and Medicare taxes on a dollar-for-dollar basis. The employees' and employer's portions of social security and Medicare taxes plus the amount that has been withheld for federal income taxes becomes the total Form 941 taxes that the employer will deposit.

Employer Tax Deposits

Tax deposits must be made according to an IRS timetable. If an employer does not follow this timetable, the employer may be subject to penalties and interest for making a late payroll tax deposit. The IRS does not treat the matter of late payroll tax deposits lightly, given the fact that the employer is a trustee of these employee taxes.

The due dates of Form 941 tax deposits depend on how an employer is classified by the IRS. (The IRS refers to employers as *depositors*.) According to IRS rules, depositors will be placed into one of two categories when making Form 941 tax deposits: **monthly** or **semiweekly**. Monthly depositors are placed on a different deposit schedule than are semiweekly depositors. The way to determine if an employer will be a monthly or semiweekly depositor is based solely on the dollar amount of the employer's Form 941 tax liability during a certain period of time. This time period is called the **look-back period.** The look-back period for each calendar year is actually a June through July fiscal year that begins 18 months before January of depositor's calendar year. So, the fiscal look-back period ends on July 31, six months before January of the depositor's calendar year. For example, the IRS has defined the look-back period for 2002 as one fiscal year, beginning on July 1, 2000, and ending on June 30, 2001, as shown in Figure 13–1.

For the 2002 calendar year, the IRS will calculate the total amount of Form 941 tax liability for each of the four quarters as shown in Figure 13–1. If the total tax liability for this look-back period is *less than $50,000,* the employer is considered a **monthly depositor.** If the amount is *$50,000 or more* during this period, the employer is considered a **semiweekly depositor.**

Q&A

Q: What is Form 941?

A: The IRS Form 941 reports the liability and deposits for federal income, social security, and Medicare taxes for each calendar quarter. Chapter 15 in Section F discusses this form in detail.

Using this rule, a new employer who was not in existence during the 2002 look-back period is automatically classified as a monthly depositor. This is due to the fact that the employer had no tax liability during the look-back period.

Q&A

Q: Is the look-back period effected by how often I pay employees?

A: No, the look-back period has nothing to do with how often you pay employees. It is based solely on the amount of your payroll tax liability for a given look-back period.

F I G U R E   13–1

The 2002 Look-Back Period

3rd Quarter	4th Quarter	1st Quarter	2nd Quarter
July-September	October-December	January-March	April-June
2000		*2001*	

An employer that has been classified as a monthly depositor will have to deposit all Form 941 taxes accumulated during a month by the 15th of the following month. There are several exceptions to this rule, which we will discuss later in the chapter. The employer will use Form 8109, known as a *federal tax deposit coupon*, when making the payroll tax deposit at the bank. (Form 8109 is illustrated in Figure 13–10 in this chapter.)

When the employer has been classified as a semiweekly depositor, it will have to make all Form 941 tax deposits on either a Wednesday or a Friday. The day the deposit is due and payable depends on when the employer pays its employees. Figures 13-2 and 13-3 will help illustrate this point.

Wednesday Deposits

If the employer pays its employees on a Wednesday, Thursday, or Friday, the Form 941 tax deposit will be due on the following Wednesday. In Figure

F I G U R E   13–2

Wednesday Deposits—General Rule

SUNDAY	MONDAY	TUESDAY	WEDNESDAY	THURSDAY	FRIDAY	SATURDAY
Week 1						
6	7	8	9	10	11	12
			If the payday occurs on Wednesday, Thursday, or Friday of Week One . . .			
Week 2						
13	14	15	16	17	18	19
			then the payroll tax deposit is due this Wednesday.			

F I G U R E   13–3

Friday Deposits—General Rule

SATURDAY	SUNDAY	MONDAY	TUESDAY	WEDNESDAY	THURSDAY	FRIDAY
5	6	7	8	9	10	11
If the payday occurs on Saturday, Sunday, Monday, or Tuesday . . .						*then the payroll tax deposit is due on this Friday.*

13–2, a payday falling on Wednesday through Friday of the first week means the tax deposit is due on Wednesday of the second week. There are also three exceptions to the **Wednesday deposit rule,** which we will discuss later.

Friday Deposits

If the employer pays its employees on Saturday, Sunday, Monday, or Tuesday, the Form 941 tax deposit will be due on the following Friday. Figure 13–3 illustrates this general rule. Please note that we begin the week in Figure 13–3 on a Saturday instead of Sunday to better illustrate the rule. Again, as with the general rule for Wednesday deposits, there are three exceptions to the **Friday deposit rule.**

Q&A

Q: Are the semi-weekly or monthly deposit rules controlled by when a pay period ends, or when the payday actually occurs?

A: The semi-weekly and monthly deposit rules are based on the day you *pay* your employees, not the last day of the pay period. It is important to remember this point. Semi-weekly and monthly deposit rules *always* use actual paydays.

Exceptions to Deposit Rules

There are three exceptions to the two general rules stated above for Form 941 depositors. Please note that any one of these exceptions may affect either a monthly or a semiweekly depositor. These three exceptions are:

- The bank holiday exception.
- The $2,500 exception.
- The $100,000 one-day exception.

Bank Holiday Exception

Normally, if the day of the deposit falls on a federal or state bank holiday, a Saturday, or a Sunday, the deposit will be due on the next regular banking day. The IRS has created specific guidelines for monthly and semiweekly depositors.

- For monthly depositors, if the 15th of the month falls on a legal bank holiday or a Saturday or Sunday, the deposit will be due on the next banking day.

- For semiweekly depositors, if the Wednesday or Friday deposit day is a bank holiday, the IRS allows the employer to make the Form 941 deposit on the next banking day. This will always allow the employer three banking days in which to make the deposit, adjusting for a Wednesday or Friday holiday.

Example 1 and Figure 13–4 show the bank holiday exception when a Wednesday deposit is a bank holiday.

E X A M P L E   1

In looking at Figure 13–4, note that the diagram indicates that if Monday, Tuesday, or Wednesday is a legal bank holiday, the deposit is due and payable on Thursday the 17th instead of Wednesday the 16th. Thursday is the deposit date because the IRS rule states that the depositor will always be allowed three banking days in which to make the tax deposit.

F I G U R E   13–4

Wednesday Deposits and the Bank Holiday Exception

E X A M P L E   2

Figure 13–5 illustrates the deposit due date when either Wednesday, Thursday, or Friday is a bank holiday. Note that the new deposit due date is Monday the 21st, which again gives the depositor three banking days in which to make the deposit.

F I G U R E 13–5

Friday Deposits and the Bank Holiday Exception

SUNDAY	MONDAY	TUESDAY	WEDNESDAY	THURSDAY	FRIDAY	SATURDAY
Week 1						
6	7	8	9	10	11	12 ← *If the payday*
Week 2						
13	14	15 →	(16)	(17)	(18)	19
occurs this Saturday, Sunday, Monday, or Tuesday . .			*and this Wednesday, Thursday, or Friday is a bank holiday . . .*			
Week 3						
20	(21) *then the payroll tax deposit is due this Monday.*	22	23	24	25	26

The $2,500 Exception

If an employer has accumulated less than $2,500 in Form 941 tax liability by the end of a calendar quarter, the payroll tax deposit is due one month after the close of the quarter. The deposit can be sent in when filing Form 941. This rule applies to an employer that has been classified as either a monthly or semiweekly depositor. The IRS refers to this exception as the *$2,500 rule*.

Any employer who is uncertain as to whether its total Form 941 liability will exceed $2,500 in a calendar quarter should make its tax deposits using the monthly depositor rules. An employer is better off making tax deposits as a monthly depositor as opposed to finding itself underpaid at the end of the quarter with the potential of paying penalties and interest.

The $100,000 One-Day Exception

The IRS has established another exception to the general rules for employers that have large Form 941 tax liabilities. This exception, which the IRS calls the *$100,000 one-day rule,* states that any employer that accumulates a Form 941 tax liability of $100,000 or more on any one day must deposit the amount of that liability no later than the next banking day. This rule will apply to both monthly and semiweekly depositors.

In order for this rule to apply to semiweekly depositors, the $100,000 amount must be accumulated on any one day within the Wednesday through Friday or the Saturday through Tuesday payday period. A depositor may owe more than $100,000 during a week and not be subject to this exception, as we can see in Example 3 below.

E X A M P L E 3

Figure 13–6 illustrates a semiweekly depositor that accumulates a $95,000 liability on Tuesday of week 1 and a $10,000 liability on Wednesday of week 1. Because the Tuesday payday liability is a Friday deposit (of week 1) and the Wednesday payday liability is a Wednesday deposit (of week 2), the employer never reached the $100,000 accumulated liability amount on any one day, and so it does not have to make a deposit on the next banking day. The depositor will make two separate tax deposits following the general rules for semiweekly depositors.

When a monthly depositor has a Form 941 accumulated liability of $100,000 on any day, it automatically is reclassified as a semiweekly depositor for the remainder of the current year *and* will be classified as a semiweekly depositor for the next calendar year.

F I G U R E 13–6

Semiweekly Depositor with $100,000 Form 941 Liability in a Week

SUNDAY	MONDAY	TUESDAY	WEDNESDAY	THURSDAY	FRIDAY	SATURDAY
Week 1						
6	7	8 Payday #1 - $95,000 in Form 941 taxes.	9 Payday #2 - $10,000 in Form 941 taxes.	10	11 The Friday rule applies to payday #1 liability.	12
Week 2						
13	14	15	(16) The Wednesday rule applies to payday #2 liability.	17	18	19

End of Quarter Deposits

When the end of a calendar quarter falls within a Wednesday–Friday or a Saturday–Tuesday payday period, a semiweekly depositor may have to make separate Form 941 payroll tax deposits. This is because the total accumulated liability during the calendar quarter should be reported on the Form 941 prepared for that quarter, and any deposit that applies to that same quarter must be separated from the next quarter's deposits.

E X A M P L E 4

Figure 13–7 illustrates an example in which March 31 (the end of the first calendar quarter) fell on a Wednesday, and the employer had a payday on both Wednesday and Friday of that same week (week 1). Using the general rule for Wednesday deposits, one deposit should be made on Wednesday of week 2 for both the Wednesday and Friday paydays. However, because the Wednesday payday is the last day of the first quarter, the employer must use two separate federal tax deposit coupons (Forms 8109) for each of the Wednesday and Friday payday tax deposits. Note that both tax deposits would be made on the same day, Wednesday of week 2.

Thus, the Wednesday payday tax deposit applied to the first quarter of the year, and the Friday payday tax deposit applied to the second quarter. This rule is only used when two or more paydays within a Wednesday–Friday or Saturday–Tuesday payday period fall between the end of one calendar quarter and the beginning of the next quarter.

F I G U R E   13–7

End-of-Quarter Deposits

SUNDAY	MONDAY	TUESDAY	WEDNESDAY	THURSDAY	FRIDAY	SATURDAY
			Quarter ends.			
March 28	March 29	March 30	March 31	April 1	April 2	April 3
			Payday #1 occurs today.		Payday #2 occurs today.	
April 4	April 5	April 6	(April 7)	April 8	April 9	April 10
			Tax deposit is made using two separate FTD coupons.			

Payroll Tax Deposit Accuracy

As we emphasized in Chapter 1, Accuracy, Compliance, Confidentiality, and Timeliness (or *ACCT*) in payroll accounting are qualities the payroll professional should strive to achieve. When making federal payroll tax deposits, these qualities are vital. For Form 941 tax deposits, the IRS has created an **accuracy of deposits rule (98 percent rule)**. This rule states that for either a monthly or semiweekly deposit, a depositor will be considered to be in compliance with the current IRS deposit rules if both of the following are true:

- A timely deposit has been made of at least 98 percent of the Form 941 tax liability.
- Any undeposited amount is $100 or less.

Any deposit amount of $100 or less that is due and not yet paid is called a **deposit shortfall.** Obviously, when a deposit shortfall exists, it must be paid in order for the employer to avoid penalties and interest. The IRS has created what it calls **shortfall make-up dates**, which are due dates that must be met by a depositor in order to stay within the guidelines of the 98 percent accuracy rule. There are different shortfall make-up dates for monthly and semiweekly depositors.

For a monthly depositor, the shortfall make-up date is the due date of the Form 941 tax return. In most cases, this date will be one month after the end of the calendar quarter. Thus, any deposit shortfall must be paid when filing the quarterly Form 941 tax return.

The shortfall make-up dates are slightly more complicated for semiweekly depositors. When a deposit shortfall occurs within any given month, the shortfall make-up date will be either the first Wednesday or Friday that falls on or immediately after the 15th of the next month. Example 5 explains this point.

E X A M P L E 5

Figure 13–8 shows a two-month period of time. In this example, the deposit shortfall of $89.58 occurs on Friday of week 4 in the first month. In the second month, the 15th of the month falls on a Thursday, so Friday the 16th is the day that immediately follows. Friday the 16th then becomes the shortfall make-up date for the deposit shortfall that occurred during the first month. The depositor will use a federal tax deposit coupon and deposit the shortfall amount of $89.58 on the 16th.

F I G U R E   13-8

Semiweekly Shortfall Make-Up Date

First month—the deposit shortfall occurs:						
SUNDAY	MONDAY	TUESDAY	WEDNESDAY	THURSDAY	FRIDAY	SATURDAY
Week 3						
14	15	16	17	18	19	20
Week 4						
21	22	23	24	25	26 _A deposit shortfall of $89.58 occurs._	27
Week 5						
28	29	30	31			

Second month—the deposit shortfall from the first month is paid:						
SUNDAY	MONDAY	TUESDAY	WEDNESDAY	THURSDAY	FRIDAY	SATURDAY
Week 1						
				1	2	3
Week 2						
4	5	6	7	8	9	10
Week 3						
11	12	13	14	15	16 _This becomes the deposit shortfall make-up date._	17

3 DEPOSIT RULES FOR FORM 940 TAXES

The deposit rules for federal unemployment taxes are less complicated than those we have discussed for social security, Medicare, and federal income taxes. We refer to federal unemployment taxes as **Form 940 taxes** because these taxes will be reported on an annual basis when preparing a Form 940 or 940-EZ, the *Federal Annual Unemployment Tax Return.*

The rules for depositing federal unemployment taxes are as follows:

- If the accumulated liability for Form 940 taxes is more than $100 within any calendar quarter, the employer must deposit the liability no later than one month after the end of the calendar quarter.
- If, at the end of any calendar quarter, the accumulated liability for Form 940 taxes is $100 or less, no deposit is due. The employer can carry the dollar amount of this liability into the next calendar quarter. Then, in the next quarter, if the liability reaches over $100, a deposit is due one month after that calendar quarter ends.

The employer will use a federal tax deposit coupon (Form 8109) to deposit Form 940 taxes as is the case with Form 941 taxes. Again, the payroll professional should strive to make any deposit for federal unemployment taxes accurate and in a timely manner. Figure 13–9 summarizes federal unemployment tax deposit rules.

FIGURE 13–9

Calendar Quarter	Last Day of Quarter	Due date of Form 940 deposit if liability is over $100 for the quarter
1st—January, February, March	March 31	April 30
2nd—April, May, June	June 30	July 31
3rd—July, August, September	September 30	October 31
4th—October, November, December	December 31	January 31 of the next year

Q&A

Q: What is the difference between Form 940 and Form 941 taxes?

A: Form 940 taxes are federal unemployment taxes; Form 941 taxes are federal income, social security, and Medicare taxes. The IRS uses these terms because they reference the payroll tax reporting form number used by employers for reporting purposes.

4 DEPOSIT PROCEDURES USING FORM 8109

In this chapter we have referred to making a payroll tax deposit using what is known as a **federal tax deposit coupon (FTD coupon).** This is also known as **Form 8109,** which is illustrated in Figure 13–10. The FTD cou-

F I G U R E 13–10

IRS Form 8109

pon is used for depositing Forms 940 and 941 taxes, and it can be used for other types of federal tax deposits as well.

After a company has applied for an **Employer Identification Number (EIN)**, the IRS will begin sending various forms to the company. The company will receive Forms 940 and 941, which have the company's name, address, and EIN preprinted on the form. The company will also receive a book of 23 Form 8109 coupons that will have the company's EIN, name, and address preprinted on each coupon.

The IRS asks that the coupon be filled out in #2 lead pencil, so that its automatic scanning equipment can properly "read" the coupon. The essential information that is required on a preprinted coupon is the dollar amount of the deposit, the type of tax (Form 940 or Form 941), and the calendar quarter to which the deposit applies (first, second, third, or fourth). A separate coupon must be used for each type of tax that is being deposited, so two coupons must be used when an employer deposits both Form 940 and 941 taxes on the same day.

The majority of employers will make their deposits for payroll taxes by delivering them to a bank authorized to receive federal tax deposits. The employer may also deliver a payroll tax deposit to any Federal Reserve Bank (FRB) or an authorized Federal Reserve branch within the employer's geographic area. A Form 8109 must accompany any payroll tax deposit.

A payroll tax deposit should be delivered to the bank no later than the due date of the deposit. Many banks end their **banking day** at 2 P.M. or 3 P.M. local time, so the payroll professional must take care to ensure that the deposit is delivered before this time deadline. Deposits delivered after the close of a banking day may be considered by the bank to be deposited the next banking day. The IRS may judge such a deposit as being overdue and assess the employer a late-payment penalty.

Electronic Funds Transfer System

Many employers are now required to make their payroll tax deposits electronically. The IRS has a federal payroll tax deposit program in place that uses an EFT system. The Service refers to this program as **EFTPS** (Electronic Federal Tax Payment System). Employers who in calendar year 1999 had over $200,000 in *total federal tax deposits* must use EFTPS to make their deposits in 2001. The current $200,000 threshold amount was increased in 2000 from the former amount of $50,000 for 1999 and earlier years. If the employer was required to use the EFTPS system in 2000, it must continue to do so in 2001 as well.

Note that the term "total federal tax deposits" include *all* employment taxes (employee withholding, employee and employer social security and Medicare, and FUTA) *plus* the employer's corporate income taxes *and* any federal excise taxes paid during 1999. Any employer whose calendar year 1999 total federal tax deposits was less than $200,000 and who has been using EFTPS can continue to use the system on a voluntary basis.

There is a 10 percent penalty for failure to use the EFTPS system when required by these rules. Employers who do not meet the $200,000 threshold amount may voluntarily use EFTPS to remit their taxes electronically.

EFTPS allows an employer to use a PC or a touch-tone phone to make electronic payroll tax deposits. The employer can also set up EFT payroll tax deposits through its local bank. This system is based on a pilot system tested by employers in South Carolina, Florida, and Georgia during 1993 and 1994 that was known as *TAXLINK*.

5 OVERVIEW OF STATE PAYROLL TAX DEPOSIT RULES

The deposit rules for state income tax withholding vary from state to state. Generally speaking, many states will accept a deposit of state income taxes using the federal tax deposit timetable. This simplifies the depositor's task of complying with two or more different sets of deposit rules. Some states have established specific rules for their income tax deposits.

As is the case with federal payroll tax deposits, states require that any deposit for income taxes withheld from employees be accompanied by a specific state form. The function of these state forms is similar to that of the federal Form 8109. Each state will have its own version of the federal tax deposit coupon. Each state will also have its own timetable for deposits of state income taxes. A general rule can be established here: The greater the accumulated state tax liability, the sooner it should be deposited with the state.

Most states require any deposit for state income tax withholding be sent by check to the state along with the state withholding tax coupon or return. Normally, the deposit will be considered to be paid on a timely basis if the return has been postmarked on or before the due date of the deposit.

However, if the dollar amount of the state income taxes withheld exceeds a certain amount, some states require that the tax be paid to the state treasury by transferring the money directly to the state's bank account via an electronic funds transfer (EFT), similar to the federal EFTPS program. California, Colorado, and New York are examples of states that require EFT deposits if certain threshold tax liability amounts are met.

For example, in California any employer that has a liability of $50,000 or more must make current and future state tax deposits using EFT. In Colorado, if the amount of the state withholding liability is estimated to be larger than $11,000 annually, deposits must be made by EFT. For the state of New York, if the amount of taxes remitted is $400,000 or more annually, the depositor must participate in what is known as the *PromptTax Program*. Tax filers who are in the New York PromptTax Program will make their payroll tax deposits using EFT.

Remember that state laws are different from each other and are subject to change at any time. The payroll professional should consult with the revenue or income tax department of the specific states for any state income tax withholding or deposit issues.

SECTION F

Payroll Reporting Requirements

CHAPTER 14

Forms 940-EZ and 940

At this stop along our route, we discuss two taxes that an employer pays on employee earnings: federal and state unemployment taxes. We specifically discuss the payroll tax report that is prepared in conjunction with federal unemployment taxes: the Form 940-EZ and the longer Form 940. You may be fearful of learning how to prepare tax forms like the Form 940-EZ; however, once you understand the purpose of this form and where to obtain the amounts that are entered on the form itself, you will be surprised to find that this form is relatively simple to prepare.

1 THE PURPOSE OF FORM 940-EZ

The **Form 940-EZ** is called the *Employer's Annual Federal Unemployment* **(FUTA)** *Tax Return.* This return must be prepared and filed by the majority of U.S. employers who employ and pay workers whose earnings are subject to federal unemployment tax.

This return reports the amount of federal unemployment tax liability incurred by an employer during a calendar year as well as any federal unemployment tax deposits made. The amount of federal unemployment tax is calculated on the earnings of employees up to a certain maximum known as an earnings limit.

The IRS examines this return to determine if an employer has been complying with federal unemployment law in paying the correct amount of unemployment tax on its employees' earnings. Preparing and filing the Form 940-EZ also aids the payroll accountant in reconciling the amount of payroll taxes a company has paid over the year.

Any company that employs workers whose employment is covered by the Federal Unemployment Tax Act (FUTA) must pay federal unemployment taxes and file this return annually. Recall that this act is part of the Social Security Act of 1935. The term **covered employment** is defined under federal unemployment law as follows:

- The worker is classified as an *employee* using the common law test; *and*
- The company employs at least one worker for one day (or part of a day) for 20 or more weeks in the current or previous year; *or*
- The company has paid employees $1,500 or more in any calendar quarter during the current or previous year.

These requirements encompass the majority of employers today. Usually, if an employer must pay federal unemployment taxes, it must also pay into one or more state unemployment tax funds. The reporting requirements for state unemployment taxes will be discussed in Segment 5.

Types of Federal Unemployment Returns

There are two types of federal unemployment returns an employer may file: the Form 940-EZ *or* the Form 940. The *Form 940-EZ* can be prepared and filed by an employer when *all* four of the following conditions have been met:

1. The employer pays state unemployment taxes to only one state.
2. The employer has made timely payments to that state, and all taxes due to that state have been paid by the filing date of the Form 940-EZ.
3. All wages that are taxable for federal unemployment purposes are also taxable for state unemployment (SUTA) purposes.

Form 940-EZ Is a Simplified Version

The Form 940-EZ is a simplified ("easy") version of the Form 940, which is a two-page return requiring additional information from an employer. If an employer cannot meet all four conditions stated above, it must file a

Form 940 instead of a Form 940-EZ. An employer that employs workers in two or more states (and so is known as a *multistate employer*) must prepare and file a Form 940 after each calendar year. Figure 14–5 illustrates a Form 940.

2   EMPLOYEE EARNINGS RECORDS AND THE PAYROLL REGISTER

Probably the most difficult step in learning how to prepare a Form 940-EZ is knowing how to obtain the amounts that the form requires. Understanding how employee earnings records and the general ledger interact to supply the necessary amounts for this payroll tax return will make the actual preparation of the form simple.

We will make the assumption in this chapter that the payroll professional is preparing the Form 940-EZ by hand, without using a computerized payroll accounting program to calculate or print out the form.

In payroll accounting you have learned that different forms or returns must be prepared at various times during the year. The key thing to remember in preparing the federal unemployment tax return is that the form requires *annual amounts,* whereas many other returns prepared will use quarterly or pay period amounts.

Annual amounts used in preparing the Form 940-EZ can be obtained from employee earnings records and the general ledger. As we have discussed in this book, employee earnings records provide a comprehensive calendar-year history of the amounts earned by an employee. You may also recall that the general ledger is the accounting document that is utilized to maintain the current balance in each account that is used in a business. These two component parts of an accounting system will be employed to ascertain the correct amounts for the Form 940-EZ.

Specifically, the payroll professional will need the following information to prepare a Form 940-EZ:

- Wages or salaries paid during the year to employees from employee earnings records.
- Federal unemployment tax payable data from the general ledger.
- State unemployment tax payable data from the general ledger.

Employee earnings records will provide the payroll professional with the total paid to employees during the year and the amount of employee earnings subject to FUTA tax. Both amounts are required on Form 940-EZ.

Recall that one column on each employee earnings record will record the cumulative year-to-date earnings amount. This amount will be used to determine how much of the employee's earnings will be subject to federal unemployment tax. In a manual payroll accounting system, the payroll professional will examine each employee's earnings record to determine these dollar amounts.

It is important to realize that *it is the amount of wages or salaries paid, not accrued,* that is reported for the year on the Form 940-EZ. The employee earnings records are used in preparing this form because each record will show the cumulative amount of wages or salaries *actually paid* to each employee for the year. If you have reviewed Chapter 11, you may recall a journal entry was prepared to record the accrual for wages and salaries at the end of a month. An entry like the one in Chapter 11 will be made at the end of the year (if needed) to *estimate* the total wages and salaries expense for financial statement reporting. However, such an entry will not be used in preparing Form 940-EZ—only the actual dollar amounts received by employees will be reported on the Form 940-EZ and taxed by the IRS.

The general ledger can be analyzed to determine the liability for federal unemployment tax at the end of each calendar quarter. The payroll accountant will examine the general ledger accounts such as "FUTA Tax Payable" to determine the dollar amount of the liability at the end of each quarter. These amounts will be used in preparing the Form 940-EZ.

The general ledger account "SUTA Tax Payable" will also be examined to determine the amount of state unemployment tax due and paid. This information will also be reported on Form 940-EZ, as we will discuss in the next segment.

Now that we have determined where to find the amounts needed to complete a Form 940-EZ, our next step is to learn how to prepare this tax return.

3 PREPARING FORM 940-EZ

This form, as the name EZ implies, is easier to prepare than the longer and more complicated Form 940. Once you have learned how to prepare a Form 940-EZ, you will be knowledgeable about the basic steps involved in preparing a Form 940 as well.

It will be helpful for you to think of preparing the Form 940-EZ in three distinct parts. We have labeled these three parts as ①, ②, and ③, as shown in Figure 14–1. The form may be prepared starting with the top of the form and moving down. We use this approach to provide you with an organized method of preparing the form—however, once the Form 940-EZ is completed, it makes little difference which part of the form was completed first, as long as the entire form is completed before it is filed.

Draft Copies

When preparing Form 940-EZ, a photocopy of the form should be completed in pencil before the form is typed or printed in ink. Filling out a copy of the form using a pencil draft is the best way to prepare the form. The form can then be reviewed and any corrections easily made. The copy of the 940-EZ that is sent to the IRS should be either typed or printed legibly using an ink pen.

Section ①: Identification Information

In looking at Figure 14–2, you can see that the top third of the Form 940-EZ is used for employer identification purposes. Note questions A and B—these two questions are used to provide the IRS with state unemployment fund information. The IRS will verify this information with the state unemployment fund to which the employer has made tax payments to determine the final amount of federal unemployment tax due. This will be discussed further when we prepare section ② of the return.

Once a company has been given an *Employer Identification Number* (abbreviated as **EIN**), the IRS will automatically send various payroll tax forms and returns to the company after the company has filed initial returns. These returns and forms, including the Form 940 or 940-EZ, will have the identification information preprinted on the top of the form. A new employer will have to fill out this information on the first return filed with the IRS.

Section ②: Taxable Wages and FUTA Tax

The part of the Form 940-EZ that we have called Section ② is known as Part I of the form, as shown in Figure 14–3. These nine lines are used to determine the actual FUTA tax liability for the calendar year as well as and any remaining amount due to the government or any overpayment due the employer. Remember that the amounts entered on lines 1 through 9 are annual amounts.

FIGURE 14–1

Form 940-EZ

Form **940-EZ**	**Employer's Annual Federal Unemployment (FUTA) Tax Return**	OMB No. 1545-1110

Department of the Treasury
Internal Revenue Service (99)   ▶ **See separate instructions for Form 940-EZ for information on completing this form.**

Name (as distinguished from trade name)
U.S. Route 66 Trucking, Inc.   Calendar year 200X
Trade name, if any
P. O. Box 66
Address and ZIP code
Adrain, TX 79001   Employer identification number
12 3456789

T
FF
FD
FP
I
T

Answer the questions under *Who May Use Form 940-EZ* on page 2. If you cannot use Form 940-EZ, you must use Form 940.

A Enter the amount of contributions paid to your state unemployment fund. (See separate instructions.) . . . ▶ $ 10,294 97
B (1) Enter the name of the state where you have to pay contributions . . . . ▶ ....Texas
   (2) Enter your state reporting number as shown on your state unemployment tax return ▶ 302300-00-0
If you will not have to file returns in the future, check here (see Who Must File in separate instructions), and complete and sign the return. ▶ ☐
If this is an Amended Return, check here . . . . ▶ ☐

Part I   Taxable Wages and FUTA Tax

1	Total payments (including payments shown on lines 2 and 3) during the calendar year for services of employees		1	608,588 23
2	Exempt payments. (Explain all exempt payments, attaching additional sheets if necessary.) ▶	2		
3	Payments of more than $7,000 for services. Enter only amounts over the first $7,000 paid to each employee. Do not include any exempt payments from line 2. (See separate instructions.) The $7,000 amount is the Federal wage base. Your state wage base may be different. **Do not use your state wage limitation**	3	429,374 42		
4	Total exempt payments (add lines 2 and 3) . . . . ▶		4	429,374 42
5	**Total taxable wages** (subtract line 4 from line 1) . . . . ▶		5	179,213 81
6	FUTA tax. Multiply the wages on line 5 by .008 and enter here. **(If the result is over $100, also complete Part II.)**		6	1,433 71
7	Total FUTA tax deposited for the year, including any overpayment applied from a prior year		7	1,365 00
8	**Balance due** (subtract line 7 from line 6). Pay to the **"United States Treasury"** . . . . ▶		8	68 71
	If you owe more than $100, see **Depositing FUTA tax** in separate instructions.			
9	**Overpayment** (subtract line 6 from line 7). Check if it is to be: ☐ Applied to next return or ☐ Refunded ▶		9	

Part II   Record of Quarterly Federal Unemployment Tax Liability (Do not include state liability.) **Complete only if line 6 is over $100.**

Quarter	First (Jan. 1 – Mar. 31)	Second (Apr. 1 – June 30)	Third (July 1 – Sept. 30)	Fourth (Oct. 1 – Dec. 31)	Total for year
Liability for quarter	892.03	301.72	169.12	70.84	1,433.71

Under penalties of perjury, I declare that I have examined this return, including accompanying schedules and statements, and, to the best of my knowledge and belief, it is true, correct, and complete, and that no part of any payment made to a state unemployment fund claimed as a credit was, or is to be, deducted from the payments to employees.

Signature ▶ *Jim Johnson*   Title (Owner, etc.) ▶ *Controller*   Date ▶ 1-30-200X

For Privacy Act and Paperwork Reduction Act Notice, see separate instructions.   Cat. No. 10983G   Form **940-EZ**

Line 1: Total Payments The amount entered on this line represents the to-tal wages paid to employees for the year. As we discussed above, this would be the total from all employee earnings record year-to-date totals. The pay-roll professional will add together the employee earnings records totals to determine this amount.

Line 2: Exempt Payments An amount entered on this line represents amounts paid to employees that are not taxable for federal unemployment purposes. Examples of such payments would be amounts paid to workers for any injury or sickness covered under worker's compensation law, the cost of group term life insurance, or the value of meals and lodging.

F I G U R E   14–2

Form 940-EZ, Section ①

Form **940-EZ**	**Employer's Annual Federal Unemployment (FUTA) Tax Return**	OMB No. 1545-1110
Department of the Treasury Internal Revenue Service (99)	► See separate Instructions for Form 940-EZ for information on completing this form.	200X

Name (as distinguished from trade name) U.S. Route 66 Trucking, Inc.	Calendar year 200X	FF
Trade name, if any P. O. Box 66		FD
		FP
Address and ZIP code Adrain, TX 79001	Employer identification number 12 :3456789	T

Answer the questions under **Who May Use Form 940-EZ** on page 2. If you cannot use Form 940-EZ, you must use Form 940.

A   Enter the amount of contributions paid to your state unemployment fund. (See separate instructions.) . . . ► $ 10,294 | 97

B   (1) Enter the name of the state where you have to pay contributions . . . . ►   Texas

(2) Enter your state reporting number as shown on your state unemployment tax return ►   302300-00-0

If you will not have to file returns in the future, check here (see **Who Must File** in separate instructions), **and complete and sign the return.** ► ☐

If this is an Amended Return, check here . . . . ► ☐

F I G U R E   14–3

Form 940-EZ, Section ②

Part I	Taxable Wages and FUTA Tax			
1	Total payments (including payments shown on lines 2 and 3) during the calendar year for services of employees	1	608,588	23
2	Exempt payments. (Explain all exempt payments, attaching additional sheets if necessary.) ►	2		
3	Payments of more than $7,000 for services. Enter only amounts over the first $7,000 paid to each employee. Do not include any exempt payments from line 2. (See separate instructions.) The $7,000 amount is the Federal wage base. Your state wage base may be different. **Do not use your state wage limitation** 3 429,374	42		
4	Total exempt payments (add lines 2 and 3)	4	429,374	42
5	**Total taxable wages** (subtract line 4 from line 1) . . . . ►	5	179,213	81
6	FUTA tax. Multiply the wages on line 5 by .008 and enter here. **(If the result is over $100, also complete Part II.)**	6	1,433	71
7	Total FUTA tax deposited for the year, including any overpayment applied from a prior year	7	1,365	00
8	**Balance due** (subtract line 7 from line 6). Pay to the **"United States Treasury "** . . . . ►	8	68	71
	If you owe more than $100, see **Depositing FUTA tax** in separate instructions.			
9	**Overpayment** (subtract line 6 from line 7). Check if it is to be: ☐ **Applied to next return or** ☐ **Refunded** ►	9		

Line 3: Payments of More than $7,000   The amount on this line represents the total earnings of employees that are over $7,000 on an employee-by-employee basis. Any amounts paid to workers in excess of $7,000 in a year are not taxable for FUTA purposes. A quick review of how the federal unemployment earnings limit relates to this return will help in understanding how we arrive at the correct dollar amount for this line.

E X A M P L E 1

Lucky Dollar, Inc., has two employees. One works part-time,, the other full-time. The part-time worker was paid $6,500 for the year. The full-time worker was paid $24,000 for the year. The total amount paid to both employees of Silver Dollar for the year was $30,500 ($6,500 + $24,000). How much of the total wages paid to the employees of Lucky Dollar represents "payments in excess of $7,000"?

Steps to Solve Example 1

1. Determine the total wages paid to each employee during the year.

2. If an employee's earnings are over $7,000, subtract $7,000 from the total amount paid to the employee for the year. The result will be the "payments of more than $7,000."

3. The amount of any employee's earnings that is less than $7,000 for the year will not be included on this line.

Solution to Example 1

1. $ 6,500.00   wages paid to part-time employee
          $24,000.00   wages paid to full-time employee

2. $24,000.00   full-time employee's wages
          −7,000.00   current FUTA earnings limit
          $17,000.00   amount included on line 3 for Example 1

In Example 1, notice that only the full-time employee's earnings will be included on line 3. The part-time employee was not paid more than $7,000. Also note that the total Lucky Dollar paid to both employees, $30,500, is not used for the line 3 computation.

Line 4: Line 4 is simply the sum of any amounts found on lines 2 and 3.

Line 5: Total Taxable Wages This is the dollar amount of earnings subject to FUTA tax for the employer. The amount is found by subtracting line 4 from line 1. The amount on this line equals the total of the first $7,000 each employee has earned during the calendar year. If an employee did not earn $7,000 in the year, the total gross earnings for the employee would be included as part of the total amount found on line 5.

The earnings limit for federal unemployment tax purposes is the first $7,000 each employee earns in a calendar year. You may recall that by definition an **earnings limit** is the maximum amount, or ceiling, that an employee earns that will be subject to some type of payroll tax. Therefore, line 5 represents the total of the individual employee earnings limit amounts for FUTA purposes in the calendar year.

Line 6: FUTA Tax   This amount is found by multiplying line 5 by .008 (eight-tenths of 1 percent). This, then, is the total FUTA tax liability for the calendar year.

Line 7: FUTA Tax Deposits   This amount can be found by analyzing the *FUTA Tax Payable* general ledger account for debits made to it (which indicate payments of FUTA taxes) or by preparing a schedule of Form 8109 FUTA tax deposits made throughout the year.

Line 8: Balance Due   If line 7 is less than line 6, the employer still owes FUTA tax. The amount on this line should be $100 or less. If the amount is more than $100, it indicates that the employer has not complied with the FUTA tax deposit rules for the year. Please see Chapter 13 for a discussion of the FUTA tax deposit rule.

Q&A

Q: Why is $100 the threshold amount for unpaid FUTA taxes?

A: Any liability more than $100 after the end of the calendar year or after any calendar quarter indicates that the employer *is not* following the payroll tax deposit rules for federal unemployment taxes. Refer back to Chapter 13 to review the FUTA deposit rules.

Line 9: Overpayment   When line 7 is greater than line 6, the employer has paid too much in FUTA tax and is due either a refund or a credit toward the next year's FUTA tax liability. The preparer of the form should check the appropriate box to inform the IRS about the status of the overpayment.

Section ③: Quarterly FUTA Liability

The bottom third of the Form 940-EZ is used to report the quarterly FUTA liability for the employer. The amounts to be reported in Part II of this form are the FUTA liabilities at the end of each calendar quarter.

F I G U R E   14–4

Form 940-EZ, Section ③

Part II	Record of Quarterly Federal Unemployment Tax Liability	(Do not include state liability.) **Complete only if line 6 is over $100.**			
Quarter	First (Jan. 1 – Mar. 31)	Second (Apr. 1 – June 30)	Third (July 1 – Sept. 30)	Fourth (Oct. 1 – Dec. 31)	Total for year
Liability for quarter	892.03	301.72	169.12	70.84	1,433.71

Under penalties of perjury, I declare that I have examined this return, including accompanying schedules and statements, and, to the best of my knowledge and belief, it is true, correct, and complete, and that no part of any payment made to a state unemployment fund claimed as a credit was, or is to be, deducted from the payments to employees.

Signature ► *Jim Johnson*   Title (Owner, etc.) ► *Controller*   Date ► *1-30-200X*

For Privacy Act and Paperwork Reduction Act Notice, see separate instructions.   Cat. No. 10983G   Form **940-EZ**

(See Figure 14–4.) These amounts can be obtained by examining the general ledger account *"FUTA Tax Payable."*

Preparing the Form 940

If you understand the steps in preparing the Form 940-EZ, you have the basic tools required to prepare the Form 940 as well. The Form 940, shown in Figure 14–5, is a two-page form that requires more information from an employer. The form is more complex due to the fact that the employer must list specific information about state unemployment tax payments and experience or merit ratings. (This rating is discussed in Chapter 12.) This version of the form must be prepared if the company employs workers in more than one state.

4   FILING REQUIREMENTS FOR FORM 940-EZ

Whether an employer prepares a Form 940 or a Form 940-EZ, the return must be completed and sent to an area IRS office no later than one month after the end of the calendar year (January 31 of the subsequent year). If the employer has made all federal unemployment tax payments on time, the employer can file the Form 940-EZ by February 10.

The form should always be signed and dated by a responsible party of the company or its authorized agent (such as a CPA or tax attorney).

Any amount due to the government for FUTA taxes can be submitted in a check along with the form. The final FUTA tax deposit can also be made prior to submitting the return by using a Federal Tax Deposit Coupon (**Form 8109**) and depositing the amount of FUTA tax at a bank.

F I G U R E   14–5

Form 940

Form **940**	Employer's Annual Federal Unemployment (FUTA) Tax Return	OMB No. 1545-0028

Department of the Treasury
Internal Revenue Service (99)

▶ See separate Instructions for Form 940 for information on completing this form.

200X

		T
Name (as distinguished from trade name)	Calendar year	FF
Saturn Rockets, Inc.	200X	FD
Trade name, if any		FP
		I
Address and ZIP code	Employer identification number	T
1236 Pearl Street	12 3456789	
Boulder, CO 80302		

A   Are you required to pay unemployment contributions to only one state? (If "No," skip questions B and C.) . ☒ Yes ☐ No

B   Did you pay all state unemployment contributions by January 31, 200X? ((1) If you deposited your total FUTA tax when due, check "Yes" if you paid all state unemployment contributions by February 12, 200X. (2) If a 0% experience rate is granted, check "Yes." (3) If "No," skip question C.) . . . . ☒ Yes ☐ No

C   Were all wages that were taxable for FUTA tax also taxable for your state's unemployment tax? . . . . . ☒ Yes ☐ No

If you answered "No" to any of these questions, you must file Form 940. If you answered "Yes" to all the questions, you may file Form 940-EZ, which is a simplified version of Form 940. (Successor employers see **Special credit for successor employers** on page 3 of the instructions.) You can get Form 940-EZ by calling 1-800-TAX-FORM (1-800-829-3676) or from the IRS Web Site at **www.irs.gov.**

If you will not have to file returns in the future, check here (see **Who Must File** in separate instructions), **and complete and sign the return** . . . . ▶ ☐

If this is an Amended Return, check here. . . . . ▶ ☐

Part I   Computation of Taxable Wages

1	Total payments (including payments shown on lines 2 and 3) during the calendar year for services of employees	1	14,085	06
2	Exempt payments. (Explain all exempt payments, attaching additional sheets if necessary.) ▶	2		
3	Payments of more than $7,000 for services. Enter only amounts over the first $7,000 paid to each employee. (See separate instructions.) Do not include any exempt payments from line 2. The $7,000 amount is the Federal wage base. Your state wage base may be different. **Do not use your state wage limitation**.	3	4,000	00
4	Total exempt payments (add lines 2 and 3)	4	4,000	00
5	**Total taxable wages** (subtract line 4 from line 1) . . . . ▶	5	10,085	00

Be sure to complete both sides of this form, and sign in the space provided on the back.
For Privacy Act and Paperwork Reduction Act Notice, see separate instructions.   Cat. No. 11234O   Form **940**

DETACH HERE   *(continued)*

A photocopy of the 940-EZ form should always be kept on file for future reference. The payroll professional should also note on the photocopy the date the actual return was mailed to the IRS.

5   SUMMARY OF STATE UNEMPLOYMENT REPORTING REQUIREMENTS

Employers who are subject to paying FUTA taxes on the earnings of their employees must also pay state unemployment taxes as well. The term **SUTA** is the acronym that stands for *state unemployment tax acts.* All 50

FIGURE 14-5

Form 940 *(concluded)*

| Form 940 | | | | | | | | | Page **2** |

Part II   Tax Due or Refund

									1	625	27
1	Gross FUTA tax. Multiply the wages from Part I, line 5, by .062										
2	Maximum credit. Multiply the wages from Part I, line 5, by .054 . .	2		544	59						
3	Computation of tentative credit (**Note:** *All taxpayers must complete the applicable columns.*)										

(a) Name of state	(b) State reporting number(s) as shown on employer's state contribution returns	(c) Taxable payroll (as defined in state act)	(d) State experience rate period From	To	(e) State experience rate	(f) Contributions if rate had been 5.4% (col. (c) x .054)	(g) Contributions payable at experience rate (col. (c) x col. (e))	(h) Additional credit (col. (f) minus col.(g)). If 0 or less, enter -0-	(i) Contributions paid to state by 940 due date
CO	306000-001	8,398.00	Jan 200X	Dec 200X	4.4	453.49	369.51	83.98	369.51
ID	5550007600	1,687.00	Jan 200X	Dec 200X	2.5	91.10	42.18	48.92	42.18
		10,085.00						132.90	411.69

3a	Totals . . . ▶						
3b	**Total tentative credit** (add line 3a, columns (h) and (i) only- for late payments also see the instructions for Part II, line 6 . . . . ▶	3b		544	59		
4							
5							
6	**Credit:** Enter the smaller of the amount from Part II, line 2 or line 3b; or the amount from the worksheet in the Part II, line 6 instructions	6		544	59		
7	**Total FUTA tax** (subtract line 6 from line 1). If the result is over $100, also complete Part III . .	7		80	68		
8	Total FUTA tax deposited for the year, including any overpayment applied from a prior year . .	8		0	00		
9	**Balance due** (subtract line 8 from line 7). Pay to the "United States Treasury". If you owe more than $100, see **Depositing FUTA Tax** on page 3 of the separate instructions . . . . ▶	9		80	68		
10	**Overpayment** (subtract line 7 from line 8). Check if it is to be: ☐ **Applied to next return** or ☐ **Refunded** . . . . ▶	10					

Part III   Record of Quarterly Federal Unemployment Tax Liability (Do not include state liability.) **Complete only if** line 7 is over $100. See page 6 of the separate instructions.

Quarter	First (Jan. 1- Mar. 31)	Second (Apr. 1- June 30)	Third (July 1- Sept. 30)	Fourth (Oct. 1- Dec. 31)	Total for year
Liability for quarter	31.62	15.69	25.68	7.69	80.68

Under penalties of perjury, I declare that I have examined this return, including accompanying schedules and statements, and, to the best of my knowledge and belief, it is true, correct, and complete, and that no part of any payment made to a state unemployment fund claimed as a credit was, or is to be, deducted from the payments to employees.

Signature ▶ *Roger Rockets*   Title (Owner, etc.) ▶ *President*   Date ▶ *1-30-200X*

Form **940**

states and Puerto Rico have passed unemployment laws requiring that companies employing workers in those locations pay state unemployment taxes on the earnings of those workers.

All states require that companies that employ workers in their state file an unemployment tax return. For the majority of states the return must be filed one month after each calendar quarter ends. Figure 14–6 shows the due dates for calendar quarter returns.

Although the style and appearance of each state's return is different, the same basic information is requested from an employer. For state unemployment tax purposes, the following information is needed to determine the total quarterly tax liability of an employer:

- The total gross quarterly wages paid to employees in the state.
- The total quarterly wages subject to state unemployment taxes.
- The total quarterly wages exempt from state unemployment tax.

F I G U R E   14–6

Due Dates For Quarterly State Unemployment Reports

Calendar Quarter	Report Is Due By
First—January, February, and March	April 30
Second—April, May, and June	July 31
Third—July, August, and September	October 31
Fourth—October, November, and December	January 31

- The actual SUTA tax liability based on the employer's current experience or merit rating.
- The SUTA tax liability due to the state for the quarter.

As you can see by looking at the list of required information above, the state requires the same information as the IRS requires for filing a Form 940-EZ.

The states in Figure 14–7 require an employer to file a quarterly state unemployment tax return no later than one month after each calendar quarter ends. Figure 14–7 lists the specific state form that must be filed for this sample of states.

In addition to the actual unemployment tax return, a state may also require a listing of each employee by name, social security number, and the dollar amount of earnings for the quarter. This form is called a *quarterly wage report*. This report may be part of the actual return itself, or it may be a separate form that must accompany the unemployment tax return. Figure 14–7 lists the quarterly wage reports for our sample of states.

Keep in mind that the state unemployment earnings limit maximum may be different than the $7,000 federal limit. State earnings limit maximums for 2001 range from $7,000 up to $28,400.

Another difference between the Form 940-EZ and a state unemployment tax return is the rate of unemployment tax an employer will pay. Each state will assign a percentage rate to an employer based in part on the dollar amount of unemployment taxes paid to the state and the benefits paid to former employees of the employer. This rate is referred to as an **experience** or **merit rating.** This rating may change over time for an employer. Most states have set minimum and maximum rates for employers. For a further discussion of this rating, please see Chapter 12, Segment 4.

Summary of Quarterly Unemployment and Wage Reports

State	Quarterly Unemployment Report	Quarterly Wage Report
Arizona	UC-018	UC-020
California	DE6	DE6
Colorado	UITR-1	UITR-1(a)
Georgia	DOL-4, Part II	DOL-4, Part I
Illinois	UC3/40	UI40-A
New York	NYS-45	NYS-45
Texas	C-3	C-4

Please note: In this listing, some state quarterly unemployment tax reports and quarterly wage reports may be combined into a single report, or one report plus an attachment. Check with the specific state department of labor for the proper filing of these forms.

Payment of State Unemployment Taxes

Generally, the amount of state unemployment tax is due with the filing of the quarterly unemployment tax return.

Q&A

Q: Why are state unemployment tax returns filed quarterly?

A: The state unemployment fund uses the money remitted with the return to operate the fund; hence, the filing dates become quarterly as opposed to annually for the Form 940-EZ or 940.

Depending on the amount of tax due, some states may require deposits be made before the end of each calendar quarter. Certain states may also offer electronic funds transfer for SUTA tax deposits. The payroll professional should check with a particular state regarding its specific rules for SUTA tax payments.

CHAPTER 15

The Form 941

This spot on the road map is dedicated exclusively to preparation of IRS Form 941. At first sight this form may appear to be complex and difficult to prepare. However, once you understand the purpose of this form and try your hand at preparing it using the illustrations and examples in this chapter, you will find preparing the Form 941 a manageable task.

1 THE PURPOSE OF FORM 941

The preparation of payroll tax reports is an integral part of the payroll accounting process. Preparing the *Form 941*, known as the **Employer's Quarterly Federal Tax Return**, is very much a part of this process. The Form 941 is a tax return that will be prepared and filed by the majority of U.S. employers that withhold social security and federal income taxes from their employees.

The Form 941 is required by the Internal Revenue Service (**IRS**) for tax compliance purposes. The government will use the information provided on this form as a means to check and verify that payroll taxes withheld from employees and the employer's tax obligation have been paid to the government on a timely basis. As we have discussed in this book, tax compliance is a necessary part of running a business today. It is also an important function in the payroll accounting process to which we introduced you in Chapter 1.

F I G U R E 15–1

Form 941

① ② ③

Form **941**

Department of the Treasury
Internal Revenue Service

Employer's Quarterly Federal Tax Return

▶ See separate instructions for information on completing this return.

Please type or print.

OMB No. 1545-0029

Enter state code for state in which deposits were made **only** if different from state in address to the right ▶ ☐ (see page 2 of instructions).

Name (as distinguished from trade name): Mystery Investigations, Inc.
Trade name, if any

Address (number and street): 1555 Magnolia Lane

Date quarter ended: September 30, 200X
Employer identification number: 12-3456789
City, state, and ZIP code: Whodunit, MA 01268

T
FF
FD
FP
I
T

If address is different from prior return, check here ☐

IRS Use

1 1 1 1 1 1 1 1 1 1 2 3 3 3 3 3 3 3 4 4 4 5 5 5
6 7 8 8 8 8 8 8 8 8 9 9 9 9 9 10 10 10 10 10 10 10 10 10

If you do not have to file returns in the future, check here ▶ ☐ and enter date final wages paid ▶ ☐
If you are a seasonal employer, see **Seasonal employers** on page 1 of the instructions and check here ▶ ☐

1	Number of employees in the pay period that includes March 12th ▶	1	
2	Total wages and tips, plus other compensation	2	13,302 00
3	Total income tax withheld from wages, tips, and sick pay	3	1,231 00
4	Adjustment of withheld income tax for preceding quarters of calendar year	4	
5	Adjusted total of income tax withheld (line 3 as adjusted by line 4—see instructions)	5	1,231 00
6	Taxable social security wages . . . . 6a 13,302 00 × 12.4% (.124) =	6b	1,649 45
	Taxable social security tips . . . . . 6c × 12.4% (.124) =	6d	
7	Taxable Medicare wages and tips . . . 7a 13,302 00 × 2.9% (.029) =	7b	385 76
8	Total social security and Medicare taxes (add lines 6b, 6d, and 7b). Check here if wages are not subject to social security and/or Medicare tax . . . . ▶ ☐	8	2,035 21
9	Adjustment of social security and Medicare taxes (see instructions for required explanation) Sick Pay $ _____ ± Fractions of Cents $ +.01 ± Other $ _____ =	9	01
10	Adjusted total of social security and Medicare taxes (line 8 as adjusted by line 9—see instructions)	10	2,035 22
11	**Total taxes** (add lines 5 and 10)	11	3,266 22
12	Advance earned income credit (EIC) payments made to employees	12	
13	Net taxes (subtract line 12 from line 11). **If $2,500 or more, this must equal line 17, column (d) below (or line D of Schedule B (Form 941))**	13	3,266 22
14	Total deposits for quarter, including overpayment applied from a prior quarter	14	(3,266 22)
15	**Balance due** (subtract line 14 from line 13). See instructions	15	0
16	Overpayment. If line 14 is more than line 13, enter excess here ▶ $ _____ and check if to be: ☐ Applied to next return **or** ☐ Refunded.		

• **All filers:** If line 13 is less than $2,500, you need not complete line 17 or Schedule B (Form 941).
• **Semiweekly schedule depositors:** Complete Schedule B (Form 941) and check here . . . . ▶ ☐
• **Monthly schedule depositors:** Complete line 17, columns (a) through (d), and check here. . . . . ▶ ☒

17 Monthly Summary of Federal Tax Liability. Do not complete if you were a semiweekly schedule depositor.			
(a) First month liability	(b) Second month liability	(c) Third month liability	(d) Total liability for quarter
1,083.03	1,108.20	1,074.99	3,266.22

Sign Here

Under penalties of perjury, I declare that I have examined this return, including accompanying schedules and statements, and to the best of my knowledge and belief, it is true, correct, and complete.

Signature ▶ *Sam Spade*
Print Your Name and Title ▶ *Owner*
Date ▶ *10-31-200X*

For Privacy Act and Paperwork Reduction Act Notice, see back of Payment Voucher.   Cat. No. 17001Z   Form **941**

This form reports an employer's total quarterly liability for three federal taxes. The first tax is social security or FICA tax, which includes the amount withheld from employees as well as the employer's obligation. The second tax is Medicare, which again includes the amount withheld from employees as well as the employer's liability. The third tax is the federal income tax withheld from employees.

In learning how to prepare the Form 941, it will be helpful if we think of the form as being made up of three distinct sections. By breaking the form down into these three sections, our task of preparation is easier, beginning with section ① and ending with ③. Figure 15–1 shows the current Form 941 separated by section. We will discuss the preparation of these sections of the Form 941 in detail in Segment 3 of this chapter.

The Form 941 will be prepared after the end of each calendar quarter in the year. Preparing and filing the Form 941 on a timely basis is one of the goals the payroll professional strives to achieve so that the company is in compliance with the Internal Revenue laws of the United States. Each Form 941 report will cover a three-month time period, divided as shown in Figure 15–2. Keep in mind that because businesses operate using a 52-week calendar year, each calendar quarter will be 13 weeks long.

F I G U R E   15–2

Due dates for Form 941

Calendar Quarter of the Year	Quarter Includes the Following Months	Due Date of the Form 941
First	January, February, March	April 30
Second	April, May, June	July 31
Third	July, August, September	October 31
Fourth	October, November, December	January 31 (of the next year)

2   THE RELATIONSHIP BETWEEN ACCOUNTING RECORDS AND FORM 941

The difficult step in learning to prepare the Form 941 is knowing where to obtain the correct figures to complete the form. Understanding the relationship among the payroll register, employee earnings records, other accounting documents, and the Form 941 will help you learn how to find the correct amounts needed for preparing this form.

F I G U R E   15–3

Relationship between Accounting Records and Form 941

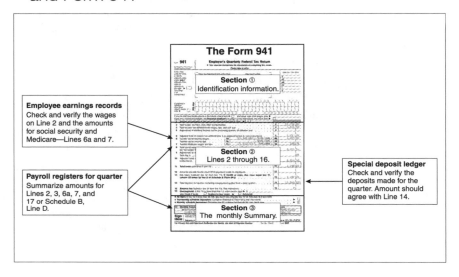

When preparing a Form 941, the payroll professional must rely on amounts obtained from payroll registers, employee earnings records, and the special tax deposit ledger (if one is used). Let's review the purpose and use of these accounting records. Keep in mind that any combination of these accounting records can be used to provide the required amounts that must be reported on the Form 941.

Figure 15–3 shows how amounts from these documents are used in preparing the Form 941. It will be helpful to refer back to this diagram when studying this segment and Segment 3.

The Payroll Register

The **payroll register** is the accounting document that provides a summary of payroll information for a given pay period. The payroll register will list all the employees who were paid for a given pay period, and it will include each employee's gross earnings, amounts withheld for taxes and various deductions, and his net pay. The payroll register is unique in that it is the only record in an accounting system that summarizes the accounting activity associated with paying employees on a pay period basis.

Q&A

Q: Which form is used to report federal unemployment taxes?

A: The Form 940-EZ (or 940), not the Form 941. Note that the Form 940-EZ (or 940) is prepared annually, whereas the Form 941 is prepared quarterly.

The information obtained from payroll register reports for any given calendar quarter can be summarized on a quarterly basis. The payroll accountant will prepare a workpaper schedule that will list the amounts of earnings and taxes withheld for each pay period. These quarterly amounts are then used in preparing portions of the 941 report. The specific information the payroll professional would be interested in summarizing is:

- Gross wages or salaries paid to employees for the quarter.
- Federal income tax withheld for the quarter.
- Social security withheld for the quarter.
- Medicare tax withheld for the quarter.

Payroll registers generated by a computerized program often will have quarter-to-date and year-to-date totals for gross earnings, taxes withheld, and earnings limits for social security purposes. If the payroll professional is working with such computer-generated payroll registers, these totals will be used in preparing portions of the form. A computerized payroll accounting program that offers such features can simplify the preparing of Form 941.

The Employee Earnings Record

The **employee earnings record** is another unique accounting document. The employee earnings record is the only document that lists the earnings of each employee on a pay period basis for a calendar year. These records will be used to determine the total amount of earnings subject to the social security earnings limit. The quarterly earnings within this limit will be used in calculating the total liability for social security taxes for each calendar quarter, which is reported on Form 941.

The Special Deposit Ledger

The payroll accountant may decide to maintain a **special deposit ledger** that will list the Form 8109 deposits made for social security, Medicare, and federal income taxes. The total of the payroll tax deposits for social security and federal income taxes for a quarter will be shown on line 14 of the Form 941.

We have briefly summarized how these accounting documents are used in the preparation of the Form 941. In order to fully understand how these accounting documents tie into preparing the Form 941, the next section will go over the mechanics involved when using payroll registers and employee earnings records to prepare this report.

3 THE STEPS TO PREPARING FORM 941

Draft Copy

When preparing Form 941, a photocopy of the form should be completed in pencil before the form is typed or prepared in ink. Filling out a pencil draft copy of the form is the best way to prepare the form. The 941 can then be reviewed and any corrections easily made. The copy that will be sent to the IRS should be either typed or printed legibly using an ink pen.

As we pointed out earlier in this chapter, in learning how to prepare the Form 941 it will be helpful if we think of the form as being made up of three distinct sections numbered ① through ③. Figure 15–1 shows the current version of the Form 941, separated by section. We will now discuss each section of the form.

Section ①: Identification Information

The first section of the Form 941 is the easiest part to prepare. This section, shown in Figure 15–4, is used to identify the company by legal name, trade name (if any), address, city, state, Zip code, Employer Identification Number (abbreviated as **EIN**), the quarter of the report, and the state code.

If the Form 941 is being prepared for the first time for a new business, the payroll professional will need to fill this section out completely. After the IRS receives the first Form 941 for a new business, computer-generated Forms 941 will be sent back to the business that will have the name, address, and EIN information preprinted on the form.

E X A M P L E 1

Mystery Investigations, Inc., is a small company that employs three people. It is located at 1555 South Magnolia Lane in Whodunit, Massachusetts 01268. The EIN for the company 12-3456789. The Form 941 will be prepared for the quarter ending on September 30, 200X.

F I G U R E 15–4

Section ①

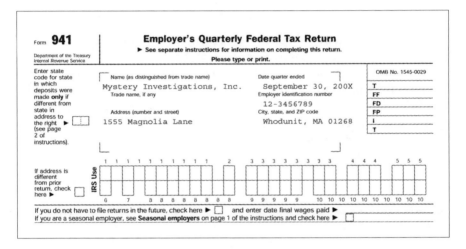

In looking at Figure 15–4, notice that the top third of the Form 941 contains a few questions that may require a response by the payroll accountant. These questions are summarized below.

Last Return If this particular Form 941 is the last one that will be filed for a business, this must be noted, along with the date the final earnings have been paid to employees. The IRS will then flag the EIN of this business as no longer in operation.

There are several reasons for filing a final return. One is that the business may be closing. Another is that the business may be merging with another, and the new business will report employee earnings using a new EIN and name.

Seasonal Employers If the business is seasonal in nature, operating for only a part of a year, it may not have to file a Form 941 for each quarter of the year. The IRS will need to know this to account for any quarters in which it did not receive a Form 941 from the business.

Line 1

This line (not shown in Figure 15–4) asks for the total number of employees of the business on the payroll as of March 12 of each year. The IRS uses this data for statistical purposes. Note that the payroll accountant will only provide this information on the first quarter's (March 31) Form 941 report.

Section ②: Lines 2 through 16

This section illustrated in Figure 15–5 will be prepared next. The purpose of this section is to calculate the amount due to the IRS for federal income and social security taxes at the end of a calendar quarter. This section will use amounts from all of the accounting documents discussed in Section 2.

Completing lines 2 through 16 of the Form 941 will provide the IRS with several different types of information, listed by line in Figure 15–5. We continue with our preparation of the third-quarter Form 941 return for Mystery Investigations, Inc.

E X A M P L E   2

The following dollar amounts shown in Figure 15–5 have been obtained from the payroll registers and employee earnings records for Mystery Investigations, Inc., as of September 30 (the end of the third quarter). To simplify our illustration, amounts have been rounded to the nearest dollar. All employees' year-to-date wages as of September 30 are under the current year social security earnings limit. The company pays its three employee semimonthly on the 15th and last day of each month.

The accountant for Mystery Investigations, using the information in Figure 15–6, has completed lines 2 through 13 of Form 941, as shown in Figure 15–5.

Using the summary found in Figure 15–7 as our guide, we will now discuss how to calculate the dollar amounts for each line in Section ②.

Section ② for Mystery Investigations, Inc.

2	Total wages and tips, plus other compensation			**2**	13,302	00
3	Total income tax withheld from wages, tips, and sick pay			**3**	1,231	00
4	Adjustment of withheld income tax for preceding quarters of calendar year			**4**		
5	Adjusted total of income tax withheld (line 3 as adjusted by line 4—see instructions) . . .			**5**	1,231	00
6	Taxable social security wages	**6a** 13,302 00	× 12.4% (.124) =	**6b**	1,649	45
	Taxable social security tips	**6c**	× 12.4% (.124) =	**6d**		
7	Taxable Medicare wages and tips . . .	**7a** 13,302 00	× 2.9% (.029) =	**7b**	385	76
8	Total social security and Medicare taxes (add lines 6b, 6d, and 7b). Check here if wages are not subject to social security and/or Medicare tax . . . . ▶ ☐			**8**	2,035	21
9	Adjustment of social security and Medicare taxes (see instructions for required explanation) Sick Pay $ _____ ± Fractions of Cents $ _+.01_ ± Other $ _____ =			**9**		01
10	Adjusted total of social security and Medicare taxes (line 8 as adjusted by line 9—see instructions)			**10**	2,035	22
11	**Total taxes** (add lines 5 and 10)			**11**	3,266	22
12	Advance earned income credit (EIC) payments made to employees			**12**		
13	Net taxes (subtract line 12 from line 11). **If $2,500 or more, this must equal line 17, column (d) below (or line D of Schedule B (Form 941))**			**13**	3,266	22
14	Total deposits for quarter, including overpayment applied from a prior quarter			**14**	(3,266	22)
15	**Balance due** (subtract line 14 from line 13). See instructions			**15**	0	
16	**Overpayment.** If line 14 is more than line 13, enter excess here ▶ $ _____ and check if it to be: ☐ Applied to next return **or** ☐ Refunded.					

Line 2

The payroll professional will list the total earnings paid to employees for the quarter on line 2. This amount can be found by adding together the gross earnings found on each payroll register for the quarter.

The majority of the time, line 2 will list the earnings for the quarter. On occasion however, line 2 will also contain other types of compensation that employees may receive, such as reimbursement for business expenses or for cafeteria-plan out-of-pocket costs.

Lines 3 through 5

These lines deal with the amount of **federal income tax** that has been withheld for the quarter. The amount of income tax listed on line 3 will include the amounts withheld from wages and salaries only. Any federal income tax withheld for other reasons, such as gambling winnings or **backup withholding**, will be reported on another IRS form known as Form 945 (not illustrated). The dollar amount for line 3 can again be found by summing the amount of federal income tax withheld from each payroll register for the quarter, or the "federal income tax withheld" amounts on each employee earnings record for the quarter.

FIGURE 15–6

Third-Quarter 200X Payroll Register Information for Mystery Investigations, Inc.

Pay Period	Holly				Maria				Jason			
	Wage	FIT	Social Security	Medicare	Wage	FIT	Social Security	Medicare	Wage	FIT	Social Security	Medicare
7-15	$1,159	$117.00	$ 71.86	$ 16.81	$ 508	$ 60.00	$ 31.50	$ 7.37	$ 520	$ 24.00	$ 32.24	$ 7.54
7-31	1,206	126.00	74.77	17.49	512	60.00	31.74	7.42	507	21.00	31.43	7.35
8-15	1,182	123.00	73.28	17.14	507	60.00	31.43	7.35	535	24.00	33.17	7.76
8-31	1,096	108.00	67.95	15.89	610	75.00	37.82	8.85	568	30.00	35.22	8.24
9-15	1,150	117.00	71.30	16.68	505	60.00	31.31	7.32	539	24.00	33.42	7.82
9-30	1,219	126.00	75.58	17.68	473	55.00	29.33	6.86	506	21.00	31.37	7.34
Totals	$7,012	$717.00	$434.74	$101.69	$3,115	$370.00	$193.13	$45.17	$3,175	$144.00	$196.85	$46.05

F I G U R E   15–7

Summary of Information Found on Lines 2 through 16
of Form 941

Line number(s)	Description of information
2	Total wages, tips, etc., paid to employees for the quarter.
3, 4, 5	Federal income taxes withheld and any adjustments from prior quarters for income taxes.
6a, 6b, 7, 8, 9, 10	Social security and Medicare tax liability.
11	Total federal income, social security, and Medicare taxes.
12	Earned Income Credit advanced to employees during the quarter.
13	Net liability for Form 941 taxes.
14	Total of Form 941 tax deposits for the quarter.
15	Balance due for 941 taxes for the quarter.
16	Overpayment of 941 taxes for the quarter.

Line 4: Line 4 will be used to adjust the amount of federal income tax withheld for previous quarters of the year. If line 4 is used, it is recommended that a Form 941c also be prepared and attached to the Form 941. Segment 5 will discuss how to correct errors made in federal income tax withholding on the Form 941, using Form 941c.

Line 5: Line 5, the adjusted total of federal income tax withheld, is merely the result of netting lines 3 and 4 together. If there is no adjustment amount on line 4, line 5 will be the same amount as is found on line 3.

Lines 6a through 10: Social Security Taxes

The payroll accountant will use these lines to arrive at the total social security tax liability for the quarter. Keep in mind that when we use the term *total liability,* we are referring to the combined total of the **social security taxes** withheld from employees for the quarter *and* the employer's portion of social security tax.

Calculating Lines 6a and 7: Note that this section of the form requires that we report the total earnings subject to social security and Medicare taxes *and* the social security and Medicare tax liability for the quarter. The *earnings* are shown in the center column of lines 6a, 6b, and 7, whereas the *tax* on the earnings will be shown in the right-hand column of the form. Both the earnings and the social security and Medicare taxes must be shown on the form.

Line 6b will be used only by an employer to report any tip income that will be subject to social security and Medicare taxes. We will not deal with this line in this chapter. Please look at Section C, Chapter 9, for a discussion of the payroll accounting for food and beverage establishments and reporting FICA taxes on tip income.

The earnings of employees will be subject to an **earnings limit** for purposes of figuring the social security taxes to be withheld. The social security *earnings limit maximum* for each employee in 2001 is $80,400. This limit has risen each year for the last several years.

Line 6a: Earnings Limit Amount   The amount of earnings that should be reported in the center column of line 6a is the *total* of employee earnings for the quarter that, on an individual employee basis, is less than $80,400 for 2001. In order to find this amount, the payroll professional should examine the employee earnings records to find out if the earnings paid to each employee during the quarter are under the $80,400 earnings limit for social security purposes. Based on this information, the payroll professional can then calculate the total amount of the wages and salaries that, on an individual employee basis, is less than the 2001 social security earnings limit.

The procedure involved to determine the total earnings that are within the social security earnings limit can be a time-consuming and tedious task if a computerized payroll accounting program is not being used. Many computerized programs will track each employee's earnings on a year-to-date basis, and can easily produce a summary total of the social security earnings limit amounts for each quarter that can be used on lines 6a and 7 of the 941 form. Example 3 helps illustrate this point.

E X A M P L E 3

Build-a-Business, Inc., is a consulting firm that employs five people: two office staff and three professionals. Payroll information has been obtained for the third quarter of 200X as shown in Figure 15–8.

F I G U R E   15–8

Third-Quarter Payroll Information for
Build-a-Business, Inc.

Employee	June 30 year-to-date wages or salaries paid	Wages or salaries paid during the third quarter
Todd	$ 55,217.83	$26,821.14
Fred	48,914.12	18,015.10
Nathan	37,571.12	13,895.03
Tammy	13,865.97	6,981.14
Connie	12,506.27	6,235.82
Totals	$168,075.31	$71,948.23

Based on the third-quarter payroll information, what dollar amount would a payroll accountant show for "Taxable social security wages" on line 6a?

Steps to Solve Example 3

1. Determine on an employee-by-employee basis if the wages and salaries paid for the quarter are over or under the social security earnings limit by taking the prior quarter's year-to-date wages or salaries and adding the amount paid to the employee during the current period.

2. Any individual employee's current quarterly wages or salaries that are under the limit will be included in the "earnings" column of line 6a.

3. If a portion of an employee's wages or salaries is within the earnings limit for the current quarter, include only that portion under the earnings limit maximum by subtracting the prior quarter's year-to-date earnings from the social security earnings limit maximum. The result is the amount includable in the line 6a "earnings" column.

4. Once the wages or salaries amount within the social security earnings limit has been found for each employee, add the individual totals together to arrive at the column total for line 6a.

Solution to Example 3

The payroll accountant, in following the four steps above for Build-a-Business, has prepared a workpaper schedule to show the dollar amount to include in the line 6a "earnings" column in Figure 15–9.

FIGURE 15-9

Third-Quarter Payroll Information for Build-a-Business, Inc.

Employee	A June 30 Year-to-Date Wages or Salaries Paid	B Wages or Salaries Paid During the Third Quarter	C September 30 Year-to-Date Wages or Salaries (A + B)	D Amount over $80,400 Social Security Earnings Limit, if Any ($80,400 − A)	E Amount of Third-Quarter Wages or Salaries Included in Line 6a Earnings Column (Amount in D or B)
Todd	$ 55,217.83	$26,821.14	$ 82,038.97	$80,400 − $55,217.83	$25,182.17
Fred	48,914.12	18,015.10	66,929.22	N/A	18,015.10
Nathan	37,571.12	13,895.03	51,466.15	N/A	13,895.03
Tammy	13,865.97	6,981.14	20,847.11	N/A	6,981.14
Connie	12,506.27	6,235.82	18,742.09	N/A	6,235.82
Totals	$168,075.31	$71,948.23	$240,023.54	N/A	$70,309.26

Line 6a: Social Security Tax Once the earnings that are under the social security earnings limit have been found and entered in the center column of line 6a, calculating the actual tax is simple. The earnings amount will be multiplied by the tax rate of 12.4 percent to arrive at the total social security tax liability for the quarter.

Note that the 12.4 percent rate for social security tax is the combined total of 6.2 percent for the employees' contribution and 6.2 percent for the employer's contribution (.062 + .062 = .124).

Please note that there is no earnings limit for Medicare tax. Before 1994 there was an earnings limit maximum for Medicare taxes as there is to-day for social security taxes. With the *Revenue Reconciliation Act of 1993* this limit was eliminated. This means that Medicare tax will be paid on all wages and salaries paid to employees each quarter and year.

Line 7: Earnings Amount The amount of earnings that should be re-ported in the center column of line 7 is the dollar total of employees' earn-ings for the quarter that are taxable for Medicare purposes.

Line 7: Medicare Taxes As is the case with line 6a, once the Medicare earnings have been found and entered in the center column of line 7, calcu-lating the Medicare tax is simply a matter of multiplying this amount by 2.9 percent and entering the result in the right-hand column on line 7.

The 2.9 percent amount used on line 7 represents the combination of the employee (1.45 percent) and employer (1.45 percent) portions of the Medicare tax for the quarter (.0145 + .0145 = .029).

Line 8: This line is merely the total of the tax amounts entered on lines 6b, 6d, and 7b. It represents the *total* social security and Medicare tax liability for the quarter, before any adjustments are made.

Line 9: The major use for this line will be to adjust the total social secu-rity and Medicare tax liability for any *differences* between the actual lia-bility shown on line 17(d) in Section ③ and the amount computed on lines 6b, 6d, and 7b.

Line 9 can be used for rounding differences, FICA adjustments due to sick pay, or for differences due to other circumstances. For example, a FICA **rounding difference** is created due to the fact that the calculation for the employees' and employer's FICA uses a different dollar amount for earnings in the calculation. The employee's FICA to be withheld on a pay period basis uses the employee's gross earnings for that pay period.

The employer's liability for FICA for the same pay period is calculated based on *the gross earnings for all employees for the pay period.* Calculating the employer's portion based on the total earnings of all employees while calculating each employee's liability using each employee's individual gross earnings amount causes the rounding difference.

The rounding difference becomes apparent when the Form 941 is prepared for a quarter. Recall that we said that the amount found on line 13 must match the amount found on line 17(d). If the difference between lines 13 and 17(d) is due to FICA rounding, the amount found on line 13 must be corrected to match the total on line 17(d) of the monthly summary. To correct the FICA liability, the amount of the adjustment is entered on line 9 in the "Fractions of Cents" column.

A FICA sick pay adjustment occurs when an employer has a third-party insurance company pay employees for sick leave compensation. In such cases FICA is withheld from the employee by the insurance company and the employee's earnings are included for social security and Medicare purposes on lines 6a and 7—so the FICA liability reported is too high. An amount entered in the "Sick Pay" column of line 9 will correct this situation.

Under other special circumstances an adjustment may be entered in the "Other" column by an employer.

E X A M P L E 4

The accountant for Mystery Investigations, Inc. has calculated amounts for line 17(a) through (d) of the third-quarter 941 form. Based on the total employee and employer liability for the quarter, we find that the total dollar amount of social security and Medicare taxes is $2,035.22. Using the total earnings paid for the quarter of $13,302.00 we find that in multiplying this figure by 15.30 percent the total FICA (social security and Medicare) is $2,035.21. The difference of 1 cent represents rounding due to calculating FICA based on the total earnings for the quarter, rather than on individual employee gross amounts each pay period. This 1-cent amount should be entered as a positive number on line 9 of Form 941 in the "Fractions of Cents" column as shown in Figure 15–10.

F I G U R E   15–10

Example 4

6	Taxable social security wages	**6a**	13,302 00	× 12.4% (.124) =	**6b**		1,649	45
	Taxable social security tips	**6c**		× 12.4% (.124) =	**6d**			
7	Taxable Medicare wages and tips . . .	**7a**	13,302 00	× 2.9% (.029) =	**7b**		385	76
8	Total social security and Medicare taxes (add lines 6b, 6d, and 7b). Check here if wages are not subject to social security and/or Medicare tax . . . . ▶ ☐				**8**		2,035	21
9	Adjustment of social security and Medicare taxes (see instructions for required explanation) Sick Pay $ _____ ± Fractions of Cents $ +.01 ± Other $ _____ =				**9**			01
10	Adjusted total of social security and Medicare taxes (line 8 as adjusted by line 9—see instructions)				**10**		2,035	22

Line 10: This line is the total of the social security tax liability found on line 8, as adjusted by any amount found on line 9. This adjusted total will be used in computing line 13.

Line 11: Total Taxes for the Quarter

This line is computed as the total of the amounts found on lines 5 and 10. The total taxes are then made up of the total liability for social security and Medicare plus the total federal income taxes withheld for the quarter from employees.

Line 12: Advanced Earned Income Credit

If any employees have received any advances of earned income credit for the quarter, this amount must be reported on line 12. The amount of the advanced earned income credit can be found by examining the payroll registers for the quarter and calculating a total for the amounts advanced to employees. Refer to Section B, Chapter 5, for a complete discussion of the **earned income credit** and how an employee may become eligible to receive this credit each pay period as a payroll advance.

Line 13: Net Taxes

This line is calculated by taking the amount on line 11 and subtracting any amount found on line 12. Arriving at the amount on line 13 is a basic exercise in subtraction, but understanding what the dollar amount represents on the form is important.

Monthly Depositors and Lines 13 and 17(d) Line 13 is the actual liability for employee and employer social security, Medicare, and employee federal income taxes for the quarter. This is the total quarterly liability for which the business is responsible, and that should be remitted to the IRS. The business is placed in a situation of being responsible for employee taxes it has withheld from paychecks as well as its own obligation for social security and Medicare taxes. This is why line 13 is important, as it determines the business's "tax bill" for the quarter.

For "monthly" depositors, the amount on line 13 must match the amount found on line 17(d); others will use a separate form called Form 941 Schedule B, discussed later in this section. When the amounts differ due to FICA rounding, sick pay, or other FICA adjustments, the difference must be shown on line 9. When the adjustment has been entered on line 9, line 10 must be recalculated. The new total on line 10 will then be used in calculating lines 11 and 13 of Section ②.

Line 14: Total Tax Deposits
This line is the total of the social security, Medicare, and federal income taxes that have been deposited for the quarter. If the payroll accountant uses the special-deposit ledger, this amount can be found by calculating the quarterly total of the Form 8109 deposits made for these two taxes.

Lines 15 and 16
Lines 15 and 16 represent any balance due for taxes or an overpayment of taxes for the quarter. To find the amount for either line 15 or line 16, the payroll accountant must subtract line 14 from line 13. If the result is a positive amount (or balance due), enter the amount on line 15. If the result is a negative amount (or overpayment), enter this amount as a positive number on line 16. There will only be one dollar amount found on either line 15 or line 16—not both lines.

Line 15 Should Be Less than $2,500 Any amount found on line 15 means that the business owes the IRS for social security, Medicare, and federal income taxes for the quarter. This amount *should always be less than $2,500.* The reason for this is that if the liability for these taxes is $2,500 or more, the business has not made its payroll tax deposits on a timely basis. This impacts the business because the IRS may assess interest and penalties due to the underpayment of these payroll taxes. These rules are discussed in Section E, Chapter 13.

The amount of the balance due as indicated on line 15 can be paid by check and sent in with the Form 941, or it can be deposited using a Form 8109, as discussed in Section E, Chapter 13.

Any amount found on line 16 indicates that the business has for some reason paid more than its liability for taxes for the quarter. One possible cause for an overpayment would be a miscalculation of a payroll tax deposit made during the quarter. An adjustment amount from line 4 may also cause an overpayment of taxes for the quarter.

Any overpayment as indicated on line 16 can be refunded by the IRS or it can be applied against the next quarter's tax liability. The payroll professional should indicate this preference by checking the appropriate box on line 16.

Section ③: The Monthly Summary of Federal Tax Liability

You will notice that directly beneath line 16 are two additional boxes that relate to Form 941 tax deposit information. The IRS requests that the employer specify if it is a monthly or semiweekly depositor for Form 941 taxes.

If the employer has been classified as a monthly depositor, the payroll professional will complete line 17, boxes (a), (b), (c), and (d). The amounts found in the first three boxes should match the amounts of the monthly Form 941 tax deposit made using the federal tax deposit coupons (Form 8109).

Line 17

This section of the form, called the *Monthly Summary of Federal Tax Liability,* is shown in Figure 15–11. The purpose of the monthly summary is to show the total dollar amount of liability for social security and federal income taxes for each month of the quarter for monthly depositors.

The federal tax liability shown in the monthly summary is often referred to as the *Record of Federal Tax Liability* (**ROFT**). It is comprised of three amounts:

- The amount of social security taxes withheld from employees each month.
- The amount of federal income taxes withheld from employees each month.
- The amount of social security taxes that the employer matches with employee contributions each month.

E X A M P L E   5

Mystery Investigations, Inc., has withheld the following dollar amounts from its employees for the third quarter of the year. As shown in Example 1, the company pays its employees semimonthly on the 15th and last days of the month. Mystery Investigations has been classified as a "monthly" Form 941 tax depositor for the year.

F I G U R E   15–11

Example 5

- **All filers:** If line 13 is less than $2,500, you need not complete line 17 or Schedule B (Form 941).
- **Semiweekly schedule depositors:** Complete Schedule B (Form 941) and check here . . . . ▶ ☐
- **Monthly schedule depositors:** Complete line 17, columns (a) through (d), and check here. . . . . ▶ ☒

17 Monthly Summary of Federal Tax Liability. Do not complete if you were a semiweekly schedule depositor.			
(a) First month liability	(b) Second month liability	(c) Third month liability	(d) Total liability for quarter
1,083.03	1,108.20	1,074.99	3,266.22

Sign Here — Under penalties of perjury, I declare that I have examined this return, including accompanying schedules and statements, and to the best of my knowledge and belief, it is true, correct, and complete.

Signature ▶ *Sam Spade*   Print Your Name and Title ▶ *Owner*   Date ▶ 10-31-200X

For Privacy Act and Paperwork Reduction Act Notice, see back of Payment Voucher.   Cat. No. 17001Z   Form **941**

To properly prepare this summary, the payroll professional would sum the three columns of taxes for each month of the quarter. Line 17 is broken into three separate column amounts that represent each month during a calendar quarter. Column (a) is the first month of the quarter, column (b) is the second month, and column (c) is the third month of the quarter. The total of columns (a) + (b) + (c) is entered in column (d) of line 17.

If the employer has been classified as a semiweekly depositor, line 17 of Form 941 is not prepared. An additional form must be completed by a semiweekly depositor, which is known as Form 941, Schedule B (not illustrated in this book). This form is an expanded version of the monthly summary that lists the Form 941 tax liability on a daily basis, rather than monthly, on line 17 of Form 941.

$100,000 Liability

Form 941 Schedule B also must be prepared if the total liability for FICA and FIT taxes is $100,000 or more on any payday. Recall that the $100,000 one-day rule (discussed in Chapter 13) gives an employer one banking day on which to deposit any Form 941 tax liability that is $100,000 or more on the previous day.

The Importance of Lines 13 and 17 or Schedule B, Line D

For monthly depositors, the amount listed on lines 13 and 17 or Schedule B, line D, is critical to preparing the rest of Form 941 because it is the *total Form 941 tax liability* for the quarter. What this means is that the total computed tax liability for the quarter, which will be entered on line 11 in section ② of the form, must match the amount found on lines 13 and 17(d) or Schedule B, line D. Figure 15–12 is an index showing how the Form 941 quarterly tax liability should be reported on the form for various types of Form 941 depositors.

F I G U R E   15–12

Index to Reporting the Quarterly Tax Liability on Form 941

Criteria	Location Where Liability Should Be Recorded
▪ Employer has less than a $2,500 liability at the end of the quarter.	Do not complete Line 17 of Form 941 or Schedule B.
▪ Employer has made deposits using the "monthly" rules.	Complete Line 17, "Monthly Summary of Federal Tax Liability." Do not use Schedule B.
▪ Employer has made deposits using the "semi-weekly" rules.	Complete Form 941 Schedule B. Do not complete Line 17.
▪ Employer has a $100,000 "one-day" Form 941 liability.	Complete Form 941 Schedule B. Do not complete Line 17.

Researching Over- and Underpayment of Taxes

The payroll professional should analyze any amount found on line 15 or line 16 and find the reason for any overpayment or underpayment of taxes for the quarter. This should be done to help in verifying the amounts and to eliminate the possibility that a mistake was made while preparing lines 2 through 14 of the form. It will be well worth the time spent to determine if a mistake was made in preparing or calculating the amounts found on the form, because it is easier to correct the form before it is sent to the IRS than afterward.

4 FORM 941 FILING REQUIREMENTS

Once the draft copy of the Form 941 has been reviewed for accuracy and checked for math errors, a copy can be typed or legibly written in ink and sent to the IRS. It is important that the copy submitted to the IRS is clear and readable. This will help the IRS to match amounts found on the Form 941 with tax deposits and W-2 forms submitted after the end of the year.

The form must be signed and dated by a responsible party of the business, such as a corporate officer or a treasurer. Under certain circumstances the payroll professional may also sign the form. In signing the form, the person who signs the form attests that it is accurate, correct, and complete.

The payroll professional should always make a photocopy of the form that is being sent in to the IRS. Such photocopies for each quarterly report should be maintained in a file for future reference. The mailing date of the return should be noted on the photocopy for future reference.

Depending on where the corporate office of the employer is domiciled (or located) and if any amount is due with the Form 941, the form will be sent to one of 10 different IRS addresses in the United States. The voucher Form 941-V (not illustrated) should also be attached and sent along with the return itself if any payment of taxes is due. If the payroll professional is in doubt as to the correct mailing address, he should check the instructions found on the back of the IRS printed Form 941 (which lists the various addresses) or call a local IRS office for address verification.

Filing Date: General Rule

As we pointed out in Figure 15–2, the Form 941 should be sent to the IRS no later than 30 days following the last day of each calendar quarter. As the figure shows, the filing dates for the report are April 30, July 31, October 31, and January 31. This is the general rule for filing the Form 941.

Exception: The 10-Day Rule

An exception exists to the general rule. If all of the required payroll deposits were made on time for the total amount of the tax liability for the quarter, an extra 10 days is granted for filing of the form. This means that the filing dates for the report can be extended to May 10, August 10, November 10, and February 10.

5 CORRECTING ERRORS ON FORM 941

One area of emphasis in this chapter has been the need for accuracy when preparing the Form 941. It is obvious that correcting errors found on the draft copy of the Form 941 is much easier than attempting to correct any errors found *after* the form has been sent in to the IRS.

Errors may have been made that may not become apparent until after the form has been filed. When this is the case, the payroll professional should use a form known as *Form 941c (Statement to Correct Information Previously Reported on the Employer's Federal Tax Return),* shown in Figure 15–13.

The Form 941c has been divided into five parts. Part I requests specific information regarding the quarter to which the adjustment relates, as well as a signature and certification that the return is correct and accurate. Part II will be used to correct amounts reported for income taxes. Part III will be used to correct an error made in figuring the social security taxes for the quarter. Part IV will be used for any Medicare (or HI FICA) tax adjustment. Part V is used to explain why the adjustments have been made.

In situations where taxes have been overcollected, the employer may have to refund the excess amounts to the employees affected. Note that Part I requires that the employer state how a situation such as this has been handled.

Procedures for Filing Form 941c

After a draft copy of the Form 941c has been prepared and checked, a typed or handwritten ink copy should be completed, dated, and signed. A photocopy of the Form 941 that is being amended should be securely attached to the Form 941c. Across the top of the photocopied Form 941 a phrase such as "See amended Form 941c attached" should be typed in the event that the two documents are separated.

The Form 941c should be sent to the same IRS office to which the Form 941 was sent. The payroll professional should make photocopies of both returns and retain them in a separate file for future reference.

6   OTHER QUARTERLY TAX RETURNS FOR CERTAIN EMPLOYERS

As was pointed out in Segment 1, the majority of businesses will complete and file a Form 941. However, certain businesses or employers are required to file a different version of the standard Form 941. The factors that determine what version of Form 941 must be filed depend on the type of activity in which the business is engaged as well as the domicile of the business. Figure 15–14 summarizes the different versions of Form 941 and what types of businesses are required to use them.

F I G U R E 15–13

Form 941c Page 1

Form **941c**	**Supporting Statement To Correct Information**	OMB No. 1545-0256
	Do Not File Separately	Page No.
Department of the Treasury Internal Revenue Service	▶ File with the employment tax return on which adjustments are made.	

Name   **Employer identification number**

Telephone number

A This form supports adjustments to: **Check one box.**

- ☐ Form 941
- ☐ Form 941-M
- ☐ Form 941-SS
- ☐ Form 943
- ☐ Form 945

B This form is filed with the return for the period ending (month, year) ▶

C Enter the date you discovered the error(s) reported on this form. (If you are making more than one correction and the errors were not discovered at the same time, please explain in Part V.) . . . ▶

Part I — Signature and Certification (You **MUST** complete this part for the IRS to process your adjustments for overpayments.)

I certify that **Forms W-2c,** Statement of Corrected Income and Tax Amounts, have been filed (as necessary) with the Social Security Administration, and that (check appropriate boxes):

☐ All overcollected income taxes for the current calendar year and all social security and Medicare taxes for the current and prior calendar years have been repaid to employees. For claims of overcollected employee social security and Medicare taxes in earlier years, a written statement has been obtained from each employee stating that the employee has not claimed and will not claim refund or credit of the amount of the overcollection.

☐ All affected employees have given their written consent to the allowance of this credit or refund. For claims of overcollected employee social security and Medicare taxes in earlier years, a written statement has been obtained from each employee stating that the employee has not claimed and will not claim refund or credit of the amount of the overcollection.

☐ The social security tax and Medicare tax adjustments represent the employer's share only. An attempt was made to locate the employee(s) affected, but the affected employee(s) could not be located or will not comply with the certification requirements.

☐ None of this refund or credit was withheld from employee wages.

Sign Here   Signature ▶   Title ▶   Date ▶

Part II — Income Tax/Backup Withholding Adjustment

	(a) Period Corrected (Quarterly returns, enter date quarter ended. Annual returns, enter year.)	(b) Withheld Income Tax Previously Reported for Period	(c) Correct Withheld Income Tax for Period	(d) Withheld Income Tax Adjustment
1				
2				
3				
4				
5	Net withheld income tax/backup withholding adjustment. If more than one page, enter total of all columns (d) on first page only. Enter here and on the **appropriate** line of the return with which this form is filed . . . . ▶			**5**

Part III — Social Security Tax Adjustment (Use the tax rate in effect during the period(s) corrected. You must also complete Part IV.)

	(a) Period Corrected (Quarterly returns, enter date quarter ended. Annual returns, enter year.)	(b) Wages Previously Reported for Period	(c) Correct Taxable Wages for Period	(d) Tips Previously Reported for Period	(e) Correct Taxable Tips for Period	(f) Social Security Tax Adjustment
1						
2						
3						
4						
5	Totals.—If more than one page, enter totals on first page only. ▶					
6	Net social security tax adjustment. If more than one page, enter total of **ALL** columns (f) on first page only. Enter here and on the appropriate line of the return with which this form is filed . . ▶					**6**
7	Net wage adjustment. If more than one page, enter the total of **ALL** lines 7 on first page only. If 5(c) is smaller than 5(b), enter difference in parentheses . . . . ▶					**7**
8	Net tip adjustment. If more than one page, enter the total of **ALL** lines 8 on first page only. If 5(e) is smaller than 5(d), enter difference in parentheses . . . . ▶					**8**

For Paperwork Reduction Act Notice, see page 3.   Cat. No. 11242O   Form **941c**

F I G U R E   15–13

Form 941c Page 2

Form 941c   Page **2**

Part IV	Medicare Tax Adjustment

	(a) Period Corrected (Quarterly returns, enter date quarter ended. Annual returns, enter year.)	(b) Wages and Tips Previously Reported for Period	(c) Correct Taxable Wages and Tips for Period	(d) Medicare Tax Adjustment
1				
2				
3				
4				
5	Totals.—If more than one page, enter totals on first page only . . ▶			
6	Net Medicare tax adjustment. If more than one page, enter total of **ALL** columns (d) on first page only. Enter here and on the appropriate line of the return with which this form is filed . . . . . ▶			6
7	Net wage and tip adjustment. If more than one page, enter the totals for **ALL** pages. If 5(c) is smaller than 5(b), enter difference in parentheses . . . . ▶			7

Part V	Explanation of Adjustments

F I G U R E   15–14

Other Versions of the Federal Quarterly Tax Return

Form number	Type of business that will use the form
941PR	Employers whose corporate office is located in Puerto Rico
941SS	Employers located in Guam, American Samoa, the Virgin Islands, or the Northern Mariana Islands
943	Agricultural employers who pay cash to employees eligible for social security benefits

In examining Figure 15–14, you will see that agricultural employers and employers located outside the continental United States will use a special version of the Form 941.

Domicile of the Business

Businesses whose corporate or main offices are located outside of the 50 states must use a special version of Form 941 to report federal income taxes and FICA payroll taxes. Forms 941PR and 941SS apply to businesses located on islands that are political subdivisions of the United States.

The special versions of the Form 941 are similar to the standard form with which this chapter deals. The special versions will have additional questions relevant to the type of employer or the domicile of the employer.

In looking at Figure 15–14, you can see that the great majority of businesses in operation today in the United States will use the standard version of the Form 941.

Delinquent Payroll Tax Deposits and Form 941M

If an employer has not made federal income, social security, and Medicare tax deposits or the employer has not filed Form 941 when required to do so, the IRS may require the employer to report social security, Medicare, and federal income tax liabilities on a monthly basis. The special form that is used in this situation is *Form 941M, Employer's Monthly Federal Tax Return.*

This form is similar to the Form 941, with the major exception that it will only report monthly amounts for the federal income taxes and FICA payroll tax liabilities. An employer in this situation must comply with the appropriate payroll tax deposit rules as well as filing requirements in order to avoid legal action by the IRS.

Besides an employer having to file Form 941M, an additional penalty may apply. If responsible individuals connected with an employer willfully do not withhold Form 941 taxes or deposit the taxes withheld, the IRS may levy a penalty called the *trust fund recovery penalty.* The penalty may be assessed to any responsible individuals who are connected with either accounting for, collecting, or paying Form 941 taxes. The penalty assessed is the total dollar amount of unpaid Form 941 taxes. The assessment of such a penalty shows the intent of the IRS to collect Form 941 taxes from employers.

The easiest way for an employer to avoid problems with the IRS is to make the required payroll tax deposits on time and file all appropriate tax reports when they are required. Employers who do comply with IRS payroll tax rules will not have to file the Form 941M. The IRS treats noncompliance with payroll tax rules as a serious matter. The best way for the employer to avoid these problems is to follow the rules.

CHAPTER 16

Forms W-2, W-3, 1096, and 1099

Hey, this is our last stop on our payroll roadmap. Congratulations, it's the final destination in our journey! And it's fitting that we end our journey with a discussion of the important Forms W-2, W-3 and 1099. If our payroll person has done his job accurately, completely, and timely, completing these forms will be simple—more important, it will signify that the payroll is complete for another year. But then, there's always a next year in payroll, so we can start all over again . . .

1   REPORTING EMPLOYEE EARNINGS

All workers who have earnings or have had federal income or FICA taxes withheld from their pay must receive a federal form known as the *W-2, Wage and Tax Statement.* The purpose of **Form W-2** is to summarize the earnings information for each employee of a company and to report amounts withheld for income and FICA taxes to the government. Certain other amounts deducted from earnings may be noted and summarized on the W-2 as required. As you are probably aware, this form is used by individuals in filing their own federal and state income tax returns.

The amounts reported on the Form W-2 span a calendar year, from January 1 to December 31. The amounts shown on a W-2 are the actual amounts paid, not accrued, to an employee for the year. The same holds true for amounts withheld. If an employee worked less than a full year, the em-

Distribution of an Employee's Form W-2

W-2 copy	Copy is distributed to	The copy's purpose
A	Social Security Administration office	Data is entered into SSA computer system
B	The employee	For individual's federal tax return filing
C	The employee	For employee's records
D	The employer	For employer's records
1	The state, county, or locality	For state, county, or locality records
2	The employee	For filing with state, county, or locality tax returns, if required

ployee will still receive a W-2 with the earnings information for the time period the employee worked for the employer.

This form must be given to each employee on or before January 31 each year. A copy of each W-2 is sent to the Social Security Administration (SSA) as well as to the state and local governments that tax the income of workers. Figure 16–1 shows the distribution of the Form W-2 to the employee and governments.

Each employee will receive several duplicate copies of the W-2. These copies are labeled Copy B, Copy C, and Copy 2. The employee will attach Copy B to his federal income tax return, while Copy 2 will be filed with a state income tax return. Copy C should be retained by the employee with a copy of his income tax return. When required, the employee will file a Copy 2 with the county or locality where the employee lives when the employee's earnings are taxed at a local level. Figure 16–2 shows the distribution of the W-2 copies the employee receives.

Due Dates for the W-2

Calculating and preparing the Form W-2 becomes a task of most payroll departments. The employees should receive their copies of the Form W-2 no later than January 31 of each year. If the employee terminates employment prior to December 31, the Form W-2 may be sent to the employee the earlier of either 30 days after the date of termination or January 31, at the employer's option.

F I G U R E 16–2

Distribution of Employee W-2 Copies

W-2 Copy	Copy distribution
B	Employee will file with Form 1040, 1040A, or 1040EZ tax returns by April 15 or extended due dates.
C	Employee will keep with a copy of annual income tax return after filing.
2	Employee will file with a state, county, or local tax return by April 15 or extended due dates.

However, if an employee specifically requests his W-2 form after termination, the employer must give it to the employee within 30 days or January 31, whichever is earlier. Some states also require that state copies of the W-2 form be given to terminated employees no later than 30 days after the date of termination. See Segment 4 for more information about state requirements.

The company must send copies of all W-2 forms prepared to a regional Social Security Administration office no later than the last day of February of each year. An employer can request additional time by filing a *Form 8809, Request for Extension of Time to File Information Returns.* The 8809 form must be submitted on or before the last day of February in order to receive a valid extension of time to file the W-2 forms.

2 PREPARING W-2 FORMS

In order to learn how to prepare these forms, we will assume that the payroll professional is preparing a W-2 form and W-3 transmittal form by hand, without using a computer software program. In reality, most companies today rely heavily on the capabilities of computers in preparing W-2 forms. There are a number of software programs available that simplify the preparation process and assist the payroll professional in verifying and reconciling the W-2 amounts with other payroll records.

Form W-2 is a Multicopy Form

As you can see from looking at Figures 16-1 and 16-2, several copies of each W-2 form must be prepared. The form is available in quantity from the

IRS or office supply stores, in either a multipart carbon format or NCR (no-carbon-required) format.

Many payroll accounting software programs feature W-2 print options. Such programs are capable of printing W-2s using laser or dot-matrix printers. Using software programs to print W-2 forms ensures accurate preparation and a substantial time savings over preparation by hand.

Accuracy

Each W-2 form should be typed neatly, without any dollar signs or commas in the figures. All amounts entered on W-2s should use the decimal point (0.00). It is important that the form be accurately prepared and proofread before it is distributed to the employee and government entities. It is relatively easy to catch and correct errors before the form is sent out to employees and the government. Correcting a W-2 form after it has been distributed is time-consuming and inconvenient for everyone concerned.

First we will prepare a W-2 form for a single employee. Then, in Segment 3, we will learn about preparing the W-3 transmittal form for the employees' W-2s.

In a manual accounting system, the payroll accountant will use the completed **employee earnings records** with year-to-date totals as the primary source of information for each Form W-2. Each employee earnings record at year-end contains the needed information for completing the employee's Form W-2, because it is a historical summary of the payroll activity for each employee for the year.

Let's look at the employee earnings record for David Adams, an employee of U.S. Route 66 Trucking, Inc. Figure 16–3 shows the completed record for this employee as of the end of 2001.

The payroll accountant will transfer the end-of-year totals for this employee to his Form W-2. The completed Form W-2 for David Adams is shown in Figure 16–4. Please note that the IRS has broken the form W-2 into *boxes*, which require a specific item of information.

You will note that some of the information found on the Form W-2 is not found on the employee earnings record. Let's examine the Form W-2 box by box to determine the correct source for each item of information requested.

box a   This box can be used by a preparer to identify each W-2 form by number. Its use is optional.

Employee Name Adams, David					Hire Date 06/21/97			Date Terminated _____				Emp. I.D. No. 4199	

| Dept. No. 0645   Rate of Pay $14.84/Hour   SSN 908-75-2625 | | | | | | | Married/Single S | | | | W-4 Allow. 0 | | |

TIME CARD AND EARNINGS DATA

							DEDUCTIONS				
Week No. & End Date	Total Regular Hours/ Rate of Pay	Regular Earnings	Total Overtime Hours/ Rate of Pay	Overtime Earnings	Gross Earnings	Year-to-Date Earnings	OASDI FICA	HI FICA	FIT	SIT	Net Pay
#49 -12/9	40/14.84	593.60	8.5/22.26	189.21	782.81	32,873.06	48.53	11.35	162.13	37.99	522.81
#50 -12/16	40/14.84	593.60	9.4/22.26	209.24	802.84	33,675.90	49.78	11.64	168.61	38.99	533.82
#51 -12/23	40/14.84	593.60	9.7/22.26	215.92	809.52	34,485.42	50.19	11.74	168.92	39.33	539.34
#52 -12/30	40/14.84	593.60	0.0/22.26	00.00	593.60	35,079.02	36.80	8.61	109.31	28.50	410.38
4th Qtr. Totals		7,716.80		1,175.96	8,892.76	35,079.02	551.35	128.95	1,637.58	426.96	6,147.92
Year-to-date Totals		30,867.20		4,211.82	35,079.02	35,079.02	2,174.90	508.65	6,459.71	1,684.21	24,251.55

F I G U R E   16–4

Form W-2

a Control number	22222	Void ☐	For Official Use Only ► OMB No. 1545-0008		
b Employer identification number 12-3456789				**1** Wages, tips, other compensation $ 35,079.02	**2** Federal income tax withheld $ 6,459.71
c Employer's name, address, and ZIP code				**3** Social security wages $ 35,079.02	**4** Social security tax withheld $ 2,174.90
U.S. Route 66 Trucking, Inc. P. O. Box 66 Adrian, TX 79001				**5** Medicare wages and tips $ 35,079.02	**6** Medicare tax withheld $ 508.65
				7 Social security tips $	**8** Allocated tips $
d Employee's social security number 908-75-2625				**9** Advance EIC payment $	**10** Dependent care benefits $
e Employee's first name and initial David	Last name Adams			**11** Nonqualified plans $	**12a** See instructions for box 12 $
1671 S. Pearl Street Colorado Springs, CO 80902				**13** Statutory employee ☐ Retirement plan ☐ Third-party sick pay ☐	**12b** $
				14 Other	**12c** $
					12d $
f Employee's address and ZIP code					

15 State Employer's state ID number CO	04-7655152	16 State wages, tips, etc. $ 35,079.02	17 State income tax $ 1,684.21	18 Local wages, tips, etc. $	19 Local income tax $	20 Locality name
		$	$	$	$	

Form **W-2** Wage and Tax Statement   **2001**   Department of the Treasury—Internal Revenue Service

Copy A For Social Security Administration—Send this entire page with Form W-3 to the Social Security Administration; photocopies are **not** acceptable.

Cat. No. 10134D

For Privacy Act and Paperwork Reduction Act Notice, see separate instructions.

box b   This is the federal **EIN** given to the company by the IRS.

box c   The name and address of the employer must be given. The name of the business should match the name associated with the Employer Identification Number (EIN).

box d   Each individual employee's social security number must be entered in this box. It is critical that the correct employee's number is entered here.

box e   The employee's name should be entered in this area.

box f   The employee's home address should be printed in this area.

box 1   The total gross earnings for the year must be entered in this box. This includes wages, salaries, commissions, advances, and other types of income.

box 2   The amount of federal income tax withheld for the year must be entered in Box 2.

box 3   The amount of earnings subject to social security tax must be entered in this box.

box 4   The amount of social security tax is entered in this box.

box 5   The total gross earnings subject to Medicare tax is listed in this box.

box 6   The amount of Medicare tax withheld must be entered in this box.

box 7   The dollar amount of tip income subject to social security tax will be entered in this box.

box 8   An amount may be entered in this box for employees of food and beverage establishments where an amount has been allocated for tip income. Chapter 9 discusses allocated tips.

box 9   Any advance earned income credit payments made to employees throughout the year must be listed in box 9. Section B, Chapter 5, discusses the advance earned income credit.

box 10   This box is used to report employer-paid dependent care benefits. The amount listed would be for benefits provided to the employee by the employer. The fair (or current) market value of the benefits should be shown in the box. If an employee is reimbursed for child day care from a §125 cafeteria plan, the dollar amount of the reimbursement must also be listed in Box 10.

box 11   This box is used to report the dollar amount contributed to a nonqualified plan.

box 12   This box is comprised of four sections labeled **a, b, c,** and **d.** This box is used to report a number of special amounts reported to the IRS. If used, each box will contain an alphabetic code (A through H, and J through S for the 2001 reporting year), followed by a dollar amount. For example, the codes below are used to report the following amounts:

- Code A—Uncollected social security or RRTA tax on tips.
- Code B—Uncollected Medicare tax on tips.
- Code C—Cost of group-term life insurance over $50,000.
- Code J—Nontaxable sick pay.

Please refer to the instructions for Forms W-2 and W-3 before reporting any dollar amount connected with special reporting.

box 13 This is a multipurpose box that can be used to report the following amounts:

- If the employee is a statutory employee (such as certain insurance representatives), this box should be checked.
- Contributions to various retirement plans.
- Sick pay received under a plan where an employee has made contributions toward this benefit previously.

box 14 This box is used to report the lease value of a vehicle provided to an employee. It can also be used for other special information to be given to an employee.

box 15 The two-letter postal code abbreviation of the state in which income tax was withheld and the employer's state identification number may be entered in this box.

box 16 The amount of earnings subject to state income taxes should be entered in this box.

box 17 Any state income tax withheld will be shown in this box.

box 18 The amount of earnings subject to local or county income taxes should be entered in the box.

box 19 Any amount withheld for local or county income taxes should be entered in this box.

box 20 The name of the locality or county where taxes have been withheld should be listed in the box.

Please keep in mind that the 24 active boxes found on Form W-2 will satisfy the special needs of most any employment situation. Several of these boxes will not be used in most employment situations.

Earnings Limits Are Reflected on Form W-2

In looking at Figure 16–4, please note that Boxes 1, 3, 5, and 7 all deal with the total wages or earnings of the employee. Box 1 is the gross wages or earnings of the employee, without regard to any earnings limits for social security taxes. Any amount found in Box 3 is affected by the current earnings limit maximum for social security taxes. Box 5 should be the same amount as is entered in Box 1. The total of Boxes 3 and 7 should not exceed the social security earnings limit for the year.

For 2001, the maximum dollar amount that would be found in Box 3 is $80,400, which is the social security earnings limit maximum. In theory, an employee could have a different dollar amount in Box 3 while Boxes 1 and 5 would have the same dollar amount.

Please note that Boxes 4 and 6 are used to report the amount of social security and Medicare tax withheld from the employee for the year. The dollar amount of tax in Box 4 should be based on the social security earnings limit found when totaling Boxes 3 and 7. The amount found in Box 6 should be the Medicare tax taken as a percentage of the earnings found in Box 5.

State and Local Taxes

Boxes 15 through 20 are used to report any state or local taxes withheld from the employee. Boxes 15 and 20 should list the state or local taxing authority. Boxes 16 and 18 should show the dollar amount of wages that are being taxed for state or local purposes.

The Form W-2 is simple to prepare. Remember, however, that it is an important form in that it reports the earnings and withholding amounts for each worker employed by the company, which is reported to several government entities. Accuracy in preparing this form—as well as having the forms ready for distribution to employees and the government by the prescribed deadlines—cannot be stressed enough. We will now look at the process involved in submitting W-2 forms to the government.

3 PROCEDURES FOR SUBMITTING W-2 FORMS AND THE W-3 FORM

The employer must prepare and submit an additional form along with the "A" copy of each W-2 to the **Social Security Administration**. This form, shown in Figure 16–5 and called the **Form W-3**, *Transmittal of Income and Tax Statements*, summarizes the individual dollar amounts found on each individual W-2 form. This form is used by the Social Security Administration to reconcile the individual dollar amounts found on each W-2 after this information is entered into the administration's computer system.

All the W-2 forms for a particular employer identification number (EIN) should be submitted to the government in one batch along with the W-3 form. In a situation where the employer has a large number of W-2 forms to submit, the IRS will accept the shipment in separate packages when they are shipped at the same time.

F I G U R E   16–5

The Form W-3

Forms Are Sent to the Social Security Administration

As shown in Figure 16–1, W-2 Copy A is the copy that will be sent to a regional Social Security Administration data operations center. There are currently four centers that serve employers, based on the location of the employer.

It is the Social Security Administration, not the IRS, that originally receives the earnings data for each employer. The data is entered into the SSA's computer system so that the contributions made for FICA purposes can be recorded. The IRS is allowed to share the data from the Social Security Administration under a special agreement. This is one way in which the IRS verifies the amounts found on an employee's Form 1040, 1040A, or 1040EZ.

The W-3 is merely a summary total of the individual amounts found on each employee's W-2 form. The Social Security Administration uses the amounts found on the W-3 form to verify that it has entered the correct amounts into its computer system from each W-2 submitted.

Reconciling Form W-3 Amounts

Before the W-2s and W-3 are sent to the SSA, the payroll professional should reconcile the amounts found on the W-3 for earnings and federal income and social security taxes with the quarterly amounts found on the 941 forms for the employer. Specifically, the amounts entered into the following boxes on the completed Form W-3 should agree with the quarterly totals for the four 941 forms for the year:

- Box 1: Wages, tips, and other compensation.
- Box 2: Federal income tax withheld.
- Box 3: Social security wages.
- Box 4: Social security (OASDI) tax withheld.
- Box 5: Medicare wages and tips.
- Box 6: Medicare (HI) tax withheld.
- Box 7: Social security tips.

Reconciling these amounts with the four totals found on the 941 forms before submitting the W-2s and W-3 will verify the accuracy of the W-2 amounts. Any differences found between the W-2s and the 941 forms should be checked. In most cases, there should not be any dollar differences upon reconciling the amounts. If there is, the payroll professional should identify the reason for the difference and be prepared to justify the difference to the IRS at a later date if the employer is audited.

The W-3 differs slightly from the W-2 in its appearance. Looking at Figure 16–5, note that in the upper left-hand corner Box b asks for the kind of payer. The employer will check off the correct box, as determined by the type of quarterly federal tax return that the employer sends to the IRS. Refer to Chapter 13 for a discussion of these different types of quarterly tax returns.

The total number of W-2 forms being submitted to the SSA should be indicated in Box c. This allows the SSA to verify that all W-2 forms have been entered into its computer system.

4   STATE AND LOCAL REPORTING REQUIREMENTS

When state and/or local income taxes are withheld from employee earnings, the employer usually sends the state or local taxing authority all "Copy 1" copies of the W-2 forms for reporting purposes.

States generally require that the employee file a state tax return after the end of the year to verify the earnings and determine the actual income tax due to the state. On a local level, some local and county governments may also require the filing of a separate return—workers who reside in the states of Michigan and Ohio are familiar with such city and county tax returns. However, a local or county government may tax income and not have a return filing requirement.

There are currently 41 states that require income tax withholding on employee earnings. Nine states (Alaska, Florida, Nevada, New Hampshire, South Dakota, Tennessee, Texas, Washington, and Wyoming) do not require withholding and have no income tax laws.

State Versions of Form W-2

Some state and local governments may require that employers use their own version of the Form W-2. In such cases the employer must prepare not only the federal W-2s but also the state or local version of the form as well.

State W-2 Due Dates

Most states have adopted a January 31 due date for providing W-2 forms to employees. A few states may extend the due date to February 15.

State due date rules vary when an employee terminates employment and requests his W-2 forms. The majority of states require that the employee receives his W-2 forms within 30 days of the employee's request (or January 31, whichever date is first) for the forms. Arizona's time period is 15 days. Several states (Arkansas, Kansas, Maryland, New Mexico, South Carolina, Utah, Vermont, Virginia, Washington D.C., and Wisconsin) require that the forms be given to the employee immediately upon request.

State Form W-2 copies and any state versions of the Form W-3 will be due on different dates, depending on the state's filing rules. Several states have adopted a January 31 due date, while many use the last day of February (which is the federal filing deadline). Colorado's and Nebraska's due date is March 15, while New Jersey's is February 15.

When reporting earnings to a state, county, or local government, the payroll professional should always check with the specific government or municipality involved for the current reporting requirements and due dates.

5 FORMS 1096 AND 1099

Our discussion of payroll accounting and administration would not be complete without mentioning two other forms used in payroll accounting and administration. The Form 1099 Miscellaneous Income is used to report sources and types of income other than wages and salaries. According to IRS rules, if a recipient receives $600 or more in nonemployee income, the payee should prepare a Form 1099. Typically, the form would be used to report income given to independent contractors (called "nonemployee compensation" or "other" income) as well as rents or royalties. Figure 16–6 shows the Form 1099. Please note that the form provides for federal income tax withholding on such income.

There are several different types of Forms 1099. For example, a different Form 1099 will be used to report interest income (Form 1099-INT) or pension plan distributions (Form 1099-R).

The Form 1099 must be sent to the IRS no later than February 28 for the previous calendar year. A Form 1099 must be accompanied by a transmittal form called the Form 1096 (not illustrated). The two forms function together the same way the Forms W-2 and W-3 do, and basically serve similar purposes.

F I G U R E   16–6

Form 1099-MISC

Note that employee earnings (i.e., wages and salaries) should *not* be reported on Form 1099. From a payroll accounting standpoint, only other income or nonemployee compensation (i.e., independent contractor income) should be reported on the Form 1099 and the 1096 transmittal.

Payroll Resources

APPENDIX 1

Payroll Tax Calendar and Summary Information Tables

PAYROLL ADMINISTRATION TAX DEPOSIT AND FILING CALENDAR

Use this generic tax calendar as a guide to filing deadlines and requirements for the various forms and reports used in payroll administration. This chart is not all inclusive; your specific situation may call for the filing of other forms at various times. For a complete calendar-year listing, obtain IRS publication 509, *Tax Calendars*.

Generic Payroll Administration Tax Deposit and Filing Calendar			
Month	**Activity**	**Form(s) Used**	**Notes**
January	Make monthly Form 941 payroll tax deposit for December of preceding year (if monthly depositor).	8109	Due by 15th of the month.
	Give wage and tax statement to employees.	Form W-2	Due by January 31.
	Deposit federal unemployment tax (FUTA) if it is more than $100.	8109	Due by January 31. A good idea would be to make deposit *before* filing Form 940-EZ or Form 940.
			(continued)

325

Generic Payroll Administration Tax Deposit and Filing Calendar			
Month	**Activity**	**Form(s) Used**	**Notes**
January	File *Annual Unemployment Tax Return.*	Form 940-EZ (one state employer) or Form 940 (multistate employer)	Due by January 31.[1] Pay any remaining FUTA (under $100) with form or make deposit using Form 8109.
	File *Employer's Quarterly Federal Tax Return.*	Form 941 (and 941-B if applicable)	Due by January 31.[1]
	File *Annual Return of Withheld Federal Income Tax.*	Form 945	Due by January 31.
	Employees who receive tips directly from their customers should figure a monthly tally of their tips when the amount is $20.00 or more. The amount of tips for each month should be reported to their employer.	Form 4070	Employers should receive completed and signed Forms 4070 from their employees no later than 10 days after the end of the month. If the tenth day of the month is a legal holiday, the employees should submit the forms on the next business day.
February	Ask employees to return any new W-4 forms for current year, if employee claimed an exemption from withholding the previous year.	Form W-4	Complete by February 15.
	Make monthly Form 941 payroll tax deposit for January (if monthly depositor).	8109	Due by 15th of the month.
	File copy A of any Form 1099 along with Form 1096.	Form 1099 (Copy A) and Form 1096	Due by February 28. Send to nearest IRS Service Center.
	File copy A of all W-2 forms along with Form W-3.	Form W-2 (Copy A) and Form W-3.	Due by February 28. Send to Social Security Administration.
	File *Employer's Annual Information Return of Tip Income* (if employees receive tip income subject to threshold amounts).	Form 8027. (Use Form 8027-T if submitting more than one return with same EIN.)	Due by February 28. Send to IRS Service Center, Andover, MA

Generic Payroll Administration Tax Deposit and Filing Calendar			
Month	**Activity**	**Form(s) Used**	**Notes**
February	Employees who receive tips directly from their customers should figure a monthly tally of their tips when the amount is $20.00 or more. The amount of tips for each month should be reported to their employer.	Form 4070	Employers should receive completed and signed Forms 4070 from their employees no later than 10 days after the end of the month. If the tenth day of the month is a legal holiday, the employees should submit the forms on the next business day.
March	Make monthly Form 941 payroll tax deposit for February (if monthly depositor).	8109	Due by 15th of the month.
	Employees who receive tips directly from their customers should figure a monthly tally of their tips when the amount is $20.00 or more. The amount of tips for each month should be reported to their employer.	Form 4070	Employers should receive completed and signed Forms 4070 from their employees no later than 10 days after the end of the month. If the tenth day of the month is a legal holiday, the employees should submit the forms on the next business day.
April	Make monthly Form 941 payroll tax deposit for March (if monthly depositor).	8109	Due by 15th of the month.
	Deposit federal unemployment tax (FUTA) if it is more than $100.	8109	Due by April 30.
	File *Employer's Quarterly Federal Tax Return.*	Form 941 (and 941-B if applicable)	Due by April 30.[1]
	Employees who receive tips directly from their customers should figure a monthly tally of their tips when the amount is $20.00 or more. The amount of tips for each month should be reported to their employer.	Form 4070	Employers should receive completed and signed Forms 4070 from their employees no later than 10 days after the end of the month. If the tenth day of the month is a legal holiday, the employees should submit the forms on the next business day.
May	Make monthly Form 941 payroll tax deposit for April (if monthly depositor).	8109	Due by 15th of the month. *(continued)*

Generic Payroll Administration Tax Deposit and Filing Calendar			
Month	**Activity**	**Form(s) Used**	**Notes**
May	Employees who receive tips directly from their customers should figure a monthly tally of their tips when the amount is $20.00 or more. The amount of tips for each month should be reported to their employer.	Form 4070	Employers should receive completed and signed Forms 4070 from their employees no later than 10 days after the end of the month. If the tenth day of the month is a legal holiday, the employees should submit the forms on the next business day.
June	Make monthly Form 941 payroll tax deposit for May (if monthly depositor).	8109	Due by 15th of the month.
	Employees who receive tips directly from their customers should figure a monthly tally of their tips when the amount is $20.00 or more. The amount of tips for each month should be reported to their employer.	Form 4070	Employers should receive completed and signed Forms 4070 from their employees no later than 10 days after the end of the month. If the tenth day of the month is a legal holiday, the employees should submit the forms on the next business day.
July	Deposit federal unemployment tax (FUTA) if it is more than $100.	8109	Due by July 31.
	File *Employer's Quarterly Federal Tax Return.*	Form 941 (and 941-B if applicable)	Due by July 31.[1]
	Make monthly Form 941 payroll tax deposit for June (if monthly depositor).	8109	Due by 15th of the month.
	Employees who receive tips directly from their customers should figure a monthly tally of their tips when the amount is $20.00 or more. The amount of tips for each month should be reported to their employer.	Form 4070	Employers should receive completed and signed Forms 4070 from their employees no later than 10 days after the end of the month. If the tenth day of the month is a legal holiday, the employees should submit the forms on the next business day.
August	Make monthly Form 941 payroll tax deposit for July (if monthly depositor).	8109	Due by 15th of the month.

Generic Payroll Administration Tax Deposit and Filing Calendar			
Month	**Activity**	**Form(s) Used**	**Notes**
August	Employees who receive tips directly from their customers should figure a monthly tally of their tips when the amount is $20.00 or more. The amount of tips for each month should be reported to their employer.	Form 4070	Employers should receive completed and signed Forms 4070 from their employees no later than 10 days after the end of the month. If the tenth day of the month is a legal holiday, the employees should submit the forms on the next business day.
September	Make monthly Form 941 payroll tax deposit for August (if monthly depositor).	8109	Due by 15th of the month.
	Employees who receive tips directly from their customers should figure a monthly tally of their tips when the amount is $20.00 or more. The amount of tips for each month should be reported to their employer.	Form 4070	Employers should receive completed and signed Forms 4070 from their employees no later than 10 days after the end of the month. If the tenth day of the month is a legal holiday, the employees should submit the forms on the next business day.
October	Deposit federal unemployment tax (FUTA) if it is more than $100.	8109	Due by October 31.
	File *Employer's Quarterly Federal Tax Return*	Form 941 (and 941-B if applicable)	Due by October 31.[1]
	Make monthly Form 941 payroll tax deposit for September (if monthly depositor).	8109	Due by 15th of the month.
	Employees who receive tips directly from their customers should figure a monthly tally of their tips when the amount is $20.00 or more. The amount of tips for each month should be reported to their employer.	Form 4070	Employers should receive completed and signed Forms 4070 from their employees no later than 10 days after the end of the month. If the tenth day of the month is a legal holiday, the employees should submit the forms on the next business day.

(continued)

Generic Payroll Administration Tax Deposit and Filing Calendar			
Month	**Activity**	**Form(s) Used**	**Notes**
November	Make monthly Form 941 payroll tax deposit for October (if monthly depositor).	8109	Due by 15th of the month.
	Ask employees to prepare and submit a new Form W-4 for the next year if their withholding allowance status has or will change.	Form W-4	A good idea to have all changes before December 31 for the next year's payroll.
	Employees who receive tips directly from their customers should figure a monthly tally of their tips when the amount is $20.00 or more. The amount of tips for each month should be reported to their employer.	Form 4070	Employers should receive completed and signed Forms 4070 from their employees no later than 10 days after the end of the month. If the tenth day of the month is a legal holiday, the employees should submit the forms on the next business day.
December	Make monthly Form 941 payroll tax deposit for November (if monthly depositor).	8109	Due by 15th of the month.
	Eligible employees must complete new *Earned Income Credit Advance Payment Certificate*.	Form W-5	Due no later than December 31. Current year's certificate expires on December 31 and cannot be used for next year.
	Employees who receive tips directly from their customers should figure a monthly tally of their tips when the amount is $20.00 or more. The amount of tips for each month should be reported to their employer.	Form 4070	Employers should receive completed and signed Forms 4070 from their employees no later than 10 days after the end of the month. If the tenth day of the month is a legal holiday, the employees should submit the forms on the next business day.

Notes: Each month semiweekly Form 941 tax depositors will make their deposits on Wednesdays and/or Fridays depending on their payroll frequency. See IRS Publication 509 for a complete semiweekly tax deposit calendar.

1. The IRS grants an additional 10 days to file the return to any employer who has deposited all Form 941 (or Form 940) taxes when due and who is not underpaid with the filing of the return.

Reference Guide to Federal Forms: Preparation and Filing Requirements (IRS Forms unless Noted Otherwise)		
Form Number	**Form Title**	**Who Should Prepare and/or File**
940	Employer's Annual Federal Unemployment Tax Return	Employer files annually with IRS. Used by multistate employers.
940-EZ	Employer's Annual Federal Unemployment Tax Return	Employer files annually with IRS. Used by single-state employers.
941	Employer's Quarterly Federal Tax Return	Employer files after each calendar quarter to report social security, Medicare, and federal income taxes.
Schedule B (Form 941)	Employer's Record of Federal Tax Liability	Used by "semiweekly" and "$100,000 one-day" depositors.
941c	Supporting Statement to Correct Information	Used by employer to amend a prior quarter's Form 941.
945	Annual Return of Withheld Federal Income Tax	Used by employer or payor to report any federal income tax withheld from nonpayroll sources.
1096	Annual Summary and Transmittal of U.S. Information Returns	Used as a transmittal form when submitting any 1099 forms to the IRS.
1099	Income Information Returns	This series of information returns are used to report various types of income to the IRS. Form 1099-MISC will report nonemployee compensation and rent or royalty income. Other types of forms include Form 1099-INT (interest income), 1099-DIV (dividends), and 1099-R (pension and annuities).
4070	Employee's Report of Tips to Employer	Employee will prepare and give to employer each month when no other method of reporting tips is provided to employees by employer.
8027	Employer's Annual Information Return of Tip Income and Allocated Tips	Employer files annually with IRS when employees receive tips during the year.
8109	Federal Tax Deposit (FTD) Coupon	Employer uses when making federal payroll tax deposits.

(continued)

Reference Guide to Federal Forms: Preparation and Filing Requirements (IRS Forms unless Noted Otherwise)		
Form Number	Form Title	Who Should Prepare and/or File
I-9	Employment Eligibility Verification Form	Used by employer to verify that worker is eligible to work in the U.S. Issued by the Immigration and Naturalization Service (INS).
SS-4	Application for Employer Identification Number	Will be completed to assign an EIN (Employer Identification Number) to a new business.
SS-5	Application for a Social Security Card	Must be completed by a worker who does not have an SSN. Administered by the Social Security Administration (SSA).
SS-8	Determination of Employee Work Status for Purposes of Federal Employment Taxes and Income Tax Withholding	Used by worker or employer to determine worker classification.
W-2	Wage and Tax Statement	Employer prepares to report the earnings and withholding of its employees.
W-3	Transmittal of Wage and Tax Statements	Summary of W-2 amounts used for data entry reconciliation by SSA.
W-4	Employee's Withholding Allowance Certificate	Information used by employer in calculating employee's income tax withholding.
W-5	Earned Income Credit Advance Payment Certificate	Filed by employee to claim advance EIC from an employer on pay period basis.

Summary of Form 941 (Soc. Sec., Medicare, Fed. Income) Tax Deposit Rules		
Type of Depositor	**Payday Period**	**Day Deposit Is Due**
Monthly	Anytime during a calendar month	By the 15th of the following month
Semiweekly	Wednesday, Thursday, and/or Friday	The following Wednesday
Semiweekly	Saturday, Sunday, Monday, and/or Tuesday	The following Friday

If the day the deposit is due is a Saturday, Sunday, or federal/state bank holiday, the deposit will be due the next banking day. Form 8109 is used to make the actual deposit at a bank.

Summary of Form 940 (Federal Unemployment Tax) Tax Deposit Rules		
Amount of Form 940 Tax Liability	**When Is the Deposit Due?**	**Form Used in Depositing Taxes**
$100 or less during the calendar year.	Deposit can be made when filing the Form 940 by January 31.	Form 940-EZ, Form 940, or Form 8109
$100 or less during a calendar quarter.	No deposit is necessary. Deposit liability can be carried into the subsequent calendar quarter.	N/A
Over $100 during a calendar month or quarter.	Deposit the amount due no later than one month after the calendar quarter ends.	Form 8109

Summary of Current 2001 Tax Rates and Earnings Limits for Social Security, Medicare, and Federal Unemployment Taxes		
Type of Tax	**Attribute**	**Explanation**
Social Security (FICA)	Employee and employer rates	6.20% for employee and employer.
Social Security (FICA)	Earnings limit maximum	$80,400 for 2001 calendar year. This changes each year.
Medicare	Employee and employer rates	1.45% for employee and employer.
Medicare	Earnings limit maximum	None. All earnings are taxed.
Federal Unemployment (FUTA)	Employer rate	.8% (.008) if all state unemployment taxes are paid timely.
Federal Unemployment (FUTA)	Earnings limit maximum	$7,000 during calendar year.

Conversion Chart from Minutes to Hundredths of an Hour			
Minutes	**Hundredths**	**Minutes**	**Hundredths**
01	0.02	31	0.52
02	0.03	32	0.53
03	0.05	33	0.55
04	0.07	34	0.57
05	0.08	35	0.58
06	0.10	36	0.60
07	0.12	37	0.62
08	0.13	38	0.63
09	0.15	39	0.65
10	0.17	40	0.67
11	0.18	41	0.68
12	0.20	42	0.70
13	0.22	43	0.72
14	0.23	44	0.73
15	0.25	45	0.75
16	0.27	46	0.77
17	0.28	47	0.78
18	0.30	48	0.80
19	0.32	49	0.82
20	0.33	50	0.83
21	0.35	51	0.85
22	0.37	52	0.87
23	0.38	53	0.88
24	0.40	54	0.90
25	0.42	55	0.92
26	0.43	56	0.93
27	0.45	57	0.95
28	0.47	58	0.97
29	0.48	59	0.98
30	0.50	60	1.00

Converting from the 12-Hour to the 24-Hour Time System			
12-Hour Time	**24-Hour Time**	**12-Hour Time**	**24-Hour Time**
1:00 P.M.	13:00	7:00 P.M.	19:00
2:00 P.M.	14:00	8:00 P.M.	20:00
3:00 P.M.	15:00	9:00 P.M.	21:00
4:00 P.M.	16:00	10:00 P.M.	22:00
5:00 P.M.	17:00	11:00 P.M.	23:00
6:00 P.M.	18:00	12:00 midnight	00:00

Note that the time notation for the hours between 1 A.M. and 12 noon (or 12 P.M.) are the same for both the 12- and 24-hour (military) time systems. As shown above, time notation differences occur between 1 P.M. and 12 midnight.

Use this table to convert from the continental 12-hour time notation to the 24-hour (or military) time system if you are using an older model time clock.

2001 WITHHOLDING ALLOWANCE TABLE

Use this table to determine the correct dollar amount of withholding allowances claimed by an employee when calculating the employee's federal income tax using the percentage method. Please note that the amounts found in this multiplication table are updated annually. Refer to IRS Publication 15 (*Circular E*) for the current calendar year withholding allowances.

Pay Period	Withholding Allowance Amount based on the Number of Allowances Claimed on Form W-4									
	1	2	3	4	5	6	7	8	9	10
Daily or Misc.	11.15	22.30	33.45	44.60	55.75	66.90	78.05	89.20	100.35	111.50
Weekly	55.77	111.54	167.31	223.08	278.85	334.62	390.39	446.16	501.93	557.70
Biweekly	111.54	223.08	334.62	446.16	557.70	669.24	780.78	892.32	1,003.86	1,115.40
Semimonthly	120.83	241.66	362.49	483.32	604.15	724.98	845.81	966.64	1,087.47	1,208.30
Monthly	241.67	483.34	725.01	966.68	1,208.35	1,450.02	1,691.69	1,933.36	2,175.03	2,416.70
Quarterly	725.00	1,450.00	2,175.00	2,900.00	3,625.00	4,350.00	5,075.00	5,800.00	6,525.00	7,250.00
Semiannually	1,450.00	2,900.00	4,350.00	5,800.00	7,250.00	8,700.00	10,150.00	11,600.00	13,050.00	14,500.00
Annually	2,900.00	5,800.00	8,700.00	11,600.00	14,500.00	17,400.00	20,300.00	23,200.00	26,100.00	29,000.00

Information
Resources List

Here are some of the various resources available to help you with payroll accounting and administration. This listing is broken into sections by activity or topic.

This listing is by no means complete; please consider it as a *starting point* for your journey. Note that addresses, phone numbers, and web domain names are believed to be current at time of publication and are subject to change.

FEDERAL GOVERNMENT AGENCIES

Electronic Payroll Tax Deposits (EFTPS)

Many employers are now required to make their payroll tax deposits electronically. The IRS has a federal payroll tax deposit program in place that uses an EFT system. The Service refers to this program as **EFTPS** (Electronic Federal Tax Payment System). Employers who in calendar year 1999 had over $200,000 in *total federal tax deposits* must use EFTPS to make their deposits in 2001. An employer may also choose to voluntarily participate in the EFTPS program. For more information about EFTPS, contact the IRS at 1-800-555-4477 or 1-800-945-8400.

The INS

The Immigration and Naturalization Service (not the IRS) is responsible for the Form I-9. The INS Form I-9 can be downloaded as an Adobe pdf file. On

the Internet, use the link www.ins.usdoj.gov/graphics/formsfee/forms/i-9.htm
to download the form.

The IRS on the Web

The Internal Revenue Service publishes many excellent resources in the areas of payroll administration and accounting. These publications are available from the IRS using any number of methods. For example, the IRS has a
highly useful web site which an employer can utilize to find current tax and
payroll information as well as download IRS forms, Publications, and Instructions in several different electronic file formats (among which is the
Adobe® pdf file format, which can be read with Adobe Acrobat® Reader
software).If you have not already used the IRS website, the authors suggest
you visit it at www.irs.gov. Internet FTP services are also available from
the IRS at ftp.irs.gov.

Other Ways of Obtaining IRS Information

Certain IRS forms can be obtained via fax by calling 703-368-9694. Call
this number from your fax machine and follow the instructions to have
forms faxed back to you. If you prefer to phone the IRS, forms, publications, and automated instructions can be obtained by calling
1-800-TAX-FORM (1-800-829-3676). This number is available 24 hours
per day, 7 days a week. If you want to have the IRS send forms to you, use
IRS Form 7018-A (found in the back of Circular E, also known as IRS Publication 15).

Form 941TeleFile

The IRS has also established a program where an employer can electronically file its Form 941, *Quarterly Federal Tax Return.* Using TeleFile, an
employer can call a toll-free 800 number and use the keys on a touch-tone
phone to complete the return. This service is available to any monthly depositor once an employer has filed a Form 941 with the IRS. The IRS will
return specific instructions along with the next quarter's Form 941 about
Form 941TeleFile.

Form 941 e-File

The IRS also allows an employer to electronically file Form 941 through its
e-file program. Contact the IRS at 1-800-829-1040 or visit the IRS on the

web at www.irs.gov/elec_sys/efile-bus.html to obtain specific information about how the program works.

IRS Publications

As part of your tool kit, you will want to have current copies of the following IRS Publications:

- **Circular E (Publication 15).** Known as the Employer's Tax Guide, this indispensable publication contains current wage-bracket and percentage method tax withholding tables along with advance EIC payment tables. It also offers other important information about payroll taxes, deposits, and general legal issues.
- **Supplement to Circular E (Publication 15–A).** This publication, known as the *Employer's Supplemental Tax Guide,* contains information about worker classification, fringe benefits, and alternative withholding methods.
- **Publication 15-T.** This IRS publication is also known as "New Withholding Tables for 2001 (for Wages Paid After June 30, 2001)." This is a special mid-year bulletin that reflects amended wage-bracket and percentage withholding tables as required under the Economic Growth and Tax Relief Reconciliation Act of 2001. This publication will be used for the payrolls occurring from July 1 through December 31, 2001, only.
- **Publication 509.** This is the IRS calendar-year *Tax Calendars,* providing you with specific information about payroll tax deposit due dates and tax report filing deadlines. Updated annually.

Here is a brief list of other payroll related IRS publications you may need:

- **Circular A (Publication 51).** The *Agricultural Employer's Tax Guide* should be used by agricultural employers. Some regulations differ between agricultural and nonagricultural employers, and the Circular A provides accurate guidance in these areas.
- **Publication 334.** The *Tax Guide for Small Business* is published annually and covers the tax aspects of small business operation.
- **Publication 535.** *Business Expenses.*
- **Publication 553.** *Highlights of [current year] Tax Changes.*
- **Publication 583.** *Starting a Business and Keeping Records.*
- **Publication 1635.** *Understanding Your EIN.*

The Small Business Administration (SBA)

The Small Business Administration is a federal agency that offers assistance to small businesses and individuals who wish to start a small business. The SBA operates a toll-free hotline it calls the "Answer Desk." The number for the SBA Answer Desk is 1-800-8-ASK-SBA (or 1-800-827-5722). The SBA also teams up with other groups to offer business assistance. The SBA Internet web site is www.sba.gov.

The SSA

The Social Security Administration will provide workers with social security numbers. Call a local SSA office or call 1-800-772-1213 to obtain a Form SS-5.

PROFESSIONAL ORGANIZATIONS

There are many fine professional organizations dedicated to furthering the goals of payroll accounting and administration as well as adjunct areas in this field.

Payroll Accounting and Administration
- American Payroll Association (APA). Contact this group at (212) 686-2202.
- American Society of Payroll Management (ASPM). Contact this organization at (800) 684-4024.
- Canadian Payroll Association (CPA). Contact this group at (416) 487-3380.

Pension Administration (§401(k) and §125 Plans)
- American Society of Pension Actuaries (ASPA). Contact at (703) 516-9300.

NEWSLETTERS AND MAGAZINES
- *Cafeteria Plan Alert* (§125 plans), published quarterly by Mayer Hoffman McCann, L.C., CPAs. 1-800-876-7548. Their website is www.125plan.com.

- *PayTech,* published by the American Payroll Association. (212) 686-2202.
- *Pension Plan Administrator* (§401(k) plans), published by Panel Publishers. 1-800-638-8437.

BULK FORMS

Local office supply stores stock continuous part forms used to prepare W-2 and 1099 forms. You may also want to check a mail-order supply company such as Visible at 1-800-262-4460 (or at http://www.visibletax.com) for information and/or a catalog.

HR FORMS AND EMPLOYMENT POSTERS

HR Direct specializes in human resources forms, posters, and other items used in HR and payroll administration. Call 1-800-346-1231 for information and/or a catalog.

THE "E" PAYROLL TOOLKIT IS NOW ON THE INTERNET

As part of our effort and commitment to keep you informed and aware of major changes in payroll accounting and administration, Penn & Pearl Publishers LLC has established a special Internet web site for your use. You can now log on to either **http://www.epayrolltoolkit.com** or **http://www.payrolltoolkit.com** to find updates to various federal rates, amounts, and other relevant information found in this book. Stop by on the Web and check out the new "e" version of The Payroll Toolkit!

State Resources Listing of Internet Web Addresses

Now with the power of the Internet, obtaining state payroll tax information is now easier and faster than ever before. We have elected to list the web addresses for each state's "Department of Revenue" and "Department of Labor or Employment" (which may have different titles in some states).

In many cases, some tax forms may also be available for download from these state agencies in Adobe® pdf or a text file formats. Many sites also have contact information so you can address specific questions and issues with state agency personnel. The links will be especially useful to inform you of up-to-date payroll tax information and changes in rules and law.

Please keep in mind that these links are current as of the time of publication. Many will change over time as states revise their web sites. If a link is no longer used, log on to any major search engine and search for: *[Name of State] Department of Revenue*, or *[Name of State] Unemployment Insurance*.

State	Department of Revenue Web Address	Department of Labor and Employment /Unemployment Taxes Web Address
Alabama	http://www.ador.state.al.us	http://webserver.dsmd.state.al.us/dir
Alaska	http://www.revenue.state.ak.us	http://www.state.ak.us/local/akpages/LABOR/home.htm
Arizona	http://www.revenue.state.az.us	http://az.jobsearch.org/
Arkansas	http://www.state.ar.us./dfa/	http://www.state.ar.us/esd/ark_esd.html
California	http://www.boe.ca.gov For the California State Board of Equalization.	http://wwwedd.cahwnet.gov/
	http://www.ftb.ca.gov For the California Franchise Tax Board.	
Colorado	http://www.state.co.us/gov_dir/revenue_dir/home_rev.html	http://www.state.co.us/gov_dir/labor_dir/labor_home.html
Connecticut	http://www.dir.state.ct.us/index.html	http://www.ctdol.state.ct.us/
Delaware	http://www.state.de.us/revenue/index.htm	http://de.jobsearch.org/
Florida	http://sun6.dms.state.fl.us/dor/	http://www.floridajobs.org/
Georgia	http://www2.state.ga.us/Departments/DOR/	http://www.dol.state.ga.us/
Hawaii	http://www.state.hi.us/tax/tax.html	http://www.hawaii.gov/workforce
Idaho		http://www.doe.state.id.us/
Illinois	http://www.revenue.state.il.us/	http://il.jobsearch.org/
Indiana	http://www.ai.org/dor/publications/legal/index.html	http://www.bloomington.in.us/employment/
Iowa	http://www.state.ia.us/government/drf/index.html	http://www.state.ia.us/government/des/
Kansas	http://www.ink.org/public/kdor/	http://www.hr.state.ks.us/
Kentucky	http://www.state.ky.us/agencies/revenue/revhome.htm	http://ky.jobsearch.org/
Louisiana	http://www.rev.state.la.us/	http://www.ldol.state.la.us/
Maine	http://janus.state.me.us/revenue/	http://www.state.me.us/labor/ucd/homepag1.htm
Maryland	http://www.comp.state.md.us/default.asp	http://www.dllr.state.state.md.us/
Massachusetts	http://www.state.ma.us/dor/dorpg.htm	http://ma.jobsearch.org/
Michigan	http://www.treas.state.mi.us/	http://www.mesc.com/
Minnesota	http://www.state.mn.us/ebranch/mdor/	http://mn.jobsearch.org/

State	Department of Revenue Web Address	Department of Labor and Employment /Unemployment Taxes Web Address
Mississippi	http://www.mstc.state.ms.us/	http://www1.pcsvcs.com/~mesclmi/
Missouri	http://www.dor.state.mo.us/	http://www.dolir.state.mo.us/
Montana	http://www.state.mt.us/revenue/	http://jsd.dli.mt.gov/
Nebraska	http://www.nol.org/home/NDR	http://www.dol.state.ne.us/
Nevada	http://tax.state.nv.us/	http://www.state.nv.us/detr/detr.html
New Hampshire	http://www.state.nh.us/revenue/index.htm	http://www.nhworks.state.nh.us/
New Jersey	http://www.state.nj.us/treasury/taxation/	http://wnjpin.state.nj.us/
New Mexico	http://www.state.nm.us/tax/	http://gsd.state.nm.us/dol/dol_esd.html
New York	http://www.tax.state.ny.us/	http://www.labor.state.ny.us/
North Carolina	http://www.dor.state.nc.us/	http://www.esc.state.nc.us/
North Dakota	http://www.state.nd.us/taxdpt/	http://www.state.nd.us/jsnd/lmi.htm
Ohio	http://www.state.oh.us./tax/	http://www.state.oh.us/obes/
Oklahoma	http://www.oktax.state.ok.us/	http://www.oesc.state.ok.us/
Oregon	http://www.dor.state.or.us/default.html	http://www.emp.state.or.us/
Pennsylvania	http://www.revenue.state.pa.us/	http://www.state.pa.us/PA_Exec/Labor_Industry/
Rhode Island	http://www.doa.state.ri.us/tax/	http://www.det.state.ri.us/
South Carolina	http://www.doa.state.ri.us/tax/	http://scjob.sces.org/
South Dakota	http://www.state.sd.us/revenue/Revenue.html	http://www.state.sd.us/dol/
Tennessee	http://www.state.tn.us/revenue	http://www.state.tn.us/employsecurity/
Texas	http://www.window.state.tx.us/m23taxes.html	http://www.twc.state.tx.us/
Utah	http://www.tax.ex.state.ut.us/	http://udesb.state.ut.us/
Vermont	http://www.state.vt.us/tax/index.htm	http://www.det.state.vt.us/
Virginia	http://www.tax.state.va.us/	http://www.state.va.us/vec/vec.html
Washington	http://dor.wa.gov/index.asp	http://www.wa.gov/esd/
Washington, D. C.	http://cfo.washingtondc.gov/services/tax/about/index.shtm	http://does.dc.gov/
West Virginia	http://www.state.wv.us/taxrev/	http://wv.jobsearch.org/
Wisconsin	http://www.dor.state.wi.us/	http://badger.state.wi.us/0/agencies/dilhr/dlirhome.html
Wyoming	http://revenue.state.wy.us/	http://wyjobs.state.wy.us/

GLOSSARY

A

Accuracy of deposits rule (98 percent rule) This IRS rule allows a depositor some margin for error in the accuracy of Form 941 deposits. It states that if any underdeposited amount does not exceed the greater of 2 percent of the actual liability or $100 *and* any deposit shortfall is paid by a shortfall make-up date, the IRS will consider the depositor to be in compliance with federal payroll tax deposit rules.

ACH ACH is the acronym that stands for *automated clearing house*. This is the entity that is responsible for electronically transmitting funds between banks. The ACH will use the Federal Reserve telecommunications network for transmitting funds between financial institutions. There are over 40 local and regional ACHs in the United States.

After-tax deduction This is a deduction that is made from the gross earnings of an employee. An after-tax deduction offers no tax savings to an employee. Labor union dues and charitable contributions are two typical examples of after-tax deductions.

Age Discrimination in Employment Act This law prohibits employment discrimination against individuals who are over 40 years old. It also prohibits a company from establishing a mandatory retirement age.

Allocated tips The term *allocated tips* refers to an amount that is calculated based on a percentage of the gross receipts of a food or beverage establishment. A prorated allocated amount of tips may be distributed to an employee who reported less than the allocated amount to his employer.

American Payroll Association APA is the nationwide association of payroll accountants and administrators that is dedicated to the setting of guidelines and standards for the payroll profession.

American Society for Payroll Management ASPM is a nationwide association dedicated to furthering payroll administration.

American Society of Pension Actuaries ASPA is a nationwide association dedicated to furthering the pension administration profession.

Antidiscrimination laws These federal laws have been enacted to prohibit discrimination in the areas of hiring and promoting employees in the workplace. These laws include, but are not limited to, the Civil Rights Act, The Americans with Disabilities Act, and the Age Discrimination in Employment Act. Some states have also passed state-specific antidiscrimination legislation.

B

Backup withholding Backup withholding is a term that refers to federal income taxes that have been withheld on wages (or other forms of income) where the employee (or recipient) of the income has not furnished the employer or payer with a social security number or other recognized identification number. It would be a rare occurrence in payroll accounting where an employee would not have a social security number. Backup withholding is reported on Form 945. (See Form 945.)

Banking day   A banking day is an established time each business day before which bank transactions are considered to be completed on that day. Generally, a banking day will end at 2 or 3 P.M. local time. Business transacted after this time is usually considered to be the next day's business.

Bases of accounting   The two major bases or methods of accounting are the *cash basis* and *accrual basis*. If the cash basis is used, accounting transactions will follow the flow of cash in a business. When the accrual basis is used, revenues will be recorded when earned and expenses recorded when incurred, as opposed to when received or paid.

Before-tax deduction   This is a deduction that is made before any taxes are calculated or withheld from an employee. The effect of such a deduction is that taxes will be calculated and paid on a lesser amount of the earnings of the employee. A before-tax deduction offers a tax savings to an employee. Contributions to a retirement plan and medical insurance premiums may be deducted before taxes.

biweekly pay period   A biweekly pay period occurs once every two weeks, or 26 times per year. See also *pay period.*

Bonus   A bonus is income that is paid to an employee as an incentive for performance on the job or for achieving specific goals that the management of a company sets. The amount of a bonus is income to the employee and will be added to the regular and overtime earnings of an employee.

C

Cafeteria plan   This plan is technically known as a Section 125 (§125) plan. It offers a variety of benefits to employees that can be deducted on a before-tax basis. This type of plan is also referred to as a *flexible benefit plan.* Another version of this plan is called a *flexible spending arrangement.*

Calendar quarter   A calendar quarter is a three-month time period, or 13 weeks in length. Calendar quarters are January through March, April through June, July through September, and October through December.

Calendar year   A calendar year begins on January 1 and ends on December 31. Contrast this to a fiscal year. A fiscal year is any year that runs for any 12 consecutive months.

Canadian Payroll Association   The CPA is a group dedicated to furthering the payroll accounting and administration profession in Canada.

Certified Payroll Professional (CPP) examination   This examination is administered annually by the APA; it tests a candidate's knowledge of payroll accounting and administration concepts, theories, and practices.

Circular E   Circular E is also known as Publication 15, *Employer's Tax Guide.* This IRS publication provides useful information about calculating federal income and social security taxes. The IRS publishes this guide each December for use the next calendar year.

The Civil Rights Act This law prohibits discrimination in the area of employment due to race, religious beliefs, sex, or national origin.

Commissions Commission income is income earned for transacting business on behalf of a company, with the goal being to close a sale. Commission income is taxable for federal, social security, and state income tax purposes.

Common law test The common law test is used to determine if a worker is an employee of a business. There are four major points of law used in this test to make the determination. This test is used by the federal, state, and local governments as well as courts of law. This test is used under FUTA to determine if a worker will be covered under the law for unemployment purposes.

Comp time Compensation time (or *comp time*) denotes overtime hours that are worked and "banked" by employees and then taken later as paid time off. Comp time offers the advantage of smoothing out a business's labor costs, because overtime hours are tracked for use as paid time off instead of paid directly to employees. Comp time is popular in the accounting and legal professions.

Covered employment This term describes the criteria used to determine if an employee's earnings will be subject to federal unemployment tax. It is a legal definition found in the Federal Unemployment Tax Act.

Credit See *tax credit.*

Cross-foot This is an accounting term that means to add or subtract amounts found in a row horizontally.

Current Tax Payments Act This tax act originally was signed into law in 1942. It required that the majority of employers had to withhold federal income taxes on a pay period basis. This law is now part of the Internal Revenue Code of 1986. Forty-one states have also passed similar laws requiring employers to withhold state income taxes.

D

De minimis exception This rule is now called the $2,500 quarterly liability exception. If a depositor's Form 941 tax liability is less than $2,500 at the end of a calendar quarter, the deposit will be due one month after the end of the calendar quarter. This is an exception to the federal payroll tax deposit rules for monthly and semiweekly depositors.

Deposit shortfall The term *deposit shortfall* refers to the amount of underdeposited Form 941 taxes. This amount must be deposited according to a specific timetable to avoid IRS underpayment penalties.

Draw A draw is a monetary advance given to salespeople that will be paid back at a later date when future sales have been completed. Draws are generally netted against commissions earned on a monthly or quarterly basis.

E

Earned income credit Earned income credit (EIC) is a credit advanced to working taxpayers who support a dependent, or to low-income workers without any dependents. An individual taxpayer may receive the earned income credit in advance if he has what the IRS terms a *qualifying child.* Congress has granted this credit to taxpayers who maintain support of a qualifying child and whose earned and adjusted gross income is a certain amount or less for one qualifying child (or a slightly greater maximum amount for two or more qualifying children) each year.

Earnings limit   An earnings limit is the maximum amount of an individual's earnings in a calendar year that will be subject to being taxed for federal, social security, or state unemployment purposes.

EEOC (Equal Employment Opportunity Commission)   This federal agency is charged with enforcing various laws in employment situations, such as the Civil Rights Law and Equal Pay Act.

EFT   EFT stands for *electronic funds transfer*. The EFT system allows for the direct deposit of employee paychecks and other transfers of funds between banks and financial institutions in the United States.

EFTPS   See *Electronic Federal Tax Payment System.*

EIC   See *earned income credit.*

EIC percentage method   This method of calculating the amount of EIC that may be advanced to an eligible employee relies on IRS tables and several calculations that the payroll accountant must perform. The IRS tables may be found in IRS Circular E.

EIC wage-bracket withholding method   This is a method of calculating the amount of EIC that may be advanced to an eligible employee by an employer. The method relies solely on tables for the computation. These tables are found in IRS Circular E.

Eighth monthly period   This term refers to a month that has been divided into eight time periods of approximately three days each. Some state payroll tax deposits will be made according to this schedule.

Eight percent (8 percent) rule   This is a general IRS rule used to determine the amount of allocated tips for a food or beverage establishment. The general rule states that 8 percent of the gross receipts of a food or beverage establishment will be allocated as tips to employees.

EIN   EIN is the acronym that stands for Employer Identification Number. It is sometimes abbreviated as FEIN, for Federal Employer Identification Number. The EIN is issued by the IRS to a company, and it must be used for reporting purposes. The EIN must be used on Forms 941, 8109, W-2, and W-3. A company may also have a state EIN which may be a different number from the federal EIN.

Electronic Federal Tax Payment System (EFTPS)   A program sponsored by the IRS. Certain employers whose calendar year 2000 *total of federal tax deposits* (i.e., deposits for employment taxes, excise taxes, and corporate income taxes) was more than $200,000 must use EFTPS to make their calendar year 2001 payroll tax deposits electronically. Any employer whose total calendar year 1999 federal tax deposits were less than $200,000 can still voluntarily use EFTPS beginning in 2000 and later years.

Employee   An employee is a worker who is under *the direct supervision and control* of his employer. A worker usually will be classified as an employee by applying the common law test. *Control* is the key term in classifying a worker as an employee. An employee may work for one company and be leased to another, or the employee may work for a temporary agency and be assigned to a number of different employers over a period of time.

Employee benefits Costs and expenses that an employer pays on behalf of its employees are known as employee benefits (or *fringe benefits*). If an employer pays the medical insurance premiums of an employee, it is considered a benefit. Other common benefits include holiday and sick-leave pay.

Employee earnings record This accounting document provides a comprehensive history of the earnings of an employee during a calendar year. An employee earnings record will be maintained for each employee who is paid during the year. The record will generally show quarterly and year-to-date earnings amounts. It is used in conjunction with the payroll register.

Employer's quarterly federal tax return The Employer's Quarterly Federal Tax Return, commonly known as the Form 941, is used to report the total employer liability for social security and Federal income taxes each calendar quarter.

Employment application This document is completed by candidates for a job within a company. There are no rules as to its appearance, although certain questions that may discriminate against potential candidates may not be asked.

Employment laws These federal, state, and local laws directly affect how employees are hired and paid. Figure 1–1 in Chapter 1 illustrates a sample of the various laws affecting payroll accounting.

Employment tax An employment tax or *head tax* is levied on employees by certain localities for working in those localities. Such taxes are called occupational taxes, license fees, or earnings taxes.

Equal opportunity employer An employer that holds itself to be an equal opportunity employer makes a conscious effort to prevent discrimination in hiring and promotion practices, per the Civil Rights Act of 1964.

Equal Pay Act This law (considered an antidiscrimination law) prohibits discrimination based on the gender of employees.

Escheat laws These state laws govern the disposal and distribution of unclaimed property. The disposition of any unclaimed earnings of employees are regulated by escheat laws. Escheat laws are not uniform but vary somewhat by state.

Exempt employee An exempt employee is an employee who will not be paid overtime earnings for hours worked in excess of 40 per workweek. Federal wage and hour law provides rules for classifying an employee as *exempt*.

Experience or merit rating This term is used to describe the process by which an employer is assigned a specific percentage rate for state unemployment tax. The rate given to an employer depends on the dollar amount of benefits paid to former employees and the amount of state unemployment taxes paid by an employer over a certain period of time. The state will use a formula to determine the rate for an employer. The rate may change depending on benefits paid out and the amount of unemployment tax paid to the state.

F

Fair Labor Standards Act The Fair Labor Standards Act (FLSA) is a major federal law that regulates employee compensation. Included in the act are regulations regarding minimum wage, overtime, discrimination, child labor, and record keeping. This law is also known as the Federal Wage and Hour Law.

Federal income tax   Federal income tax refers to the tax that must be paid on income earned by employees. The requirement to tax income was passed into law on March 1, 1913, and was ratified as the 16th constitutional amendment. During World War II, the government required that income taxes be withheld on employee earnings by employers. The total of federal income taxes withheld for a quarter by an employer must be reported on the Form 941.

Federal tax deposit coupon   This form is also called Form 8109. It will be used for federal income, social security, Medicare, and federal unemployment tax deposits and can also be used for the payment of other types of federal taxes.

Federal Wage and Hour Law   See *Fair Labor Standards Act.*

FEIN   Acronym that stands for Federal Employer Identification Number. See *EIN.*

FICA   This acronym stands for Federal Insurance Contributions Act, which is part of the Social Security Act of 1935. The law provides old age, survivors, and disability insurance for workers, which is known as social security. This term is used interchangeably with the term *Social Security taxes.*

Fiscal year   A fiscal year is any year that runs for any 12 consecutive months.

FLSA   See *Fair Labor Standards Act.*

Foot   This is an accounting term that means to add or subtract the amounts found in a column vertically.

Form 940   Form 940, *Employer's Annual Federal Unemployment Tax Return,* is filed on an annual basis after December 31 of each year by any employer who pays state unemployment taxes into two or more state funds. Form 940 reports the amount of federal unemployment taxes paid or due on employee earnings on a calendar-year basis.

Form 940-EZ   Form 940-EZ, *Employer's Annual Federal Unemployment Tax Return,* is filed on an annual basis after December 31 of each year by any employer who pays state unemployment taxes into only one state fund. Form 940-EZ reports the amount of federal unemployment taxes paid or due on employee earnings on a calendar-year basis. Less complex than Form 940, it is for employers who pay into more than one state unemployment fund.

Form 941   The Form 941 is known as the *Employer's Quarterly Tax Return.* It is used to report the total employer liability for social security and federal income taxes each calendar quarter.

Form 941-C   Called the *Statement to Correct Information,* this form is used to correct errors made on previously filed 941 forms. This form must be filed with a Form 941—it cannot be filed separately.

Form 945   The Form 945 is called the *Annual Return of Withheld Federal Income Tax.* This return must be filed by January 31 of each year by any employer that has withheld federal income tax from a nonpayroll source. Federal income tax withholding from nonpayroll sources include pensions, annuities, IRAs, gambling winnings, military retirement pay, and backup withholding. An employer must file form 945 only if tax withholding has occurred from these nonpayroll sources.

Form 1096   The Form 1096, *Annual Summary and Transmittal of U.S. Information Returns,* is used to transmit various 1099 forms to the IRS. (See Form 1099-MISC.) These forms must be submitted to an IRS district office no later than the last day of February for the prior calendar year.

Form 1099-MISC This form (known as an information return) is used to report payments made to independent contractors when the payment made is $600 or more in a calendar year. It can also be used for other types of payments made such as royalties, rents, commissions, fees, prizes, and other income. The form should be issued annually to recipients of such payments by the last day of February for any payments made in the prior calendar year.

Form 4070 The Form 4070 is called *Employee's Record of Tips to Employer*. It is used by an employee to report tips to his employer over the period of one month or less. Use of this form is optional if the employer has established another method for reporting tips. This form is contained in IRS Publication 1244.

Form 8027 This form is called the *Employer's Annual Information Return of Tip Income and Allocated Tips*. It will be filed by a food and beverage establishment to determine the amount of tips to be allocated to all tipped employees on an annual basis.

Form 8109 This form is commonly referred to as the *Federal Tax Deposit Coupon*. It is used for deposits of federal taxes, including federal unemployment taxes.

Form SS-4 The Form SS-4 is known as the *Application for Employer Identification Number*. This form must be completed by a new business (employer) in order for the IRS to assign an EIN (Employer Identification Number).

Form SS-5 The Form SS-5 is known as the *Application for a Social Security Card*. This form should be completed by any worker who does not have a social security number. The form is available from the Social Security Administration.

Form SS-8 The Form SS-8 is known as *Determination of Employee Work Status for Purposes of Federal Employment Taxes and Income Tax Withholding*. This form can be filled out by a worker or an employer to determine whether the worker(s) should be classified as an employee or an independent contractor for income tax withholding purposes. The four- page form consists of 20 questions that the IRS will use in making its determination.

Form W-2 This form is also called the *Wage and Tax Statement*. It is issued annually to any employee who earned wages or had federal income or social security taxes withheld during the year. It is a multipart form that is distributed to the employee, employer, Social Security Administration, and state, county, or local taxing authorities.

Form W-3 This form is known as the *Transmittal of Income and Tax Statements*. It will be submitted along with one or more W-2 forms for a given employer identification number. The form is used by the Social Security Administration to reconcile the amounts found on the individual W-2 forms for a given EIN.

Form W-4 This form is known as the *Employee's Allowance Withholding Certificate*. A new employee will fill this form out, providing the payroll professional with information needed to calculate the employee's income tax withholding. An employee can revise a W-4 form at any time. Some states require that a separate state form be completed for state income tax withholding purposes.

Form W-5 The Form W-5 is known as the *Earned Income Credit Advance Payment Certificate*. This form must be completed, dated, and signed by an employee who wishes to have the basic portion of the earned income credit advanced to him on a paycheck basis. A new W-5 form must be completed each year by the employee in order to receive the advanced credit for that year.

Friday deposit rule   For semiweekly payroll tax depositors, this rule states that for the Saturday–Tuesday payday period, any federal income and social security tax liability is due and payable the following Friday.

Fringe benefits   See *employee benefits.*

FUTA   This acronym stands for *Federal Unemployment Tax Act,* which is another part of the Social Security Act of 1935. It established unemployment insurance for unemployed workers, and required states to set up unemployment funds to handle contributions from employers and claims from unemployed workers. FUTA law requires that employers pay federal unemployment tax and file a Form 940 or 940-EZ after the end of each year.

G

GAAP   This is the acronym for *Generally Accepted Accounting Principles.* These standards or rules in part govern how accountants will record business transactions.

General ledger   The general ledger is the accounting book that is used to maintain the current balance for each account used in a business. The general ledger is also referred to as the *book of final entry.* The current balance is frequently referred to as a *running total.* The general ledger can be used to obtain and verify amounts that will be reported on Form 941.

Gross earnings   This refers to the total of all regular, overtime, and other earnings and compensation an employee will earn within a pay period. This key amount will be used in computing federal, social security, state, and local taxes.

H

HI   HI stands for hospital insurance, and is more commonly known as Medicare. The current percentage rate for HI is 1.45 percent.

I

I-9 Form   The Immigration and Naturalization Service requires every new employee of a company to fill out this form. It serves to verify the identity of the employee and the employee's eligibility to work in the United States.

Imprest checking account   A checking account that is known as an imprest account is established and used by a business for one specific purpose, such as the payroll checking account. Imprest accounts will be maintained with cash transfers from a general checking account.

Independent contractor   A person who performs services or provides a combination of goods and services to another person, business, or independent contractor is called an *independent contractor.* The independent contractor is considered to be independent from the person or business that requests the services, and the independent contractor may be considered to be self-employed.

Internal control   The term *internal control* refers to checks and balances that are built into an accounting system that will protect the system from waste, fraud, and inefficiency. Simple measures such as cross-footing amounts and requiring posting references are examples of building internal control into the accounting system. Segregation of job duties and maintaining a separate checking account for payroll checks are other examples of good internal control.

Internal Revenue Code These federal laws govern taxation. As applied to payroll accounting, certain sections of the code directly govern the collection and remittance of income taxes on a federal level.

International Society of Certified Employee Benefit Specialists (ISCEBS) This group is a nonprofit educational association whose mission is to provide educational opportunities to individuals holding the CEBS designation.

Interstate commerce Interstate commerce is an activity that is conducted between two businesses located in different states. This concept is used to determine if an employer will be subject to the Fair Labor Standards Act. A firm that does business with other companies outside of its own domicile is engaged in interstate commerce. This designation is important to determine if the business must pay minimum wage and overtime to its employees.

Involuntary deductions This term refers to amounts that will be withheld from employees' earnings due to a legal order from a court of law, a labor union agreement, or a tax levy. The specifics of the deduction are set forth in a legal document. There are labor laws that set limits on the total amount of involuntary deductions that can be withheld from an employee each pay period.

Involuntary unemployment This term is used to describe a situation in which a worker becomes unemployed through no fault of the worker. Typically, corporate downsizing efforts, layoffs, or the employer going out of business are the main reasons for a worker to become involuntarily unemployed.

IRS IRS is the acronym for Internal Revenue Service. The IRS is the branch of government responsible for administration and enforcement of tax laws and the collection of taxes from employers and individuals.

L

Labor distribution This is a term used in conjunction with preparing a payroll register. The *labor distribution* section of a payroll register is the section of the register where each employee's gross earnings will be debited to an expense account. This distribution will allow for easier preparation of journal entries.

Labor union agreement Generally, this is an agreement between a labor organization and a specific company or a group of companies. Such agreements will provide additional guidance as to how employees are to be paid, their working conditions, and their benefits. Such agreements supplement employment laws for an employer subject to such an agreement.

Look-back period A look-back period is a fiscal year that begins on July 1 and ends on June 30. The look-back period for a current calendar year will be the prior July 1–June 30 fiscal year. The amount of federal income, social security, and Medicare taxes paid during this period of time will determine a depositor classification under IRS payroll tax deposit rules.

M

Magnetic media This term is used by the Social Security Administration to refer to electronic methods of storing W-2 information. The typical methods of storage are magnetic computer tape or floppy disk. If 250 or more W-2 forms are submitted under one EIN, the SSA requests that the forms be submitted in magnetic media format.

Marital status The marital status of an employee is requested on the Form W-4. It will be used to determine the income tax to be withheld on an employee's earnings each pay period.

Medicare tax Medicare tax (technically known as hospital insurance) is used to pay medical expenses for retired and disabled individuals who have paid into the fund. The current rate paid by employees is 1.45 percent on all earnings. This amount must be matched by a worker's employer on a dollar-for-dollar basis. Some people refer to this tax as social security, although it must be accounted for and tracked separately by an employer.

Minimum wage A company that must comply with federal wage and hour law is required to pay an hourly worker a minimum amount. This is referred to as the minimum (or federal) wage. The worker must be classified as nonexempt, and the employer must be engaged in interstate commerce. For 2001, the minimum wage is $5.15 per hour.

Monthly depositor Per IRS payroll tax deposit rules, a monthly depositor will deposit any federal income, social security, and Medicare taxes accumulated during a month by the 15th of the next month.

N

Net earnings Sometimes called take-home pay, net earnings means the amount of money an employee actually receives for a pay period after taxes and deductions have been withheld from gross earnings. This will be the amount of the employee's paycheck each pay period.

New hire reporting Employers who hire new workers must now report specific information within a 7- to 20-day time period to the state in which the employer is domiciled. This is according to a federal law known as the Personal Responsibility and Work Opportunity Act of 1996. See Section 8 in Chapter 2 for more information.

Nonexempt employee A nonexempt employee is an employee who will be paid overtime earnings for the hours worked in excess of 40 hours per workweek. Federal law provides rules for classifying an employee as nonexempt or exempt.

Nonresident employee (state) Nonresident employees are employees who work in one state and live in another state. These employees may be on temporary assignment working in a distant state from their home, or they may live in a state adjacent to the state in which they work. State rules for income tax withholding for nonresident employees vary with each state.

O

OASDI The term stands for *old age, survivors, and disability insurance*. This is more commonly known as social security. The percentage rate for OASDI in 2001 is 6.20 percent on all wages earned up to $80,400.

Offset amount The offset amount is used in the percentage method of withholding. It is a dollar amount that will be subtracted from the earnings of an employee to arrive at the amount that will be used to calculate the amount of income tax.

On-the-job activities On-the-job activities are the activities for which an employee is paid. These activities are usually outlined in a job description. Payroll professionals distinguish between on-the-job, before-the-job, and after-the-job activities so the employees can properly be paid for their work and work-related activities.

Overtime Overtime or premium pay are earnings paid to employees who work in excess of 40 hours in a workweek. As a general rule, employees are eligible for overtime pay if they are classified as nonexempt employees. Some employees, by virtue of their job duties or job title, are considered exempt from being paid overtime.

P

Pay period A pay period is a recurring period of time that has a specific starting and ending date that is used to track the hours worked by employees. Pay periods can be daily, weekly, biweekly, semimonthly, monthly, or quarterly.

Pay-as-you-go withholding Withholding from employees for income or social security taxes that occurs each pay period is known as pay-as-you-go withholding. This method of withholding started in 1943 for federal income taxes. Most states also assess income taxes in a similar way.

Payday period This is the period of time in which a payday occurs for a semiweekly depositor. According to current IRS deposit rules, there are two semiweekly payday periods: Wednesday through Friday and Saturday through Tuesday.

Payroll accounting The activity of calculating the earnings of employees and the related withholding for taxes and other deductions, recording the results of payroll activities, and the preparation of required payroll tax returns (federal, and state or local).

Payroll administration The activities of managing employee personnel and payroll information and compliance with federal and state or local laws. Such activities may encompass interviewing and hiring workers, maintaining personnel records, and monitoring that a business complies with federal labor and antidiscrimination laws that pertain to employment.

Payroll professional An individual who works in the area of payroll accounting and administration. Such individuals may also have financial, managerial, or human resource duties in addition to payroll accounting and administration.

Payroll register The payroll register is the accounting document that provides a summary of the payroll information for a certain pay-period. The payroll register will list all employees who were paid during the pay-period, along with their gross earnings, taxes withheld, and various deductions.

Pegboard system This is a manual payroll system that allows the payroll accountant to write out an employee's paycheck and simultaneously complete the employee's earnings record and record the payroll information in a payroll register.

Percentage method The percentage method of income tax withholding relies on a series of calculations and an IRS table to arrive at the amount of income tax to be withheld. This method is more accurate than its counterpart, the wage-bracket method, but requires more time on the part of the accountant to calculate and arrive at the amount of withholding. Most states have their own version of the percentage method of withholding.

Personnel file This is the permanent record that contains pre-employment and post-hiring information for an employee. Included in the file will be an employment application or résumé, I-9 and W-4 forms, hiring notice, and so on.

Piece-rate calculation method The piece-rate method compensates employees for every unit produced or assembled. This method is used by manufacturing companies or business engaged in assembling products for sale. Employees paid under the piece-rate method generally are eligible for overtime and must be paid at least minimum wage for all hours worked.

Profit-sharing plans Profit-sharing plans are established by employers to allow employees to share in the profits of a company on a systematic basis. These plans are designed to reward employees for efficient, productive work. Income from profit-sharing plans can be paid directly to employees or may be used to fund retirement plans.

Publication 15 See *Circular E.*

Publication 1244 This IRS publication is called the *Employee's Daily Record of Tips and Report of Tips to Employer.* It is a booklet of 4070 forms used by a employee to report tips to his employer. See *Form 4070.*

R

Record, employee earnings See *employee earnings record.*

Record retention Federal laws require that employee personnel and payroll records be retained for a minimum of two to four years. Some professionals suggest that all employee records be kept indefinitely in the event of legal action brought about by former employees.

Register, payroll See *payroll register.*

Reserve ratio method This is one of four methods used by states to determine the rate of unemployment tax for an employer. The reserve method is used by most states at present. The ratio is calculated by a state department of labor and employment, which assigns the rate to an employer for state unemployment taxes.

résumé This document is created by an individual looking for a position with a company. Although there are no absolute rules about the contents of a résumé, the candidate's name, address, experience and references are often listed.

ROFT ROFT is an acronym used by the IRS that stands for Record of Federal Tax Liability. An employer will use the ROFT to report the social security and Federal income tax liability on a monthly basis at the bottom of Form 941.

Rounding differences Rounding differences occur when the employer's social security tax liability is calculated on the gross earnings of all employees for a pay period, whereas the individual employee's social security tax liability is calculated only on his gross earnings for a pay period. The difference in the dollar amount of earnings used for calculation purposes causes a difference in the amount of social security taxes.

S

SS-8 See Form SS-8.

Salaries Salaries are earnings paid the employees on a weekly, biweekly, semimonthly, or monthly basis. Salaried employees may be paid overtime depending on how they are classified (i.e., exempt or nonexempt).

Salary reduction plan This type of plan is technically known as a *Section 401(k),* (§401(k)), or *salary deferral plan.* An employee who participates in this type of plan will have a certain percentage deducted from earnings and placed into this plan. The amount deducted is not subject to federal income tax but is taxable for social security purposes.

Schedule EIC Schedule EIC is called the *earned income credit*. It must be prepared by an eligible taxpayer who is entitled to receive the earned income credit. Any employee who files a Form W-5 must file a Schedule EIC with his individual income tax return.

Schedule SE This IRS form is called "SE" as in *Self-Employment Tax*. It will be used by any self-employed individual who has net earnings of $400 or more during the year. SE tax will be computed on this amount, subject to FICA earnings limits. SE tax will be reported on page 2 of Form 1040.

SE Tax SE tax must be paid by the majority of self-employed individuals whose net earnings from their self-employment activities exceed $400 in a year. SE tax is used to provide social security benefits for these individuals.

Section 125 plan See *cafeteria plans*.

Section 401(k) plan See *salary reduction plans*.

Self-employed A person is considered to be self-employed if that individual is engaged in a trade or business for profit. Independent contractors are considered to be self-employed for tax purposes.

Semimonthly pay period A semimonthly pay period will occur twice each month or a total of 24 times each year. See also *pay period*.

Semiweekly depositor According to the IRS payroll deposit rules, a semiweekly depositor will make any federal income, social security, and Medicare tax deposits on either a Wednesday or a Friday. The deposit date is determined by the day the earnings are paid. If the payday period is Wednesday through Friday, the deposit is due on the following Wednesday. If the payday period is Saturday through Tuesday, the day of the deposit is Friday.

SEP This acronym stands for *Simplified Employee Pension*. This is a pension plan that in some respects is similar to a §401(k) plan, but is streamlined for use by small businesses.

Shortfall make-up date This is the date that any underdeposited federal income, social security, and Medicare taxes are due. This date will be different for monthly and semiweekly depositors.

SIMPLE This acronym stands for *Savings Incentive Match Plan for Employees*. It is a type of pension plan that is similar in some respects to a SEP, but it offers several features not available with a SEP.

Small Business, Health Insurance, and Welfare Reform Acts of 1996 Signed into law in 1996, these congressional bills impact payroll accounting and administration in that the federal minimum wage is increased, the training wage for youth is re-enacted, and a small employer with fewer than 100 workers can establish a small business pension plan (which is similar to a traditional §401(k) plan).

Social Security Act The Social Security Act of 1935 (abbreviated as SSA) was the first comprehensive federal program that established benefits for workers' retirement, or untimely disability or death. The Federal Insurance Contributions Act is one major provision of the SSA. This law was passed as part of the Roosevelt Administration's attempt to ease the economic hardship caused by the Great Depression. Two parts of this law, the Federal Unemployment Tax Act and the Federal Insurance Contributions Act, have had a major impact on payroll accounting and administration. The act has been revised on several occasions since 1935.

Social Security Administration (SSA)   This federal agency was created as a result of the Social Security Act of 1935. It oversees the social security fund, which pays benefits to eligible individuals. The agency is also responsible for maintaining a database of taxpayer earnings information. W-2 forms must be sent to the SSA for processing purposes.

Social security taxes   These taxes are also referred to as *FICA (Federal Insurance Contributions Act) taxes.* Amounts withheld for these taxes support three major programs known as insurance: old age, survivors, and disability.

Special-deposit ledger   The special-deposit ledger is used by the payroll professional to track the dates and dollar amounts of payroll taxes deposited during the year. It can be used to obtain the total amount of taxes deposited for a quarter on Form 941.

Special journal   An accounting book of original entry, where source information will first be entered into the accounting system. A payroll register technically can be classified as a special journal.

Special-purpose ledgers   A special-purpose ledger can be used to provide specific information about an account or group of related accounts. In payroll accounting, the tax deposit ledger for federal or state deposits is an example of a special-purpose ledger. Special-purpose ledgers should be used when they enable a savings of time or the accounting system can be made to be more efficient.

SS-8   See *Form SS-8.*

State unemployment tax credit   This credit, also known as the *normal credit,* offsets the 6.2 percent rate for FUTA tax for any employer who pays into one or more state funds and has made timely payments into these funds. The credit is 5.4 percent, which reduces the rate of FUTA an employer will pay to .8 percent.

Supplemental wages   This term is used to denote compensation that is paid in addition to an employee's regular wages or salary. Examples of supplemental wages include (but are not limited to) commissions, bonuses, tips, vacation pay, sick leave, severance pay, awards, and prizes. Generally, federal withholding can be made at a flat rate of 27.5 percent in addition to social security, Medicare, and other state or local taxes. Tip income and vacation pay may be treated as supplemental wages at the employer's option.

SUTA   This is an acronym for *state unemployment tax acts.* All states, Puerto Rico, the Virgin Islands, and Guam have passed legislation that governs unemployment taxes, benefits, and other types of insurance such as workers' compensation and disability insurance.

T

Tax credit   A tax credit is a dollar amount that is allowed to be netted against the amount of tax due. One dollar of tax credit will offset one dollar of tax. Congress allows tax credits under certain circumstances and in specific tax situations.

Tax-deferred deduction   A deduction that is tax-deferred means that no income taxes will be paid on the amount at the time it is deducted. Income taxes will eventually be paid on the deduction at a later date. Social security taxes will be paid on the deduction at the time the amount is withheld from pay.

Tax-exempt deduction   A deduction that is tax-exempt means that no income or social security taxes will be paid on the amount at the time it is deducted or at a later date. The deduction can be made free of any tax impact.

Tax liability, federal   The term *federal tax liability* refers to the total employer obligation for social security (employee and employer portions) and Federal income tax on a pay period basis. This obligation will be reported in the section of the Form 941 known as the record of federal tax liability (ROFT).

Taxes, Form 940   This term is used to refer to federal unemployment taxes. An employer will pay federal unemployment taxes on worker earnings and file either a Form 940 or 940-EZ, *Employer's Annual Federal Unemployment Tax Return*, on an annual basis after December 31 of each year. Federal unemployment taxes must be deposited according to the IRS deposit rules using an 8109 form.

Taxes, Form 941   This term refers to federal income, social security, and Medicare taxes. An employer will file a Form 941, the Employer's Quarterly Federal Tax Return, each calendar quarter to report the amounts withheld and due for these taxes. Form 941 taxes will be deposited using Form 8109 according to IRS payroll tax deposit rules.

Taxes, head   See *employment tax.*

Taxes, occupational   See *employment tax.*

Taxes, social security   Social security taxes or FICA taxes are paid by employees (and matched by their employers) to provide benefits when the employee retires or is disabled. They are paid to the employee's surviving family in the event of the employee's untimely death. This tax technically is known as *OASDI tax.*

Ten-day Rule   The 10-day rule gives employers who have made their payroll tax deposits on a timely basis an additional 10 days after the normal due date to file their Form 941.

Time clock   A time clock is a mechanical device that will record the hours employees work. Time clocks can record time on a time card, or electronically on tape or computer disk. Time clocks generally record time using a 24-hour (military hours) day.

TIN   This acronym stands for taxpayer identification number. It is used in IRS publications and other literature. A TIN could be an individual's social security number or an employer identification number (EIN).

Tip credit   Under the Fair Labor Standards Act (FLSA), the tip credit is granted to certain employers whose employees receive tips on a recurring basis. The tip credit allows an employer to pay less than the current minimum wage to employees who receive tips that, on average, will equal or exceed the tip credit on an hourly basis. Other rules apply in order for an employer to legitimately use the tip credit.

Tip income   A tip is a gratuity given to someone for services performed. Employees who work for food and beverage establishments rely on tips to supplement the earnings they receive from their employer. Tips are taxable for FICA and income tax purposes.

Trust fund taxes   Federal, state, and local taxes withheld from employees are called *trust fund taxes* because the employer is placed in a position of trust with regard to collection and remittance for these taxes.

V

Voluntary deductions   The term *voluntary deductions* refers to deductions that are employee-authorized and -initiated. The employee will complete and sign an authorization form that provides specific information about the deduction. Charitable contributions, credit union payments, payments for medical insurance premiums, and the purchase of U.S. savings bonds are typical examples of voluntary deductions.

W

W-2 form   See *Form W-2.*

W-3 form   See *Form W-3.*

W-4 form   See *Form W-4.*

W-5 form   See *Form W-5.*

Wage and Hour Law (federal)   See *Fair Labor Standards Act.*

Wage base   See *earnings limit.*

Wage-bracket method   The federal wage-bracket method of withholding relies on a series of tables to arrive at the amount of income taxes to be withheld on an employee's earnings. The payroll professional will use the employee's marital status, number of withholding allowances, gross earnings, and pay period with the appropriate table to find the income tax to be withheld for the pay period. Most states also provide wage-bracket tables for state income tax calculations.

Wages   The term *wages* refers to the earnings of employees who are paid on an hourly or weekly basis.

Waiting period   This term is used to describe the period of time an unemployed worker must wait until he or she receives unemployment benefits. In most states this time period is one week; other states have no waiting period at all.

Wednesday deposit rule   For semiweekly payroll tax depositors, this rule states that for the Wednesday–Friday payday period, any federal income, social security, and Medicare tax liability is due and payable the following Wednesday.

Withholding allowance   Withholding allowances are dollar amounts that are subtracted from an employee's earnings in arriving at the amount subject to income taxes. The number of withholding allowances claimed by an employee on the Form W-4 will be used to determine the amount of income taxes to be withheld.

Workweek   A workweek is a fixed, recurring period of time that can start on any day of the week, and will end seven consecutive days later. Workweeks must be 168 consecutive hours or seven days in length. Overtime hours are measured relative to the total hours in a workweek.

Y

Year-to-date (Y-T-D) totals   This term refers to an amount that is tracked as a *cumulative total*, like the balance found in a general ledger account. Year-to-date totals are used in employee earnings records, on W-2 forms, and on paycheck stubs.